CONSTRUCTING SOCIAL
RESEARCH OBJECTS

D1596336

Studies in Critical Social Sciences Book Series

Haymarket Books is proud to be working with Brill Academic Publishers (www.brill.nl) to republish the *Studies in Critical Social Sciences* book series in paperback editions. This peer-reviewed book series offers insights into our current reality by exploring the content and consequences of power relationships under capitalism, and by considering the spaces of opposition and resistance to these changes that have been defining our new age. Our full catalog of *SCSS* volumes can be viewed at https://www.haymarketbooks .org/series_collections/4-studies-in-critical-social-sciences.

New Scholarship in Political Economy Book Series

CONSTRUCTING SOCIAL RESEARCH OBJECTS

Constructionism in Research Practice

EDITED BY

HÅKON LEIULFSRUD AND PETER SOHLBERG

Haymarket Books
Chicago, IL

First published in 2021 by Brill Academic Publishers, The Netherlands
© 2021 Koninklijke Brill NV, Leiden, The Netherlands

Published in paperback in 2022 by
Haymarket Books
P.O. Box 180165
Chicago, IL 60618
773-583-7884
www.haymarketbooks.org

ISBN: 978-1-64259-771-4

Distributed to the trade in the US through Consortium Book Sales and
Distribution (www.cbsd.com) and internationally through Ingram Publisher
Services International (www.ingramcontent.com).

This book was published with the generous support of Lannan Foundation and
Wallace Action Fund.

Special discounts are available for bulk purchases by organizations and
institutions. Please call 773-583-7884 or email info@haymarketbooks.org for more
information.

Cover design by Jamie Kerry and Ragina Johnson.

Printed in the United States.

10 9 8 7 6 5 4 3 2 1

Library of Congress Cataloging-in-Publication data is available.

Contents

Preface

Thanks to a generous project grant from The Norwegian Research Council and additional funding from Norwegian University of Science and Technology (NTNU), we have been able to establish a group of sociologists working with theory and theory development. This has over the years enabled us to meet, to have seminars, to offer joint PhD courses, and to develop a more explorative and creative approach to theory in interaction with our master and PhD-students. This is the final volume in a trilogy on theory exploration in research practice published by Brill based on our joint theory and methodology project.

On behalf of all the contributors to this volume we would like to acknowledge our gratitude to professor David Fasenfest as an inspiring editor of the series in which this work is published. In addition to David, we would also like to thank professor Sabrina Ramet at NTNU and Amy_46 at Wiley Editing Services for superb copy editing, and to Markus Lynum for excellent editorial assistance. It has also been a real pleasure to work with Irene Jager and the production staff at Brill. We dedicate this volume to professors Ragnvald Kalleberg (1943–2016) and Erik Olin Wright (1947–2019) – friends and collegues who have contributed in writing, discussions and inspired many of us in this collective enterprise.

Trondheim, July 2020

Figures and Tables

Figures

Tables

Notes on Contributors

Göran Ahrne
is Professor Emeritus at Department of Sociology, Stockholm University. His empirical research covers a wide variety of fields: class structure, organizations and social relations such as friendship and love. His main current research interest concerns the integration of sociological theory with organization theory by investigating how different types of social relationships are established and maintained. Parts of this research are reported on in Ahrne and Brunnson (eds.), *Organization outside organizations. The abundance of partial organization in social life* (Cambridge University Press, 2019).

Michela Betta
is Professor Emerita, Faculty of Business and Law, Swinburne University of Technology, Australia. Her main research includes management, entrepreneurship, ethics, bioethics and applied philosophy. Her most recent scientific book is *Ethicmentality – Ethics in Capitalist Economy, Business, and Society* (Springer, 2016). She is also the author of several fiction books, including *The Gatekeeper/s* (Aust'n Macauley Publisher, 2019).

Harriet Bjerrum Nielsen
is Professor Emerita at the Centre for Gender Research at the University of Oslo, Norway. Her main research interests are gender socialization, gender identity formation and gender constructions among children and adolescents. She works within a psychosocial perspective and has a special focus on the implication of social change. Her most recent book publication *Feeling gender* (Palgrave-Macmillan, 2017) is a study of gender and class in three generations of Norwegian women and men.

Michael Burawoy
is Professor of Sociology at University of California – Berkeley. Throughout his sociological career he has engaged with Marxism, seeking to reconstruct it in the light of his research and more broadly in the light of historical challenges of the late 20th and early 21st. centuries. Burawoy has developed the extended case method associated with ethnographic research, and is well known for his advocacy of public sociology. He has been President of the American Sociological Association (2003–2004); President of the International Sociological Association (2010–2014); and he is now Chair of the Berkeley Faculty Association.

Raju J. Das

is Professor Geography, Faculty of Liberal Arts and Professional Studies at York University, Toronto. He is a geographer and political economist on the editorial board of Science & Society, Professional Geographer, and Class, Race and Corporate Power. His research focuses include capitalist development and its geographical unevenness; conditions of the working class; developmental policies of the state; social capital theory and critique; Marxist political economy; and political economy and politics of India. His most recent book is Marxist Class Theory for A Skeptical World (Brill, 2017).

David Fasenfest

is Associate Professor of Sociology and Urban Affairs, College of Liberal Arts and Sciences, Wayne State University since 1998 and is Professorial Research Associate, Department of Development Studies, SOAS University of London. He is an economist and sociologist who has written numerous articles on regional and urban economic development, labour market analysis, work force development, and income inequality. He edits the journal, Critical Sociology and two Brill book series: Studies in Critical Social Science and New Scholarship in Political Economy.

Raimund Hasse

is Professor and Head of Sociology, Organization and Knowledge at the Sociological Seminar, University of Lucerne (CH). His research is informed by a neo-institutional perspective that addresses social consequences of organizational forms with a focus organizational changes in (welfare) policy and questions on economic coordination. His most recent work addresses institutional discrimination in education, the adoption of social standards, competition and the institutional character of actors.

Johs Hjellbrekke

is Professor of Sociology at University of Bergen, Department of Sociology. Director at Centre Universitaire de Norvège à Paris at FONDATION MAISON DES SCIENCES (CUNP, 2016–2020). His main research fields are in class and stratification research, elites, working life, historical sociology and history of science, and research methodology. His most recent research on social class, capital structures and social mobility is part of a larger Norwegian and European research collaboration.

Håkon Leiulfsrud

is Professor of Sociology at Norwegian University of Science and Technology (NTNU), Department of Sociology and Political Science. Before coming to

Trondheim, he worked at Stockholm University and Uppsala University. His research interests and publications are mainly in the fields of social class and social stratification, industrial relations, family and childhood, and in applications of sociological theory. His most recent book publications are Sohlberg and Leiulfsrud (eds.), *Theory in action. Theoretical constructionism,* Leiulfsrud and Sohlberg (eds.), *Concepts in action. Conceptual constructionism* (Brill and Haymarket).

Emil André Røyrvik

is Professor of Sociology at Norwegian University of Science and Technology (NTNU), Department of Sociology and Political Science. His research interests are broadly located within cultural and organizational anthropology/sociology, and his research includes the study of experts and elites, management and corporations, and contemporary forms of capitalism and financialization. Some of his recent publications include a focus on the cultural logic of quantification and measurement.

John Scott

holds Honorary Professorships at the Universities of Essex, Exeter, and Copenhagen, having previously worked as Pro-Vice Chancellor at the University of Plymouth and Professor of Sociology at the Universities of Essex and Leicester. His research has covered social stratification and the study of elites, corporate ownership and control, social network analysis, and social theory. Scott is a Fellow of the British Academy, was awarded a CBE for Services to Social Science, and is a recipient of the Distinguished Service to British Sociology Award of the British Sociological Association (he served as its president 2001–2003). His most recent publications include, *British Sociology. A History* (Palgrave Macmillan, 2020).

Peter Sohlberg

is Professor of Philosophy of Social Science at Norwegian University of Science and Technology (NTNU). Before coming to Trondheim, he has worked at Uppsala University and Stockholm University. His research interests are philosophy of science, with special focus on "knowledge-generating" research strategies in the social sciences and sociological theory. He has published within these fields, as well as in empirical sociology and social work. His most recent book publications are Sohlberg and Leiulfsrud (eds.), *Theory in action. Theoretical constructionism,* Leiulfsrud and Sohlberg (eds.), *Concepts in action. Conceptual constructionism* (Brill and Haymarket) and *Functionalist construction work in social science. The lost heritage* (Routledge, 2021).

Richard Swedberg
is Professor of Sociology at Cornell University, Department of Sociology since 2002. His two specialties are economic sociology and social theory. Before coming to Cornell, he worked at Stockholm University. His works include *Max Weber and the idea of economic sociology* (1998), *Principles of economic sociology* (2003) and *The art of social theory* (2014). Swedberg is also known for his work on social mechanisms and has written on many of the classics, including Weber, Simmel and Tocqueville. His most recent work includes sociological essays, with an emphasis on new and unorthodox ideas in social theory and economic topics.

Karin Widerberg
is Professor Emerita at Department of Sociology and Cultural Geography, Oslo University. Her main research fields are theory of science and methodology, law and ruling and understandings of gender (in general and issues related to work, sexuality and body). A key issue in Widerberg's work is the active integration between theory and empirical investigations and creative development of explorative qualitative metods (institutional etnography and memory work) on topics such as parental leave legislation, sexual harassment, the gender of knowledge, doing body/texts, the sociality of tiredness. Widerberg is a recipient of the Distinguished Service to Norwegian Sociology Award of the Norwegian Sociological Association.

CHAPTER 1

Introduction

Håkon Leiulfsrud and Peter Sohlberg

This is the third volume emanating from the theory project 'Sociological Theory and Practice Revisited' (STPR), which explores a great variety of theoretical strategies and operations in social science. Our ambition has been to inspire by example, rather than declare a convergent programmatic position; however, one stance has governed our work throughout the project, and that is the importance of active theoretical construction work in social science. We also argue that creativity in construction work cannot be easily codified into simple rules and techniques.

In relation to the construction of the research object, Pierre Bourdieu referred to Max Weber and his statement, "It is not the 'actual' interconnections of 'things' but the conceptual interconnections of problems which define the scope of the various sciences" (Bourdieu et al., 1991: 33). Despite professional training in theory and methods, it is not evident that most students (or professors) within the social sciences develop a 'theoretical eye' beyond that of a 'social engineer' or a regular 'craft-person' (Mills, 2000; Becker, 1998; Sennet, 2008). The idea of 'craft', however, is not restricted to learning 'the tricks of the trade', but also involves the skills that provide the potential to open up the ways in which we ask and solve problems. This is also in line with Bourdieu et al.'s *The Craft of Sociology*, quoted above, where the authors outlined a programme based on the extant theory in the sociological canon and how it may potentially be used to ask questions regarding relevance for an understanding of contemporary society and its issues. The epistemological and programmatic discussion in *The Craft of Sociology* is still a contribution in its own right; however, the book's most original and innovative contribution is its choice of examples and the theoretical contextualisation of them. The wealth and insight offered by these examples also support a strong argument for our approach to argue by example, rather than by some general ontological and/or epistemological principle.

Both Richard Swedberg and Michael Burrawoy (in this volume) echo a general criticism of the lack of appreciation of creative theory training in comparison to research methods in the training of younger generations of sociologists. Several of the contributors in this volume have clearly been inspired by Bourdieu and his colleagues' insistence that sociology as a craft should not stop at the level of systematic observation of social 'things' but should also be incorporated with a way of seeing that creates distance, hence the concept of a 'break' or breaking with the everyday language and immediate level of observation and interpretation.

Theory and theory construction are not essential for the discovery of new concepts or theories of our own, but rather to utilise what is already available amongst the potentially interesting theory in a field (Sohlberg and Leiulfsrud, 2017). In social science, we have a myriad of specific kinds of relations, such as power relations, relations of friendship, and hostility. These potentially interrelated concepts may be developed in theoretically substantial analyses of close interpersonal relations, while also offering examples of interconnected and interactive concepts that can be used to study the more general properties of organisations or a social field.

In contrast to those who tend to approach sociological theory and concepts as 'icons' or fixed entities, we argue that the relative value is, ultimately, to be found in theory application and practical usages. Most sociological theory textbooks are eager to map and present theory as a matrix of seemingly incompatible concepts and paradigms, as if they represented fixed entities and demarcation lines. This may, at best, be effective for teaching theory to undergraduate students who are eager for an overview but hardly gives an accurate picture of how most theory—both classical and more contemporary—has emerged in an ongoing dialogue with living or dead theorists. Neither is it very useful to persist with theory and concepts as a tribal language if we aim to encourage curiosity, creativity, and playfulness in how we construct, reconstruct, or deconstruct the sociological research object in practice (see, for example, Burrawoy and Betta, and Swedberg's chapters in this volume as examples of texts intended to give students the tools to think about theorising in practice). Much of social science continues to be based on 'spontaneous' and/or commonsensical reasoning about the social world; however, in order to avoid the epistemological obstacles represented in taken-for-granted assumptions, it is essential that we grow a critical awareness of the theoretical object and how it is linked with the language used, and that questions are asked about the limit of our interpretations of the world. The obvious question is how to put this into practice, and our answer is rather straightforward: by finding inspiration in theoretical texts, in examples that are of relevance, and in active and reflexive theory development on par with what we would normally require of a critical methodologist.

Volume III is organised into 12 chapters. In the first of two chapters written by Richard Swedberg, 'How do you Construct the Research Object in Sociology', the main focus is how the 'initial' research object is identified and constructed.

This is a theme seldom problematised since the choice of research objects is often taken for granted and habitually made. In contrast to those who argue that the sociological object exists sui generis, Swedberg's argument is that it gradually emerges during the research process. The chapter includes several examples from the sociology field that illuminate the complexity and difficulties of establishing the research object; a challenge well known to both students and scholars alike. It is also a reminder that we need to pay more attention to the *process* leading us from our initial theoretical assumptions and explanations and their consequences for the object under research. To clarify the process of construction, Swedberg introduces concepts analogous to the conventional terms 'explanandum' and 'explanans', i.e. 'observans' (to observe) and 'observandum' (the observation), to describe how we finally construct the research object. This gives a more realistic account of the early constructive stages of the research process, from the components of an explanation to the very identification of the explanandum.

Johs Hjellbrekke's chapter, 'Historical Epistemology, Sociology, and Statistics', follows Gaston Bachelard's (1884–1962) idea that facts must always be interpreted in light of the epistemological obstacles to be systematically challenged and overcome. Here, Hjellbrekke presents the historical background to an argument later found in Bourdieu et al.'s *The Craft of Sociology* that scientific facts are "conquered, constructed, and verified" (Bourdieu et al., p. 33). This chapter primarily discusses epistemological obstacles as related to statistics, but it is also evident that, prior to Thomas Kuhn, Bachelard offered a systematic account of scientific development. In the social sciences, as well as in statistics, this idea of theoretical constructions implies that taken-for-granted and commonsensical assumptions must be challenged and that the social sciences must, therefore, also be self-reflexive sciences challenging both the theoretical and methodological doxa. With a special emphasis on regression and path analyses, the chapter focuses on the methodological doxa by discussing how statistical modelling and techniques might be the origins of 'spontaneous' and/or commonsensical reasoning about the social world, thus unintentionally becoming epistemological obstacles of their own.

John Scott's chapter, 'Constructing Social Structure', reminds us that it is easy to become trapped in the idea of social structure as a metaphor for a 'social organism' with inherent functional needs and goals (cf. also Sohlberg, 2021, forthcoming). Consequently, it may be difficult to distinguish a specific sociological research object beyond systemic features with "supra-individual properties, and, perhaps, as collective entities with collective minds" (p. 38 in this volume). Like both Widerberg and Bjerrum Nielsen chapters, Scott's argument is that this scenario fails to give recognition to a sociological understanding of lived experiences. This is also an argument based on an understanding of social structure as "a combination of relational, institutional and embodied elements" (p. 39 in this volume; see also Scott, 2018). This way of seeing opens up a number of interesting sociological questions related to the shared norms and expectations framing human action, relations, and interactions, as well embodied structures expressed in "habits, tendencies, and dispositions that motivate individual actions and agency" (p. 39 in this volume). Contrary to a view where society is understood as a fully institutionalised social structure, Scott argues that we must pay closer attention to the conflicting and contradictory expectations and relations that constitute both social and system integration (Lockwood, 1992), as well as the lack of congruence between different societal levels (see also Mouzelis, 1995, who illustrated this problem).

In his chapter 'The Construction of Social Bonds', Göran Ahrne follows up Scott's proposition that the social relations at the core of how sociologists perceive society are often taken for granted and not fully substantiated. Rather than departing from an essential understanding of social relations or relations as manifested in, for example, scholarship in social network analysis, Ahrne proposes a sociology based on a relational understanding that enables us to study *what* binds people together in different types of social and organisational configurations, in a theory construction that builds on classical sociology as well as his own organisational sociology (Ahrne and Brunsson, 2019). His main concept, social bonds, remains surprisingly underdeveloped in sociology and is used in this chapter as an explorative lens to examine how they are established and what they are 'made of', presenting an effective illustration of how a seemingly homeless concept (see Volume 2) may be used as a tool to explore and construct various types of sociological research objects.

Raimund Hasse's 'Organisations as a Sociological Research Object' pursues the idea that there are almost no limits to what may constitute a research object, based upon scientific reasoning, with respect also to organisation and decision-making. In line with this, if there are no absolute truths, and if science is essentially a question of constructions, how do we know what we know? Sociological constructions are seldom just thought experiments (for a discussion of the role of thought experiments, see Betta and Swedberg's chapter in this volume) but are also grounded scientific programmes, methodology, and empirical observations. Hasse actively uses the metaphor of being 'behind the camera and in front of it' to represent the distinction between the researcher and those in front of the camera, i.e. the research objects. This is also a metaphor and argument that we, as sociologists, are not limited to one but are, in fact, various objects and that this a vital element in both the art of theory construction and in empirical analysis. In contrast to those who tend to approach the theory of organisations in a universal language of static and general functions, both Hasse and Ahrne argue that organisations still represent a relatively neglected sociological research object.

Emil R. Røyrvik's chapter 'Broken Promises and Lost Qualities' departs from a more fixed and coherent understanding of management as a research object in sociology and anthropology. Røyrvik is particularly interested in rhetorical object construction practices and how they guide sociologists and anthropologists in their ways of seeing, asking questions, and identifying problems, framed in the languages of institutional versus cultural logics. Røyrvik uses 'management by objectives' (MBO), a dominant type of management in recent years, as his case to interrogate the logics and mode of argumentation typically found in sociology and anthropology. Despite being, on the surface, rather similar concepts, his literature review reveals differences in how sociology and anthropology respectively approach the research object, illustrating how more or less implicit assumptions tend to be imported and translated into seemingly 'neutral' scientific concepts.

In her chapter 'Constructing and Researching the Object in Time and Space', Harriet Bjerrum Nielsen argues that theory construction ought to depart from how people and society are bound in time and space. Both dimensions have formed part of a general discussion as theoretical objects in sociology but with weak links to lived social structures and actors (see also Scott's chapter). Examples from Bjerrum Nielsen's own research, which followed different generational narratives over a longer period, illustrate multi-layers of time and meaning, gender relations in flux, and how a more elaborate understanding of time may inform our sociological understanding and theory construction.

The idea of theory construction, based on lived lives versus theory and on an epistemological break and distancing, is discussed and problematised by Karin Widerberg in her chapter 'Academic Star Wars: Pierre Bourdieu and Dorothy E. Smith on Academic Work'. The chapter provides the reader with an overview of Bourdieu and Smith's research programmes, with a special interest in how they constructed their sociological objects. As both sociologists tend to be identified with different research programmes and methodologies (Bourdieu with his correspondence analysis, and Smith with her institutional ethnography), despite the commonalities in their intellectual roots, they have rarely been compared. This also includes their insistence that sociological theorising should include a reflexivity of positionality and our relation to the object of study, which is, in neither case, restricted to subjectivity but to how this may be seen as part of what social structure and structurally embedded social relations entail. Similarities and differences between the two research programmes are illustrated through the use of New Public Management (NPM) in academia and academic work as an empirical case. The chapter relies heavily on descriptions of NPM in practice taken from Widerberg's own experiences as a university professor and is an example of how seemingly different theory constructions may be used to ask interesting new questions with different answers and solutions.

'Thought Experiments in Sociology', written by Michela Betta and Richard Swedberg, is another example of how we may improve our sociological imagination and theoretical vocabulary. Although the thought experiment, in contrast to the natural sciences, is rarely used explicitly in sociology, several examples can be found in the sociological canon. These examples, from Max Weber, Emile Durkheim, C. Wright Mill, and Robert. K. Merton, illustrate the usefulness of thought experiments in sociology and a way of reasoning that resonates well with Swedberg's programme of theorising (for example, see Swedberg, 2014a; 2014b).

Fasenfest and Das' chapter, 'Constructing the Conceptual Tools for the Global South', argues that we must go beyond the idea of the Global South as the ideal typical construct with a theoretical and conceptual space of its own (as in, for example, post-colonial theory). In contrast to those who claim that Marx's theoretical project is trapped in and limited to a theory of North Western Europe in a historical epoch very different from today, Fasenfest and Das focus on a more generic reading of Marx's *A Contribution to the Critique of the Political Economy* and more recent Marxist scholarship (including Das, 2017). Rather than being advocates of a singular epistemology of the Global South, they refer to epistemologies in the plural to address the specific social relations and variations within. In lieu of constructing the 'Global South' as a contrast to the 'Global North' and emphasising the difference between nations, their argument is that this is a systemic and historical feature and ongoing relation that can be found across this binary divide. This is clearly an example of a theory construction and application based on abstract theoretical constructs such as "class-exploitation, commodity, accumulation, and others" (p. 80) with the aim of understanding the complexity and variation in social relations. It is also a beneficial illustration of how Marx's theoretical framework is, and may continue to be, of relevance in a wider historical context, capturing the social and economic dynamics of the 'Global South'.

Michael Burrawoy's chapter, 'Living Theory: Reflections on Four Decades of Teaching Social Theory', touches upon several questions addressed by other authors in this volume. 'Living theory' refers to the challenges in the communication of theory, for example, how do we define sociology as an academic discipline beyond the legacy of Marx, Weber, and Durkheim? What are the options if we want to revitalise both new readings and theoretical applications of, for example, Marx (see Fasenfest and Das' chapter) into living theory? What is the role of theory and how should it be operationalised in the teaching and training of new generations of sociologists? Burawoy clearly favours an 'ethnographic approach' in contrast to a 'survey approach' in teaching and in how we learn to become theorists. This is not to say that a broader and more comprehensive knowledge of theoretical legacy and the sociological canon is unnecessary (as in 'the survey approach'), but it is a strong argument in favour of empowering students to play an active role in their own theorising (see also Swedberg in this volume). Rather than living with theory as part of the training to be a sociologist, the argument is that an active engagement with texts gives both the texts and students new energy to make sense of the world, engage in it, and find new ways of living within it.

In the postscript, we highlight the themes that have been the driving dynamics of this project. Throughout the project, we have attempted to avoid general declarations and high-flying proclamations regarding what, in essence, it means to construct the object in social science. Our primary type of argumentation has been in the form of examples rather than essential formulas. Such an approach could be seen as fragmented and superficially eclectic; however, in the epilogue, we briefly address these concerns on the basis of our experiences and discussions throughout the project. The project has not only been a book-project but also a forum for intense, stimulating, and principal discussions concerning topics that are seldom problematised in everyday academic activities. Hopefully, this stimulating milieu is reflected in the following chapters.

References

Ahrne, G. and Brunsson, N. (ed.). (2019). *Organization outside organizations: the abundance of partial organization in social life*. Cambridge, United Kingdom: Cambridge University Press.

Becker, H.S. (1998). *Tricks of the trade: how to think about your research while you're doing it*. Chicago, Illinois: Univ. of Chicago Press.

Bourdieu, P., Chamboredon, J.-C., and Passeron, J.-C. (1991). *The craft of sociology: epistemological preliminaries*. Berlin: Walter de Gruyter.

Das, R. (2017). *Marxist class theory for a sceptical world*. Leiden: Brill.

Lockwood, D. (1992). *Solidarity and schism: 'the problem of disorder' in Durkheimian and Marxist sociology*. Oxford: Clarendon.

Mills, C.W. (2000) [1959]. *The sociological imagination*. Oxford: Oxford University Press.

Mouzelis, N. (1995). *Sociological theory: What went wrong*. London and New York: Routledge.

Scott, J. (2018). "Social structure", in P. Sohlberg and H. Leiulfsrud (eds.). *Concepts in action. Conceptual constructionism*. Leiden & Boston: Brill.

Sennet, R. (2008). *The Craftsman*. London: Allan Lane.

Sohlberg, P. (2021, forthcoming). *Functionalist construction work in social science. The lost heritage*. London: Routledge.

Sohlberg, P. and Leiulfsrud, H. (2017). "Theory and theoretical operations", in P. Sohlberg and H. Leiulfsrud (eds.). *Theory in action. Theoretical constructionism*. Leiden and Boston: Brill.

Swedberg, R. (2014a). *The art of social theory*. Princeton, New Jersey: Princeton University Press.

Swedberg, R. (ed.) (2014b). *Theorizing in social science: the context of discovery*. Stanford: Stanford Social Sciences, an imprint of Stanford University Press.

CHAPTER 2

How Do You Establish the Research Object in Sociology?

Richard Swedberg

To determine the research object in a sociological analysis represents an important as well as a complex task. One reason for this is that every phenomenon, before it can be analysed and explained, has to be preceded by a process through which it is established. The way that this is done also has consequences for the explanation of the phenomenon. There exists, in brief, a distinct unity to the sociological research act.

These and related issues are explored in this chapter; and to assist in this, two new terms will be introduced. These are *observans*, meaning the process of observation, and *observandum*, the observed phenomenon. These terms complement two well-known terms in the philosophy of science, which are common also in sociology: *explanans* and *explanandum* ('the explanation' and 'the phenomenon to be explained'). Concrete examples from sociology are given throughout the chapter to illustrate the complexity of establishing the research object and that also show how this process is linked to the explanation.[1]

The terminology of explanans-explanandum was introduced by Carl Hempel and Paul Oppenheim in a famous article from 1948, which has exerted a huge influence on the philosophy of science (Hempel and Oppenheim, 1948; Salomon, 1989).[2] The article was read also by sociologists (e.g. Lazarsfeld,

---

1 As used in this chapter, the two neologisms (or protologisms) of *observans* and *observandum* have been created through intentional rhyming with *explanans-explanandum*. The terminology also has mnemonic qualities and is similar to *definiens-definiendum* (meaning how to define something, and what is defined), created from the verb *definire*, to define.

2 Before this article appeared, under the title of "Studies in the Logic of Explanation", most philosophers and scientists did not assign a central role to explanation. Many times, they did not even believe that it was possible to create scientific explanations, and that the focus of the analysis should instead be on description and observation. The situation that existed before the Hempel–Oppenheim article was published has been described in the following way: "Let's look at the dominant attitude of scientifically oriented philosophers and philosophically inclined scientists at the beginning of the twentieth century. By and large, they held that there is no such thing as scientific explanation – explanation lies beyond the scope of science, in such realms as metaphysics and theology. Karl Pearson stated it concisely: 'Nobody now believes that science explains anything; we all look upon it as a

1966: 463; Rowe, 1985). Amongst these, however, it underwent a decisive change, and took on such a general character that little was left of the original ideas of the original authors (e.g. Cohen, 1989: 192; Marshall, 1994: 167). The sociologists were, for example, not interested in the ideas of logical positivism, which were central to the argument of Hempel and Oppenheim.[3] The important notion of a covering law, the so-called DN-model (deductive-nomological model), was also ignored. All that was left of the original argument was the terminology of explanans-explanandum.[4] The reason why the sociologists liked this terminology was presumably that it constituted an easy and economical way of indicating the importance of clearly separating what is to be explained from the explanation, the explanandum from the explanans.

1   Observans – Observandum

So much for reception of the Hempel–Oppenheim article in mainstream sociology. The time has now come to engage directly with the main theme of this chapter, namely how the research object is constructed in sociology. To do so, something needs first to be said about the two terms observans and observandum. Both are homemade Latin and have been chosen in analogy with the Hempel–Oppenheim terms. '*Observans*' means 'to observe' and is the result of

---

shorthand description, as an economy of thought" (Salmon, 1999: 338). This kind of attitude changed with the publication of the article by Hempel and Oppenheim, which set off an important shift in opinion. It soon became common to see the scientific method as centred around the element of explanation (e.g. Salmon, 1989: 11; ff.: 126–135). Observation, in contrast, was viewed as considerably less important (e.g. Woodward, 2014). And the two were not connected; the explanation was independent of the observation.

3   According to logical positivism, it is imperative to express the scientific method in precise non-metaphysical language. As a result, what Hempel and Oppenheim are referring to in their article is not explanation and observation as these take place in reality, but to "the sentences" in which these are expressed in a scientific theory. They write, for example, that "by the explanandum, we understand the sentence describing the phenomenon to be explained (not the phenomenon itself); by explanans, the class of those sentences which are adduced to account for the phenomenon" (Hempel and Oppenheim, 1948: 136–137). For a discussion of the covering-law in sociology, see e.g. Gorski (2004).

4   That the terminology *explanans-explanandum* has been decoupled from logical positivism as well as the names of its two authors can be seen with the help of a few n-grams (of such terms as explanans-Oppenheim, explanans-covering law). Hempel also formulated an explanatory theory based on statistics, which was much closer to how sociologists worked at the time than the covering law theory. The so-called "inductive-statistical explanation" did not, however, have much impact; the covering law idea represented a much more innovative and influential idea (e.g. Hempel, 1965: 381–410).

a process of observation, similar to the way that '*explanans*' means 'to explain' and is the result of the process of explanation. The term '*observandum*' means 'the observation', similar to the way that '*explanandum*' means 'that which is to be explained'.

To focus on the process through which an observation is made, means that the observation, which is to be explained, is not viewed as something that is just given, natural or somehow self-evident. For one thing, when the researcher wants to study a topic, it takes some time before he or she knows what to look at and how to collect facts on the topic. Secondly, a process is involved also when it is decided what constitutes the kind of facts that are needed for the analysis to be sociological. A selection according to sociological principles has to be made; some facts need to be discarded and others selected. And thirdly, the facts that do exist about some phenomenon, are typically only available because of certain factors. Maybe some agency or group wants certain facts to be known and not others; maybe this makes some facts easier to establish and others harder. Figuring all of this out, and taking it into account, is part of the process of observation.

What has just been said needs to be explicated in some detail. First of all, there is a process involved when one 'establishes the phenomenon', to use Merton's formulation (Merton, 1987). One often begins by having some vague impressions; and from here one can go in several different directions. After some trial and error, the research object will become increasingly clear, and take such a form that it can be studied. If one starts with a given data set or with observations of one's own, this process will take different forms, but is essentially the same.

The following quote by philosopher Charles Sanders Peirce gives an indication of how complex the process of establishing the phenomenon can be; how it consists of different stages; and how it can go in different directions. One may begin the analysis, he says:

> by passively enough drinking in the impression of some nook in ... the Universe ... But attention soon passes into active observation, observation into musing, musing into a lively give and take between self and self. If one's observation and reflection are allowed to specialize themselves too much, the play will be converted into scientific study.
>
> PEIRCE, 1935: 214

The process that Peirce is describing can also be cast as a question: How do the facts come into being that make up an object of study? Much can obviously be said in answer to this question. In sociology, some of this knowledge can be found in books on methods, with their discussions of how to use techniques such as interviewing, participant observation, experiments, survey design, and so on. Statistics can also be very useful at this stage, since certain patterns can be discerned only if there is a huge number of observations (e.g. Goldthorpe, 2001). In some cases, special instruments have to be used when one makes observations, something that has been much discussed in the field of Science and Technology Studies (e.g. Shapin and Schaffer, 1985; Coopmans, Vertesi, Lynch and Wolgar, 2014).

William Whewel (1847: 233) has called the process of successive elimination, which is involved when you go from the first stage of observation to a later and more focused one, the 'decomposition of facts'. In his view, which was that of a natural scientist, observations have to be shaped in such a way that the phenomenon can be measured and quantified. To this can be added that for something to be quantified in the first place, it has to be streamlined in some fashion (or commensurated, if very different types of entities are involved – Nelson Espeland and Stevens 1998; 2008). Max Weber has also pointed out that a process of selection is always involved when one observes, both when the researcher chooses a topic and when he or she gathers information about it (e.g. Weber, 2013: 100–138).

When one goes from vague impressions to the establishment of sturdy facts in the social sciences, special attention has to be paid to *meaning*. First of all, according to Durkheim, the sociologist must break decisively with the everyday notions that people have of things and why they happen. "All preconceptions must be eradicated" (Durkheim, 1964: 31; see also Bourdieu, Chamboredon and Passeron, 1991).

Secondly, and according to Weber, a sociological analysis must in principle always take into account the meaning with which actors invest their actions. This should be done, not only when one is making observations, but also when the explanation is being constructed. Sociologists who assign importance to the way that people define the situation typically proceed in a similar way.

How the element of meaning is properly observed as well as established represents a contested issue. Weber himself, for example, suggested a few ways in which one can establish the meaning of the actors, such as through empathy and with the help of the actors' behaviour when it is rational in nature. He also emphasised that whilst the meaning of the actors has to be included in the object of study, it is only one of the factors that has to be taken into account. This goes not only for the stage of observation but also for that of the explanation.

Today's sociologists have at their disposal a number of methods that were not available in the days of Weber and Durkheim, such as the interview, participant observation, and discourse analysis, which can be used to get inside the minds of people and determine how they view things. But even if this is the case, the way that the meaning of actors can be established is still contested. The same can be said about the general importance of meaning for what is being observed, and how it should be made part of the explanation.

Let us now switch to the second set of issues that show that observation is always the result of a process; and that there exist no raw or natural facts. What is involved here is related to one factor that must not be forgotten, namely that sociology looks at a different aspect of things to, say, psychology, biology, and so on. This raises the following question which has to be addressed in every concrete piece of research: What exactly constitutes a *sociological* observandum?

No answer can be given to this question that is universally agreed upon. In modern sociology, however, it is often argued that what should be analysed and explained are *patterns of social behavior* (e.g. Merton, 1968; Zerubaval, 2007). In what follows this is also how the observandum of sociology will be defined. It should, however, also be added that the general argument of this chapter would not change, except in details, if some other way to define the sociological observandum were used.[5]

It is not enough for a sociologist, in other words, to go simply from impression to fact (Peirce, 1934; 1935) when conducting a sociological analysis. The observandum must also be aimed at existing social patterns so that the sociologist may try to single these out. In other words, a selection has to be made amongst the facts; and only behaviour that is *social* and also *repeated*, should be selected. The focus in sociology is on types and rules, not on single events or particular individuals (e.g. Weber, 1978: 19–20, 29).

It should also be noted that the use of the term 'behaviour', in the expression 'social patterns of behaviour', does not imply that the approach is behaviouristic. Exactly the opposite is true: following Weber, W.I. Thomas and others, one *always* has to include the meaning of the actors, when one establishes a social pattern. The analysis cannot be restricted to external behaviour.

It is also important that the element of 'behaviour' is understood in a broad sense. Not only open and unambiguous forms of behaviour can form a pattern. These can also come in the form of, say, categories and emotions. How to understand the interaction between what is biological and what is social is also becoming an important issue in today's sociology (see e.g. Freese and Shostak, 2009; Conlay, 2016).

---

5   One can also argue, for example, that sociology studies social facts (Durkheim), forms of social action (Weber), social forms (Simmel), the class struggle (Marx), and so on.

One sociologist who has consistently used the term 'social pattern' for the subject or observandum of sociology is Robert K. Merton. In *Social Theory and Social Structure,* he enumerates the types of facts that a sociologist should look out for, when he or she is doing research on social patterns of consequence:

In summary, then, the descriptive protocol [in a sociological analysis] should, so far as possible, include:

1. location of participants in the pattern within the social structure – differential participation;
2. consideration of alternative modes of behavior excluded by emphasis on the observed pattern (i.e. attention not only to what occurs but also to what is neglected by virtue of the existing pattern);
3. the emotive and cognitive meanings attached by participants to the pattern;
4. a distinction between the motivations for participating in the pattern and the objective behavior involved in the pattern;
5. regularities of behavior not recognized by participants but which are nonetheless associated with the central pattern of behavior.

That these desiderata for the observer's protocol are far from complete is altogether likely. But they do provide a tentative step in the direction of specifying points of observation which facilitate [the] analysis. They are intended to be somewhat more specific than the suggestions ordinarily found in general statements of procedure, such as those advising the observer to be sensitive to the "context of situation" (Merton, 1968: 114).

Of the five points that Merton makes in his discussion of the observandum in sociology, the first deals with major or central social patterns. Besides social structure, other examples that fall in this category are standard sociological concepts, such as institutions, roles and classes. The power of these patterns, Merton then goes on to say, is such that they can prevent or block attempts to form 'alternative modes of behavior'. This means that the latter can be hard to establish, but they must not be ignored.

Merton next notes that social patterns do not take the form only of patterns of behaviour in a narrow sense; they may also have important cognitive and emotional elements attached to them. He is similarly of the opinion that the meaning with which the actors invest their actions must always be studied, as part of establishing a social pattern. But he also cautions that the relationship of these meanings to actual behaviour is by no means self-evident. Certain actions and meanings usually go together, but this is not always the case. People may, for example, *not* act on their values, as Merton famously pointed out in his analysis of *The American Dilemma* (Merton, 1949; for another example of the 'attitudinal fallacy', see e.g. Jerolmack and Khan, 2014 as well as the discussion of this article in the same issue).

But as mentioned earlier in the chapter, there is more to the process of observation than establishing the phenomenon and locating the sociological observandum. There still exists one moment that the sociologist has to work through, before the observation is finished and ready to be explained. This has to do with the fact that the data that exist, as well as the possibility for the sociologist to generate new data on some pattern, are dependent on special social, economic and/or political factors. Some of these may make it hard to research some topic; others may facilitate it (e.g. 'strategic research material' – Merton, 1987). Whichever is the case, how these social, political and/or economic factors may affect the information that exists or can be generated about some phenomenon, needs to be taken into account and included in the analysis.

The last point is something about which especially Stanley Lieberson was very much concerned, namely that sociologists would work with data which were available to be analysed for reasons she or he did not know (Lieberson, 1987: 229–233).

> For example, only when the sexual mores are looser is it likely that one can do a survey of sexual mores. In a period of highly repressed sexuality it would not be easy to do such a survey – especially one that demanded official approval, access to certain types of people, funding, the ability to take a random sample, and so on.
>
> LIEBERSON, 1987: 230

By way of summarising this section, it can be said that no 'observation' can exist without first being preceded by a process of observation; and that the same goes for the research object. As has been shown, the process that is involved is quite complex. For one thing, there is what has been called 'establishing the phenomenon', in which the researcher focuses on the object of study by going from first impressions to facts. Second, since the analysis is to be sociological, the research object needs to be selected out and constituted from a sociological perspective. The process of 'establishing the phenomenon' means in other words that the phenomenon has to be *sociological.*

Thirdly, only some facts, and not others, are available to the sociologist for analysis (or can be generated with a certain research object in mind); and this is due to a process that the sociologist needs to analyse whilst understanding the various political, social, and/or economic factors that are at work here. When does this process work in his/her favor, and result in 'strategic research material'; and when does it create obstacles for the researcher? Following Merton once more, this set of issues depends on what can be called the "observability" of a phenomenon (Merton, 1968: 373–411).

2   Observandum Is Explanandum – and How This Affects the Explanans

At the outset of this chapter I wrote that explanation and observation are closely linked to one another. That this is the case is easy to see thanks to the terminology of obervans-observandum. What constitutes the explanandum in the original terminology of Hempel and Oppenheim ('the phenomenon') is by definition the same as what in this chapter has been called the observandum ('the result of observation'). This also means that the explanans is directly connected to the observans or the process of observation. There can be no explanation without there also being a process of observation.[6]

This argument also casts some new light on the suggestion that the facts in a scientific analysis are 'theory-laden' or 'theory-loaded', in the sense that they are influenced by the way that the observer looks at them (Hansen, 1958). It has, for example, been argued that if one works in accordance with a certain paradigm, one tends to view reality in a certain way (Kuhn, 1962: 126–129, 150). Where one scientist may just see a swinging stone, another may see a pendulum that traces a certain figure.

That the general perspective of a sociologist influences his or her observations is well established; and in this sense these observations are clearly 'theory-laden' (they are also influenced by the sociologist's prejudices and general being in society; see e.g. Bourdieu on reflexivity, and Weber on objectivity – Bourdieu and Wacquant, 1992; Weber, 2013).

Observations are theory-laden in another sense as well, namely because it is the task of sociologists to single out and establish social patterns of behaviour; and this means that certain theoretical assumptions have to be made in the process of observation. One assumes, for example, that sociology focuses on patterns, when the research object is decided on, and not on individual

---

6   The reader who is familiar with Hempel's work knows that he disagrees with what he terms "the paradox of theorizing" or the idea that "theoretical terms" can be fully replaced by "observational terms" (Hempel, 1965: 49, 87). This argument builds, however, on the very assumption that this chapter has tried to challenge, namely that you can draw a sharp line between observation and theory in sociology. It can be added that this distinction has for a long time been challenged in the philosophy of science.

behaviour. But what exactly is a pattern? Behaviour with meaning that is frequently repeated? And what exactly is a 'meaning', and how does it enter into action, and with what effect?

Whatever answer one gives to these questions, it is clear that without theory – here typically in the form of basic assumptions and assertions – it is not possible to do any sociological observation at all. And this, in its turn, means that explanations are not independent of observations.

There is also the fact that when the type of facts that are used in the analysis needs to be changed or complemented with new data, so may the explanation. If one finds, for example, that the phenomenon under study is not what one initially thought, one may want to go back and get some new data – and this can mean that also the explanation may have to change. One may, for example, want to study the dependence of women on their husbands in a marriage; but how one defines this dependence as one goes along (as being primarily economic, emotional or social, etc.), will influence the explanation. Again, in other words, observation and explanation are linked and not independent of one another.

If we now change from looking at the way that observation is influenced by the explanation, and instead turn to influence in the opposite direction, the following can be said. An explanation in sociology attempts to show how patterns of behaviour are generated, and how they change. This has several important consequences for the way that sociological research has to be carried out. First of all, it should be pointed out that an explanation is needed. The reason for stating this is that there exists an ambiguity with the term 'pattern', which can make it hard to differentiate between the establishment of a pattern and its explanation. The surface structure is mistaken for the deep, generative structure.

In other words, once a pattern has been established it may look to the researcher as if some social behaviour has been explained, since the data have now been cast in a sociological mold. When this is the case, there is a danger that the analysis will come to an end and not include an explanation. Analyses of big data and work in Artificial Intelligence are typically focused on patterns and can be helpful in the same way as statistics, in that they allow one to see patterns in large numbers. But they also come with a general tendency to disregard theory, including sociological theory. Such a term as 'data science', which is becoming popular, is an indication of how central data have become in modern society; it is its own subject (e.g. Lewis, 2018).

The tendency to establish social patterns without explaining them also exists in sociology. It is, for example, common in text analyses, where a number of techniques from such fields as computer science and AI are used by sociologists to map out social patterns in huge data sets. The patterns that are located in this manner exist exclusively in the use of language and are said to be expressions of roles, prejudices, ways of communicating, and so on (see e.g. Evans and Aceves, 2016). Whilst this way of proceeding can be valuable for a number of reasons, the point here is that the illusion is created that something has actually been explained.

Part of the problem here is that a number of sociological terms, such as role model, peer group, status symbol and so on, have entered the general vocabulary, which means that they need to be defined in an especially careful manner by the sociologist (e.g. Merton, 1982; Zuckerman, 1988). If this is not done, one may be tricked into believing that one is looking at a sociological phenomenon when in fact one is not. Again, the reason for this is that sociological terms that have entered the general culture 'have lost much or all of their original meaning and often acquired new meaning' (Merton and Wolfe 1984: 23). We also live, as Merton has put it, in a 'sociological culture'; and this raises a number of tricky issues as well (which unfortunately cannot be addressed here; see Merton and Wolfe, 1995: 35).[7]

That sociological theory is influenced by observation is also seen in the fact that empirical data will continually be fed into it, in the form of changes in theory that come from new analyses and their advances. Data now assume a new form, namely as theory, while they continue to have their roots in observation. Theory, to wit, is data laden.

Merton used to say that there exists a 'two-way traffic' between theory and empirical research in sociology; and this represents one way of describing their relationship (see e.g. Merton, 1968: 279, 312). One can also say that sociology is both theory-driven and data-driven, since the two at one point converge and to some extent are also part of one another. Sociology, however, cannot be exclusively theory-driven or data-driven, even if the theory part or the data part can vary in importance, depending on the situation in which sociology happens

---

7   The full quote about modern people living in a sociological culture reads as follows: "At the height of sociology's post-war popularity, Richard Rovere noted that "Those of us who have been educated in the twentieth century habitually think in sociological terms, whether or not we have had any training in sociology." This is, if anything, even more true in the 1990s. At this time Americans are exceptionally sociologically preoccupied, as they are, with questions of ethnicity, group loyalty, immigration, and lifestyles. We continue to live in a sociological culture, one important reason why sociology prospered in the United States. Sociology, moreover, has been influenced by the general culture and society. The women's movement has had a major impact on the field; the number of women sociologists has increased (Roos and Jones, 1993), and the influence of feminist ideas can be felt in nearly every area of academic sociology" (Merton and Wolfe, 1995: 35).

to find itself. According to the proponents of analytical sociology, for example, today's sociology needs much more of a sharp theoretical perspective (e.g. Hedström and Bearman, 2011). Whilst one can quarrel about the type of theory that is needed, it seems clear that modern sociology is awash in data and needs new and better theory.

But back to the main argument of the chapter. Whilst it would lead us too far astray to include a discussion here of what constitutes an explanation in sociology, two points need to be made that are relevant for an understanding of the link between the research object and its explanation, between observation and theory. The first is that a sociological explanation should be able to capture the creation and transformation of social patterns, and this means that statistics have to be used with some caution. A statistical explanation is not the same as a sociological explanation; the two follow, in principle, different logics (e.g. Goldthorpe, 2001; Hedström, 2009: 2–33, 101–113).

The second point is that the kind of explanation that is needed in sociology should ideally be able to capture the process of generating and changing social patterns in a way that is transparent. This should be done at a certain level of generality, so that the explanation can be used in empirical cases other than the ones that are analysed. Merton used the term 'social mechanism' for such general and transparent accounts of how social patterns are generated and transformed; and it represents an important part of his vision of a middle-range sociology.

Merton's study of the self-fulfilling prophecy can be cited as a fine example of this type of explanation (Merton, 1968: 475–490). But as every sociologist knows, it is very hard to discover new social mechanisms. What one usually finds is that what at first appears to be a new mechanism turns out to be a version of some basic model (e.g. Elster, 2009). This means that it may be better to try something easier. It is, for example, sometimes possible to adjust or add to some basic mechanism or to show how a new or unexpected phenomenon can be explained with the help of some existing social mechanism, and the like.

The idea that an observation has to be preceded by a process of observation is not so different from the fact that before you have an explanation, it has to be produced. One can for example view the invention of an explanation (abduction) as a case of a process that takes place in the head of the analyst, but which is otherwise analogous to what happens when he or she is observing something (e.g. Peirce, 1934: 171–172; Fann, 1970). And just like a good observer will look at things from several different angles, before settling on the right one, a good researcher will try to come up with several explanations (e.g. Stinchcombe, 1968: 13; Lave and March, 1975).

What has just been said about the way that sociologists deal with the construction of an explanation also suggests a different way of looking at the process from observans to explanans, over observandum/explanandum, to what has been presented so far in this chapter. This would be to study how this process is worked out *in actual practice* by sociologists. This means that one needs to switch from being concerned primarily with (formal) theory to (practical) theorizing. If the former can be likened to Goffman's front stage, the latter is represented by the back stage. When one theorises, one does not simply proceed from 1 to 2 to 3, with 1 standing for observans; 2 for observandum/explanandum; and 3 for explanans. In actual research, one may instead start with, say, 1; hop over 2; think a bit about 3; then go back to 2, repeat the whole thing, and so on. Similarly, what happens inside the very acts of observation (1) and explanation (3) also follows a similar non-linear logic in actual practice. The reason for this has to do with the existence of heuristic attempts, mistakes, dead ends, and so on.

3   Discussion

> What is novel here is the notion that the theory be expected to help
> us understand not only the pattern found but also the presence of
> the data and the distribution and nature of the causal variables that
> can be studied.
>
> LIEBERSON, 1987: 230

What are the practical consequences of the argument in this chapter about the research object, namely that observation is always preceded by a process of observation and that explanation and observation are closely linked to one another? A simple answer would be that more attention needs to be paid to this fact since it raises many important questions. And here the conceptual pair of observans-observandum can come in handy since they allow one to grasp this in a simple way.

To some extent, the answer to this question will also differ depending on what type of sociology is involved. In qualitative sociology, for example, the line between observation and explanation is often drawn differently from how it is done in quantitative studies. At times, it is not clearly delineated; and when this is the case, the description is more or less seen as the same as the explanation.

If we turn to quantitative sociology, it is quite common that the data sets that are being used have been put together by someone other than the analyst.

When this is the case, the process of producing the observation, and the conditions under which this takes place, is often ignored; and this may seriously compromise the analysis. Two other potential pitfalls have to do with the role of meaning, on the one hand, and the role of patterns in sociological analysis, on the other. When quantitative data are used, the element of meaning is sometimes missing or cast in such a stereotypical form that makes it easy to ignore. Both situations can result in major errors in the analysis. Some sociologists are content with simply establishing patterns and regularities, but do not show how these come into being and change; in brief, they do not show how they are generated. The idea that patterns can be used to explain other patterns is also not very helpful.

At the outset of this paper, it was mentioned that establishing the research object is a complex process that raises a number of difficult questions. Many of these have been mentioned but by no means solved. What has been provided, however, is a terminology that is hopefully useful when it comes to discussing of these issues. This terminology also shows the unity of the research act in sociology: explanans-explanandum is very closely linked to observans-observandum.

References

Beach, D. (2017). "The Analytical Core of Process Tracing", *Oxford Research Encyclopedia*. Available at http://politics.oxfordre.com/view/10.1093/acrefore/9780190228637.001.0001/acrefore-9780190228637-e-176 (accessed October 3, 2018).

Bourdieu, P, Chamboredon, J-C., and Passeron, J-C. (1991). *Sociology as a Craft: Epistemological Preliminaries*. New York: Walter de Gruyter.

Bourdieu, P. and Wacquant, L. (1992). *Invitation to a Reflexive Sociology*. Chicago: University of Chicago Press.

Cohen, B. (1989). *Developing Sociological Knowledge*. 2nd ed. Chicago: Nelson-Hall.

Conlay, D. (2016). "Socio-Genomic Research Using Genome-Wide Molecular Data", *Annual Review of Sociology* 42: 275–299.

Coopmans, C., Vertesi, J., Lynch, M., and Wolgar, S. (eds.). (2014). *Representation in Scientific Practice Revisited*. Cambridge, MA: The MIT Press.

Durkheim, E. (1964). *The Rules of Sociological Method*. New York: The Free Press.

Elster, J. (2009). *Tocqueville, The First Social Scientist*. Cambridge: Cambridge University Press.

Evans, J. and Aceves, P. (2016). "Machine Translation: Mining Text for Social Theory", *Annual Review of Sociology* 42: 21–50.

Fann. K.T. (1970). *Peirce's Theory of Abduction*. The Hague: Martinus Nijhoff.

Freese, J. and Shostak, S. (2009). "Genetics and Social Inquiry", *Annual Review of Sociology* 35: 107–128.

Goldthorpe, John (2001). "Causation, Statistics, and Sociology", *European Sociological Review* 17 (1): 1–20.

Gorski, P. (2004). "The Poverty of Deductivism: A Constructive Realist Model of Sociological Explanation", *Sociological Methodology* 34 (1): 1–33.

Hansen, N.R. (1958). *Patterns of Discovery: An Inquiry into the Conceptual Foundations of Science*. Cambridge: Cambridge University Press.

Hedström, P. and Bearman, P. (eds.). (2011). *The Oxford Handbook of Analytical Sociology*. New York: Oxford University Press.

Hedström, P. (2009). *Dissecting the Social: On the Principles of Analytical Sociology*. Cambridge: Cambridge University Press.

Hempel, C. and Oppenheim, P. (1948). "Studies in the Logic of Explanation", *Philosophy of Science* 15 (2): 135–175.

Hempel, C. (1965). *Aspects of Scientific Explanation*. New York: The Free Press.

Jerolmack, C. and Khan, S. (2014). "Talk is Cheap: Ethnography and the Attitudinal Fallacy", *Sociological Methods and Research* 43 (2): 178–209.

Kuhn, T. (1962). *The Structure of Scientific Revolutions*. Chicago: University of Chicago Press.

Lave, C. and March, J. (1975). *An Introduction to Models in the Social Sciences*. New York: University Press of America.

Lazarsfeld, P. (1966). "Philosophy of Science and Empirical Social Research", *Studies in the Logic and Foundations of Mathematic* 44: 463–477.

Lewis, M. (2018). "All the President's Data", in M. Lewis, *The Fifth Risk*. New York: W.W. Norton & Company.

Lieberson, S. (1987). *Making It Count: The Improvement of Social Research and Theory*. Berkeley, CA: University of California Press.

Marshall, G. (ed.). (1994). *The Concise Oxford Dictionary of Sociology*. Oxford: Oxford University Press.

Merton, R.K. (1949). "Discrimination and the American Creed", in R.M. MacIver (ed.). *Discrimination and National Welfare*. New York: Harper & Brothers.

Merton, R.K. (1968). *Social Theory and Social Structure*. Enlarged ed. New York: The Free Press.

Merton, R.K. (1982). "Our Sociological Vernacular", in Robert K. Merton (ed.). *Social Research and the Practicing Professions*. Cambridge, MA: Abt Books.

Merton, R.K. (1987). "Three Fragments from a Sociologist's Notebooks: Establishing the Phenomenon, Specified Ignorance, and Strategic Research Materials", *Annual Review of Sociology* 13: 1–29.

Merton, R.K. and Wolfe, A. (1995). "The Cultural and Social Incorporation of Sociological Knowledge", *American Sociologist* 26 (3): 15–39.

Nelson Espeland, W. and Stevens, M. (1998). "Commensuration as a Social Process", *Annual Review of Sociology* 24: 313–343.

Nelson Espeland, W. and Stevens, M. (2008). "A Sociology of Quantification", *European Journal of Sociology* 49 (3): 401–436.

Peirce, C.S. (1934). *Collected Papers of Charles Sanders Peirce*. Vol. V. Cambridge, MA: Belknap Press.

Peirce, C.S. (1935). *Collected Papers of Charles Sanders Peirce*. Vol. VI. Cambridge, MA: Belknap Press.

Roos, P. and Jones, K. (1993). "Shifting Gender Boundaries: Women's Inroads into Academic Sociology", *Work and Occupations* 20 (4): 395–428.

Rowe, M.E. (1985). *A Content Analysis of Citations to Four Prominent Philosophers of Science in Selected Sociology Journals*. Doctoral thesis. Department of Philosophy: North Texas State University. Available at https://digital.library.unt.edu/ark:/67531/metadc330872/ (accessed September 27, 2018).

Salmon, W. (1989). *Four Decades of Scientific Explanation*. Minneapolis, MI: University of Minnesota Press.

Salmon, W. (1999). "The Spirit of Logical Empiricism: Carl G. Hempel's Role in Twentieth-Century Philosophy", *Philosophy of Science* 66 (3): 333–350.

Shapin, S. and Schaffer, S. (1985). *Leviathan and the Airpump: Hobbes, Boyle, and the Experimental Life*. Princeton, NJ: Princeton University Press.

Stinchcombe, A. (1968). *Constructing Social Theories*. New York: Harcourt, Brace & World.

Weber, M. (1978). *Economy and Society: An Outline of Interpretive Sociology*. 2 vols. Berkeley, CA: University of California Press.

Weber, M. (2013). *Collected Methodological Writings*. London: Routledge.

Whewell, W. (1847). *History of the Inductive Sciences*. Vol. 2. A new edition, London: John W. Parker and Son.

Woodward, J. (2014). "Scientific Explanation." *Stanford Encyclopedia of Philosophy*. Available at https://plato.stanford.edu/entries/scientific-explanation/ (accessed on October 3, 2018).

Zerubaval, E. (2007). "Generally Speaking: The Logic and Mechanics of Social Pattern Analysis", *Sociological Forum* 22 (2): 131–145.

Zuckerman, H. (1988). "The Role of the Role Model: The Other Side of a Sociological Coinage", edited by H. O'Gorman. *Surveying Social Life*. Middletown, CO: Wesleyan University Press.

CHAPTER 3

Historical Epistemology, Sociology, and Statistics

Johs Hjellbrekke

Despite calls for an epistemological unity of science, often centred around Karl Popper's critical rationalism and falsificationism (Popper, 1934; e.g. Elster, 1998), the social sciences have been, and still remain, both multi-perspective sciences and sciences where different epistemological frameworks co-exist.[1] No single theory of action is commonly accepted as *the* general theory of action, and the validity of Popper's framework, when applied to objects in the *social* sciences, has repeatedly been questioned (e.g. Passeron, 1992).

The dominance of critical rationalism has been subject to variation and linked to country-specific historical scientific trajectories. For instance, when sociology was established as a university discipline in Norway, it was strongly inspired by a few select American traditions (see Hjellbrekke and Prieur, 2018). Consequently, positivist positions long reigned amongst the Norwegian 'thought collectives' (Fleck, 1935), while other schools of thought and epistemological traditions were given less attention. One of these relatively neglected epistemological frameworks was that of the French historical epistemology, originating in the works of Gaston Bachelard (1884–1962): whereas Thomas Kuhn's notion of paradigm has been highly appropriated from the natural sciences, Bachelard's idea of the dynamics of science has, probably partly due to language barriers, unfortunately, received far less attention.

For Bachelard, scientific progress is analysed as an uneven process, characterised by a series of 'ruptures' between common-sense knowledge and scientific knowledge. This commonsensical knowledge of a research object constitutes an *epistemological obstacle* that must be overcome for scientific knowledge to be gained, while in order to identify these ruptures, the study of science(s) and scientific progress must necessarily also be historical. How have specific epistemological obstacles dominated, how have they been identified, and, thereafter, how have they been overcome?

Bachelard further emphasised that each discipline constructs its own research objects (Bachelard, 1938)—the history of science is, therefore, the history of *sciences*. In sociology, this position has found one of its clearest

---

1   I would like to thank Vegard Jarness, Olav Korsnes, Mike Savage, Maren Toft, and the two editors, Håkon Leiulfsrud and Peter Sohlberg, for their valuable comments on this manuscript.

formulations in the works of Pierre Bourdieu (1930–2002), who proposed that scientific facts must be conquered, constructed, and verified (Bourdieu, Chamboredon and Passeron, 1968). Without embracing a radical constructivism, social-scientific facts are never given but must be constructed, like all other scientific facts. Given that social scientists are part of the society they analyse, this implies that the social sciences must also be reflexive sciences, that is, sciences that systematically seek to challenge the structures in their respective scientific and methodological doxa. To what degree are these doxas dominated by commonsensical understandings and perceptions of the social phenomenon under investigation? And to what degree is the research object pre-constructed by these perceptions?

The view that each discipline constructs its own research objects also has some important epistemological implications in interdisciplinary work. Tools, techniques, concepts, and theoretical and methodological approaches that have been gained or developed in one discipline might have contributed to major scientific insights within that discipline. However, when they are imported into a different science and applied to other research objects, they might not only be incompatible with fundamental properties of these objects; at worst, they can themselves become epistemological obstacles, and result in the strengthening of trivial, spontaneous, primary, and, thus, also commonsensical understandings of the objects under investigation.

To address this problem necessitates a 'double historicity'. First, the history of the imported technique or tool must be mapped out. For example, what were the research questions one once intended to be answered, and what were the main properties of the research objects under investigation? In what ways did a given technique or approach contribute to the construction of the object? Secondly, in what ways was this taken or not taken into account when the given technique or concept was imported into a different discipline, for example, sociology?

This chapter will address this issue through a historically oriented presentation of the relation between sociology and statistics. First, a general introduction to the fundamental principles of historical epistemology will be given. Thereafter, and inspired by Bachalard's historical epistemology, a brief history of statistics will be presented, before potential epistemological obstacles, stemming from the import of statistical techniques into sociology, are discussed.

1   The Historical Epistemology of Gaston Bachelard

The fundamentals of Bachelard's historical epistemology were laid out in a series of studies from 1927 onwards. In books such as *Le nouvel esprit scientifique* (Bachelard, 1934), *La formation de l'esprit scientifique* (Bachelard, 1938), *La philosophie du non* (Bachelard, 1940), and *Le rationalisme appliqué* (Bachelard, 1949), Bachelard undertook detailed, historical analyses of how natural sciences disciplines had progressed through a series of ruptures or breaks between the everyday or commonsensical knowledge of a given object and the *scientific* knowledge of the same object. Whereas the first is, to a high degree, based on spontaneous perceptions, ways of reasoning, and entities that are taken for granted, the latter must be based on the opposite. Scientific knowledge cannot simply be gained through the accumulation and generalisation of empiricist observations; to develop theoretically informed scientific knowledge, common-sense understandings and spontaneous perceptions of the research object must, instead, be challenged through the elimination of naïve-realistic, empiricist, and metaphorical elements from the concepts used in its construction.

Two notions occupy a central position in Bachelard's approach: the epistemological obstacle and the epistemological profile. The 'epistemological profile' describes the relative importance of the epistemological or philosophical basis of various forms of knowledge in the conceptualisations of a given phenomenon. In *La philosophie du non* (Bachelard, 1940), Bachelard distinguished naïve realism, empiricism, classic rationalism, complete or complex rationalism, and dialectic rationalism as bases of knowledge when analysing his own notions of 'mass' and 'energy'. Scientific knowledge must be acquired through an 'applied rationalism', that is, an a posteriori dialectical reasoning between idealism and empiricism where the scientist systematically seeks to develop dialectical alternatives to dominant understandings and perceptions of the phenomenon under scrutiny.

In this way, existing epistemological obstacles, which hinder the acquisition of scientific knowledge, are challenged and can be overcome through an epistemological break or rupture with commonsensical understandings of the research object. Put in Bourdieusian terms, the structures in the doxa are challenged. New, more precise questions can be asked, and new, scientific insights can be won. Bachelard exemplified this using numerous case studies from chemistry and physics, for example, the move from a Lavoisien to a non-Lavoisien chemistry, and the history of the understanding of electricity and how this insight came to revolutionise all hitherto known illumination techniques. In the 18th century, fire, electricity, and light were regarded as substantially equivalent; to the scholars of this time, and in the popular understanding, electricity *was* fire and light. Since all illumination techniques were based on the combustion of a substance, the first attempts at using electricity for this purpose sought to 'feed' electricity-fire-light with a substance to combust;

however, with Edison's light bulb, the principle of combustion was substituted with the principle of *non*-combustion. The dominant understanding of electricity based on primary and popular observations was, thus, substituted with a new understanding based on the principles of physics—Joule's law of heating—rather than primary observations (Bachelard, 1938).

Bachelard was not the only one to think along these lines or to emphasise the importance of the social anchoring of knowledge. In 1934, in a path-breaking study of how the understanding of syphilis had changed over the centuries, the Polish microbiologist Ludwik Fleck addressed the problem of how 'Denkstile' ('thought styles') and 'Denkkollektive' ('thought collectives') actively contributed to the discovery, but also non-discovery, of valid scientific facts. In the 15th century, what was not yet conceptualised as syphilis was generally regarded as caused by astrological constellations: '... the conjunction of Saturn and Jupiter under the sign of Scorpio and the House of Mars ... was the cause of the carnal scourge' (Fleck, 1979: 2). With the advent of biochemistry and the modern microscope, scientists' attention was turned towards the blood, and syphilis was finally understood as a blood disease. A cure, however, proved hard to find, and attempts at finding a vaccine also proved futile. Only with the arrival of modern bacteriology and the identification of the bacteria *Spirochaeta pallida* could a precise, shared understanding of the disease and its causes be established.

Compared to, and probably also *due* to the publication of Karl Popper's *The Logic of Explanation* (1935), Fleck's book went largely unnoticed for several decades, and it would take 30 years before Thomas S. Kuhn (1962) emphasised a similar position. However, Fleck's argument, that scientific facts are discovered and established by thought collectives, and that these collectives are characterised by thought styles, is not only important of itself; rather, it can also be regarded as a complementary element to Bachelard's historical epistemology. A study of epistemological obstacles must also be a historical study of how thought collectives and styles can result in discipline-specific epistemological obstacles. As Fleck pointed out, "... the more deeply one enters into a scientific field, the stronger will be the bond with the thought collective and the closer the contact with the scientist" (Fleck, 1979: 82), and when thought styles from one discipline are imposed on a research object in a different discipline, there is also the risk that it may result in new epistemological obstacles.

In the next sections, this will be discussed by examining how the relations between the social sciences and statistics have changed over time. The first step is to identify changing conceptualisations and, thus, also the changing epistemological profiles of 'statistics'.

2   Conceptualisations of 'Statistics'

In his lectures on the history of statistics, Sir Karl Pearson (Pearson, 1977) traced the term 'statistik' back to Gottfried von Achenwall, who, in 1752, used it to describe an early version of political science, or 'Statskunde' (Hacking, 1990: 25). To von Achenwall, 'statistik' was a synthesis of history and law, and quantified information and mathematical theory played no role in his descriptions of various European states. Most books on the history of statistics, therefore, have taken a different point of departure, for example, John Graunt's 1662 text 'Natural and Political Observations made upon the Bills of Mortality' (e.g. Desrosières, 1993). Graunt's work gave rise to a discipline that first was coined as 'political arithmetic', and 130 years would pass before John Sinclair adopted von Achenwall's concept in his *The Statistical Account of Scotland Drawn upon the Communications of the Ministers of Different Parishes* in 1798. The reaction from Göttingen, where von Achenwall held his chair, was negative, but from the start of the 19th century and onwards, 'statistics' was increasingly associated with analyses of various states based on quantified information about their citizens. By 1830, this understanding or 'thought style' had come to dominate in both England and France (Hacking, 1990).

Political arithmetic took inspiration from both mathematical and probability theories, but in the epistemological profile of early statistics, non-scientific elements played a major role. The development of probability theory was linked to calculations about wins and losses in gambling and insurance risk rates. Conclusions were often linked to moral judgements about gambling, insurance premiums, etc., and, briefly summarised, from 1660–1800 statistics was generally regarded as a model for enlightenment and the improvement of one's behaviour. The dominating understanding of causality was deterministic, and probability theory was, therefore, regarded as an example of the limitations of mankind's knowledge. All actions, events, and processes were, in reality, governed by laws that mankind had yet to discover (Gigerenzer et al., 1995: chapters 1–2; Hacking, 2006).

With the expansion of the modern state and its apparatus for collecting information about its citizens, this view on probability theory gradually changed. Classic probability theory was substituted by an alternative probability theory that was exclusively based on mathematics. Its epistemological profile had changed, and moral and religious elements played a far less important role: probability theory was now perceived as an analytical tool and no longer as a model for moral enlightenment. New datasets on the states' populations meant new distributions to analyse, which would not only lead to a change from a deterministic to a probabilistic understanding of causality but also to the earliest versions of sampling theory and hypothesis testing (Gigerenzer et al., 1995: op. cit.). Statistics was also partly regarded as a laboratory for social theory (Schweber, 1996: 107–128), while political and ideological elements played a central role in debates about questions regarding how to measure centrality and variation and, thus, regarding the development of the discipline.

To the 'social physicist' Adolphe Quetelet, 'l'homme moyen' was more than an ideal *type*: it was also an ideal. Individual variations around or deviations from various measures of centrality were regarded as a demonstration of the fact that individuals were lesser copies of the ideal. Thematically, the main focus was on discovering the characteristics of social groups and on the laws governing their actions (Desrosières, 1993: 94–99; Hacking, 1990: 115–124). The later eugenicist, Sir Francis Galton, held a different view. Group characteristics were of lesser importance, and the quest to identify individuals with the highest perceived genetic value meant that methods for discovering the deviations from the mean had to be developed (Porter, 1986: 129). In its epistemological profile, statistics was, therefore, still strongly influenced by 'external' elements, and the questions raised from these perspectives would have a direct impact on the development and invention of statistical measures.

When statistics was finally institutionalised as a scientific discipline between 1885 and 1935 (see MacKenzie, 1981), it also 'gained independence' from research questions originating in the state apparatus or in these early versions of social science. During these decades, statistics became a discipline comprising the methods and principles for the mathematical analysis of numerical information about the units of analysis, regardless of what these units were. Even so, many of the central contributions from these years stemmed from the circles around Karl Pearson, Egon S. Pearson, and Jerzey Neyman at the Galton Laboratories, and Ronald A. Fisher at the Rothamsted Experimental Station. Thematically, research questions in, for example, biometry, genetics, physics, chemistry, and agricultural science, dominated. Whereas Poisson, Quetelet, and Galton worked on observational data on individuals, the development of new techniques and research designs were now predominantly based on an experimental epistemology and data from experiments. The frequentist principles of hypothesis testing, where a null hypothesis is tested against an alternative hypothesis, outlined by Fisher in 1935 (Fisher, 1935: 15–17), can be said to be a 'perfect match' with Popper's claim about falsification as a scientific demarcation criterion, which was specified the very same year (Popper, 1935: 40–42). Taken together, these two schools would form a very dominant thought style and one that also would come to lead not only in experimental sciences but also in quantitative social science.

From being a discipline strongly influenced *by* the social sciences, statistics, thus, became a science that would have a strong influence *on* the social sciences in the post-war years. In sociology and political science, increasing access to data from surveys based on probability samples would strengthen the bonds between politicians and social scientists (for instance, see Savage, 2010), while the social sciences would also adopt statistical techniques and analytical designs that were developed using data from experimental studies. With this import came an inherent unity of science, epistemology, and technology, centred around the application of a few select statistical models and, in particular, the regression model and its derivative, path analysis. Elements in statistical modelling, thus, became key elements in what we might coin the methodological doxa in sociology, that is, methodological elements that we tend to take for granted or have difficulties questioning, and which, therefore, not only exert an influence on our construction of the research object but also have the capacity to effectively limit sociological theorising and reasoning. For this reason, in the post-war years, statistical models and research designs had the capacity to become epistemological obstacles of their own.

3   Statistical Modelling and Sociological Theorising

Path analysis, or causal graphs, was developed by Sewall Wright (1889–1988) in his groundbreaking work in genetics, more precisely in his study of the factors influencing the birth weights of guinea pigs (see Wright, 1921; 1934). When this research design made its way into the social sciences from the 1960s onwards, its impact was both strong and long-lasting (for instance, see Wolfle, 2003). The first attempts to apply this method in sociological studies were made by Hubert M. Blalock, who, in his influential book *Causal Inferences in Nonexperimental Research*, wholeheartedly pointed to the regression model and path analysis as the (only) way forward, proposing that sociological theories should be formulated as statistical models: "Why not formulate our causal laws and other theories in terms of these ideal models and completely isolated systems, then noting how the real world deviates from such a model?" (Blalock, 1961: 17). As aptly pointed out by Xie (2007: 146), Blalock did not stop at this and went on to make a bold claim: "It is the regression coefficients which give us the laws of science" (Blalock, 1961: 51). According to Blalock, research objects in sociology should, therefore, be constructed as statistical models; however, the limitations inherent in statistical models would also become the limitations of the sociological model.

The path diagram's appeal is understandable. They simplify complex relations, and though the calculations behind them might be complicated, the diagrams themselves are rather intuitive: they are close to our spontaneous and, thus, commonsensical understandings of causal relations and chains, in other words, exactly what Bachelard warned against in scientific reasoning. Nevertheless, Blalock paid less attention to the epistemological problems that followed with the import of these techniques into the social sciences. To analyse social phenomena as isolated systems was (and remains) highly problematic; most social phenomena are per se *open* systems (see Bhaskar, 1989), and to adopt (and adapt) the understanding of causality found in experimental studies into nonexperimental studies was not any less problematic. In an experiment, the supposed causal variable could be manipulated; in a nonexperimental study, it could not. Even so, Blalock's call for this version of 'methodological reductionism' attracted many followers.

Though Blalock was influential, the two most important publications were probably Otis Dudley Duncan's "Path Analysis: Sociological Examples" in the American Journal of Sociology (1966) and Blau and Duncan's highly influential study *The American Occupational Structure* (1967), where path analysis and the Origin-Education-Destination (or OED) model were used to analyse social and occupational mobility in the United States. In combination, Blalock and Duncan's publications formed the basis for a new school, or what Fleck coined 'thought collective', in sociology; however, just as Duncan had warned against a universal application of his socio-economic index (Duncan, 1961: 139–140), he also warned against the (over)optimistic views held by Blalock regarding path analysis and causality. To Duncan, path analysis was *not* a causal *method*: "Path analysis focuses on the problem of interpretation and does not purport to be a method for discovering causes" (Duncan, 1966: 1). This warning was repeated in Blau and Duncan (1967; see also Xie, 2007: ibid.), but whether or not it was heeded is, at best, an open question.

Despite an increasing critique against regression-based approaches to causality (e.g. Holland 1986; 1993; Freedman, 1991) and the overall applicability of the general linear model in the social sciences (Abbott, 2001), multiple examples—and too many to list here—have pointed to the contrary. Strong claims for the supremacy of the regression model over all other techniques can still also easily be found (for instance, Ringdal, 2013).[2] One unfortunate consequence of these claims calling for a 'technical unity of quantitative social

---

2 Building directly on Blalock (1961) and Simon (1977), the Norwegian sociologist Kristen Ringdal has, for instance, advocated a position where causal relations should be conceptualised in ways that are 'in harmony with our intuitive understandings of causality' and modelled as sets of linear, additive equations in closed systems, as in path analysis and LISREL-models (Ringdal, 1987: 14–15).

science', or what we might label as 'methodological reductionism', is that they also result in *theoretical* reductionism, where the sociological theory becomes synonymous with, or limited to, what can be tested by one specific statistical model. Put differently, the preferred statistical model becomes a straitjacket when theorising about social phenomena.

Relatedly, another unfortunate consequence of the dominance of this approach was that a trivial distinction based on time order was made into a central principle for reasoning about causality, or, in the words of James A. Davis:

> I will lay out four rules, but each is really only a special application of the great principle of causal order: after cannot cause before ... there is no way to change the past ... one way arrows flow with time.
>
> DAVIS, 1985: 11

In its ultimate consequence, this position invites both a self-evident and unidirectional reasoning about causality and causal processes and an almost automated classification of so-called dependent and independent variables. The theoretical poverty of this approach was criticised by Herbert Blumer as early as 1956, when, from a standpoint of symbolic interactionism, he highlighted that the 'independent' variable did not exert a direct influence on the 'dependent' variable, but that this influence was mediated by an interpretive process in most situations. To Blumer, the implication was that the sociology of variables should only be applied to phenomena that were not mediated by an interpretative process and used to objectify stable patterns of interpretations that not could be revealed by studying the agents' experiences (Blumer, 1956: 132–139). In other words, the limitations of the sociology of variables had to be acknowledged: as a general framework for building and testing sociological theories, it was insufficient.

Secondly, whenever interaction effects come into play, independent variables are no longer really independent. Their causal capacity and potential causal outcome will also be a product of their interactions with other 'independent' variables, or, as Bourdieu first pointed out in a little cited but highly important book published in 1966:

> The same causes may in each case produce different effects. ... In these circumstances, isn't it methodologically absurd to pretend to isolate the influence of this or that factor, and isn't the only reasonable enterprise to try to determine the structure of the constellation of factors that influence the birth rate at a given moment in time, in a given group of society?
>
> DARRAS, 1966: 144, author's translation

This was further outlined in Bourdieu's most famous book, *Distinction*:

> The particular relations between a dependent variable (political opin-
> ion) and so-called independent variables such as sex, age and religion,
> tend to dissimulate the complete system of relations that make up the
> true principle of the force and form specific to the effects recorded in
> such and such particular correlation.
>
> BOURDIEU, 1979: 103

The implication of this for Bourdieu was that he turned towards multiple correspondence analysis (see Hjellbrekke, 2018) in his own works, a method that
he found to be epistemologically and methodologically compatible with his
own methodological relationism (Bourdieu, 2001).

   In Scandinavian quantitative sociology, the strength of the thought collective centred around the regression model has had yet another unfortunate
consequence in that the breakthroughs obtained by way of other methodological approaches have, to a high degree, either been neglected, played a minimal
role, or only been referred to *en passant* in Scandinavian studies on similar topics. For instance, network analysis, a relational method that has led to important insights, for instance in the study of labour markets (Granovetter, 1974) and
elite integration (Useem, 1986), has, with a few noteworthy exceptions (e.g.
Grønmo and Løyning, 2003; Toubøl and Larsen, 2017) rarely been applied in
Scandinavian sociology. Just as the import from US sociology to Scandinavian
sociology in the 1960s was both selective and partial (see Zetterberg, 1966),
major advances in international sociology have not necessarily found resonance among Scandinavian scholars. Instead, dominant sociological traditions from the US would easily become even more dominant when imported
to Scandinavia, laying the groundwork for what we might call the 'big fish in a
small pond' syndrome.

4   Concluding Comments

More than 30 years ago, Andrew Abbott observed that:

> ... sociological theory and methods are divided by the unnecessarily nar-
> row approach to causality implicit in the dominant methods in the disci-
> pline. Although analysts studying social structure through network data
> and workers studying entity processes through demographic methods
> have quietly developed alternatives, all too often general linear models

have led to general linear reality, to a limited way of imagining social processes.

ABBOTT, 2001: 37

From the standpoint of Bachelard's historical epistemology, and with a focus on the relation between sociology and statistics, this chapter has sought to identify two of the problems that should be taken seriously when relations between theory and methods are addressed.

Firstly, statistical techniques are never *just* techniques but have been developed in specific epistemological contexts and to provide answers to discipline-specific research questions. For this reason, they have not only an epistemological history of their own but also consequences for how we construct our research objects. If this is not acknowledged, there is an imminent risk that the techniques themselves will become epistemological obstacles in sociological theorising.

Secondly, the methodological reductionism inherent in the calls for a 'technical' unity of science will necessarily also result in a theoretical reductionism, that is, a reductionism that can impoverish sociological theorising. Instead of being instruments for gaining knowledge, in this scenario, methods become instruments that function as limitations to our knowledge about the social world. Bachelard's historical epistemology serves as a reminder of this: that epistemological obstacles should be sought, identified, and confronted, and that methodology should not become a substitution for sociology. As pointed out by the French statistician Ludovic Lebart, "Statistics does not explain anything—but provides potential elements for explanation" (Lebart et al., 1997: 209).[3]

References

Abbott, A. (2001) [1988]. "Transcending General Linear Reality", in. Abbott, A. (ed.). *Time Matters. On Theory and Method.* Chicago: The University of Chicago Press.

Bachelard, G. (1934). *Le nouvel esprit scientifique.* Paris: Presses Universitaires de France.

Bachelard, G. (1938). *La formation de l'esprit scientifique.* Paris: J. Vrin.

Bachelard, G. (1940). *La philosophie du non.* Paris: Presses Universitaires de France.

Bachelard, G. (1949). *Le rationalisme appliqué.* Paris: Presses Universitaires de France.

Bhaskar, R. (1989). *The Possibility of Naturalism: A philosophical critique of the contemporary human sciences.* London: Routledge.

---

3 Translated from the original French text.

Blalock, H. (1961). *Causal Inference in Nonexperimental Research.* Chapel Hill, NC: University of North Carolina Press.

Blau, P. and Duncan, O.D. (1967). *The American Occupational Structure.* New York: John Wiley.

Blumer, H. (1956). "Sociological Analysis and the "Variable"", *American Sociological Review*, Vol. XXII: 683–690.

Bourdieu, P. (1984) [1979]. *Distinction.* Cambridge, MA: Harvard University Press.

Bourdieu, P. (2001). *Science de la science et réflexivité.* Paris: Raisons d'agir.

Bourdieu, P., Chamboredon, J.-C., and Passeron, J.-C. (1968). *Le métier de sociologue. Préalables épistemologiques.* Paris: Mouton.

Darras, H.J. (1966). *Le partage des bénéfices. Expansion et inégalité en France.* Paris: Éditions de Minuit.

Davis, J. (1985). *The Logic of the Causal Order.* Newbury Park: Sage Publications.

Desrosières, A. (2002) [1993]. *The Politics of Large Numbers: A History of Statistical Reasoning.* Cambridge, MA: Harvard University Press.

Duncan, O.-D. (1961). "A socio-economic index for all occupations.", in A.J. Reiss Jr. (ed.). *Occupations and Social Status.* New York: Free Press.

Duncan, O.-D. (1966). "Path Analysis: Sociological Examples.", *American Journal of Sociology* 72 (1): 1–16.

Elster, J. (1998). "A Plea for Mechanisms", in P. Hedström and R. Swedberg (eds.). *Social Mechanisms. An Analytical Approach to Social Theory.* Oxford: Oxford University Press.

Fisher, R.A. (1935). *The Design of Experiments.* Oxford: Oxford University Press.

Fleck, L. (1979) [1935]. *Genesis and Development of a Scientific Fact.* Chicago: The University of Chicago Press.

Freedman, D.A. (1991). "Statistical models and shoe leather", *Sociological Methodology* 21: 291–313.

Gigerenzer, G., et al. (1995). *The Empire of Chance.* Cambridge: Cambridge University Press.

Granovetter, M. (1974). *Getting a job. A Study of Contact and Careers.* Chicago: The University of Chicago Press.

Grønmo, S. and Løyning, T. (2003). *Sosiale nettverk og økonomisk makt. Overlappende styremedlemskap mellom norske bedrifter 1970–2000* [Social Networks and Economic Power. Interlocking Board Memberships Between Norwegian Corporations 1970–2000]. Bergen: Fagbokforlaget.

Hacking, I. (1990). *The Taming of Chance.* Cambridge: Cambridge University Press.

Hacking, I. (2006). *The emergence of probability: a philosophical study of early ideas about probability, induction and statistical inference.* (2nd ed.). Cambridge: Cambridge University Press.

Hjellbrekke, J. (2018). *Multiple Correspondence Analysis for the Social Sciences.* London: Routledge.

Hjellbrekke, J. and Prieur, A. (2018). "On the Reception of Bourdieu's Sociology in the World's Most Equal Societies", in T. Medvetz and J.J. Sallaz (eds.). *Oxford Handbook of Pierre Bourdieu*. Oxford: Oxford University Press.

Holland, P. (1986). "Statistics and Causal Inference", *Journal of the American Statistical Association* 81 (396): 945–970.

Holland, P. (1993). "Which Comes First, Cause or Effect?", in Keren and Lewis (eds.). *A Handbook for Data Analysis in The Behavioural Sciences: Methodological Issues.* Hillsdale, NJ: Lawrence Erlbaum Associates, Publishers.

Kuhn, T.S. (1962). *The Structure of Scientific Revolutions.* Chicago: Chicago University Press.

Lebart, L., Morineau, A., and Piron, M. (1997). *Statistique exploratoire multidimensionnelle.* 2eme ed. Paris: Dunod.

MacKenzie, D.A. (1981). *Statistics in Britain 1865–1930. The Social Construction of Scientific Knowledge.* Edinburgh: Edinburgh University Press.

Passeron, J.-C. (1992). *Le raisonnement sociologique. L'espace non-popperien du raisonnement naturel.* Paris: Nathan.

Pearson, K. (1977). *The History of Statistics in the 17th & 18th Centuries.* London: Charles Griffin & co. Ltd.

Popper, K. (1979) [1934]. *The Logic of Scientific Discovery.* London: Routledge.

Porter, T. (1986). *The Rise of Statistical Thinking 1820–1900.* Princeton: Princeton University Press.

Ringdal, K. (1987). *Kausalanalyse i samfunnsvitenskap* [Causal Analysis in the Social Sciences]. Oslo: Universitetsforlaget.

Ringdal, K. (2013). *Enhet og mangfold* [Unity and Diversity]. Bergen: Fagbokforlaget.

Savage, M. (2010). *Identities and Social Change in Britain since 1940. The Politics of Method.* Oxford: Oxford University Press.

Schweber, L. (1996). "L'histoire de la statistique, laboratoire pour la théorie sociale", *Revue francaise de sociologie,* XXXVII-1: 277–310.

Simon, H. (1977). *Models of Discovery: and other topics in the methods of science.* Dordrecht, Holland: Reidel.

Toubøl, J. and Larsen, A.G. (2018). "Mapping the Social Class Structure: From Occupational Mobility to Social Class Categories Using Network Analysis", *Sociology.* Available at doi.org/10.1177/0038038517704819 (accessed on May 30, 2017).

Useem, M. (1986). *The Inner Circle. Large Corporations and the Rise of Business Political Activity in the US and UK.* Oxford: Oxford University Press.

Wolfle, L.M. (2003). "The Introduction of Path Analysis to the Social Sciences, and Some Emergent Themes: An Annotated Bibliography", *Structural Equation Modelling* 10 (1): 1–34.

Wright, S. (1921). "Correlation and Causation", *Journal of Agricultural Research* 20: 557–585.

Wright, S. (1934). "The Method of Path Coefficients", *Annals of Mathematical Statistics* 5: 161–215.

Xie, Y. (2007). "Otis Dudley Duncan's Legacy: The Demographic Approach to Quantitative Reasoning in Social Science", *Research in Social Stratification and Mobility* 25 (2): 141–156.

Zetterberg, H.L. (1966). "Traditioner och möjligheter i skandinavisk sociologi" [Traditions and Possibilities in Scandinavian Sociology], In *Sociologisk Forskning* 3: 1–21.

CHAPTER 4

Constructing Social Structure

John Scott

An investigation into how a useful concept of social structure is to be constructed must take very seriously the important points made by Johs Hjellbrekke, who discusses Bachelard's anti-metaphysical approach to social scientific investigations. His argument is that metaphors may be useful guides during the early stages of a scientific study, but that each science must eventually make an epistemological break with its metaphors and actively construct its own concepts. It is undoubtedly the case that a major obstacle in the way of developing a viable concept of social structure has been an over-reliance on the misleading metaphor of the 'social organism'. The limitations of this metaphor have also been among the principal reasons why many sociologists have rejected or abandoned the concept.

This metaphor of the social organism proposed that a social structure can be seen as analogous to the physical structure of a biological organism. From this point of view, social structure is the 'skeleton' of a society and can be studied through the 'physiological' or functional processes that organise it into a collective entity with an existence *sui generis*. This is the idea that is most often invoked by proponents of structural explanations. Used unreflectively, however, with a failure to understand the proper characteristics of a social structure that differentiates it from a physical structure, the idea is seriously misleading. It is all-too-easy for critics to point to the non-observability and non-tangibility of social structures and so to reject the concept as suggesting that societies can be seen as 'living systems' with supra-individual properties and, perhaps, as collective entities with collective minds. Even those such as Dorothy Smith, discussed in Karin Widerberg's chapter, who recognise the existence of 'extra-local' social relations, may still hold that the prevailing view of social structure cannot properly grasp these relations without distorting the sociological understanding of lived experiences.

Herbert Spencer (1860; 1873–93) is generally seen as the prime culprit who popularised the idea of the social organism. It is certainly true that he started out from a metaphorical use of the notion and that he continually used the term 'social organism' in referring to societies. However, Spencer clearly recognised the issue that Bachelard was to raise later and so he explicitly discussed the differences between a biological and a sociological organism or, as he sometimes called it, 'system'. Spencer's view was that the links between the individual members of a society are neither skeletal nor physiological. These links, he argued, consist only of linguistic communication. It is the communication of meanings from one individual to another that ties them into a structure of relations and makes it possible for sociology to undertake scientific investigations that are not reducible to biology or psychology. Communicative actions produce a shared system of meanings, a 'culture', and a social consciousness that shapes individual action but does not comprise a collective 'mind'. Social structure, then, is *real*, but it *exists* only as symbolic meanings in individual minds that are sustained through linguistic communication and in the ongoing regularities of human behaviour. It is this concept of social structure that I want to unpack and develop as a valid sociological construct.

1 What Is Social Structure?

Social structure is fundamentally a matter of social relations. It is this relational concern that has underpinned the plausibility of the metaphor of the skeleton. However, I have argued elsewhere (Scott, 2001, 2017b; López and Scott, 2000) that social structure has to be seen as a combination of relational, institutional, and embodied elements. A relational structure, the primary aspect of social structure, comprises interdependencies, mutual connections, antagonisms, and recurrent practices among actors and their actions. An institutional or normative structure comprises the shared norms and expectations through which individuals define situations and orientate their actions towards each other. Relational structure results from actions undertaken in relation to norms within a particular setting and environment. In order to be effective in action, however, norms must be embodied in actors. An embodied structure comprises the habits, tendencies, and dispositions that motivate individual action and agency. Social structure exists when the shared norms held in individual minds are enacted through internalised or embodied habits of action that generate recurrent and enduring interconnections among the actors. Of these three elements, the relational is the predominant and defining aspect of social structure, as it is the relations amongst positioned actors that directly and tangibly express the structuring effects of normatively oriented actions. Social structure, it might be said, has a relational primacy. There is rarely a direct one-to-one relationship between these three elements, but all must be present in order for a sociologist to be able to refer to the existence of a social structure and to use it in an explanation of individual actions.

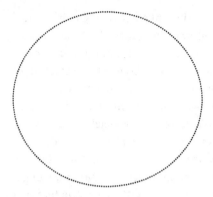

FIGURE 4.1   Example of a circle

This social structure is commonly and correctly seen as comprising the 'pattern' of social life. If we are to construct a concept of social structure as a pattern, it is necessary to ask *where* exactly that pattern can be said to exist. A pattern must be seen as something that is real, though it may not exist in physical or substantive form. It is inherent in the arrangement of the objects that form it and so is *virtual* rather than material. This can be seen by considering the simple example of a circle. The diagram in Figure 4.1 shows what everyone would agree, I assume, to be a circle, as the diagram comprises a number of dots arranged in a circular pattern. However, there is no solid line that actually *is* the circle. The circle, then, is an idea or pattern that can be found in the arrangement of the dots. As an arrangement or pattern of dots, the circle can be said to have a virtual reality. Only the dots exist, but it is 'as if' they are connected into a continuous solid line.

This argument can, however, be taken a little further. Figure 4.2 shows a circle drawn as a solid line and might be thought to 'really' be a circle in physical form. However, this is not the case. What looks like a solid line—or a dot, for that matter—is, in fact, an arrangement of ink particles on paper. If we were to put the diagram under the microscope or a strong magnifying glass—you might like to try this—it would appear disconnected rather than solid. It is in precisely the same sense that a digital image of a circle can be seen to be composed of a number of separate pixels. The circle as such—as a pattern—is distinct from the things from which it is composed, but it is real, nevertheless.

This idea is not limited to simple geometrical patterns but is fundamental to all existence. Any apparently solid object can, under detailed investigation, be shown to consist of numerous sub-atomic particles arranged in a particular way. Indeed, physicists are currently debating whether even the apparently 'fundamental' particles can be seen as substantive entities or as waves of fluctuations in a quantum reality. All the familiar objects of our everyday world,

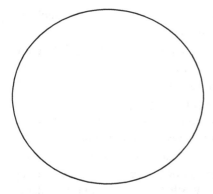

FIGURE 4.2 Second example of a circle

then, exist only as patterns of more fundamental phenomena. We grasp them through concepts and ideas that organise our perceptions by the resistance or impression they make on our senses, but they have a virtual rather than a substantive existence as distinct 'things'.

All this is, of course, also true of social structure. A social structure has a virtual reality in the interactions of communicating individuals. However, we must note that those individuals, too, have only a virtual reality. Their psychic structures—their consciousness and subjectivity—are the results of a specific arrangement of biological elements in the brain, and their biological structure is a particular arrangement of chemical and physical elements. There is, in fact, a complex hierarchy of structural levels running from the quantum level to the cultural level. This is the basis of the view of Comte and Spencer that there is a hierarchy of sciences. Each science defines its particular concepts by identifying the level at which it seeks to distinguish between a pattern and its constituent elements. A sociological definition of social structure identifies the institutional, relational, and embodied patterns that have a virtual reality in the lives of a particular population of inter-communicating individuals.

Some of the implications of this conception of social structure can be illustrated by considering what is the best-researched example of a structure in human societies. Contemporary linguistics, following Saussure (1916), have distinguished between 'speech', understood as a flow of linguistic utterances, and the 'tongue' or 'grammar' that organises the flow of utterances. Grammar, as a linguistic structure, is a collective phenomenon that is the property of a 'speaking mass', a population of speaking, communicating individuals. Although a grammar is a 'social fact' in Durkheim's sense, it does not exist as a tangible thing, separate from the subjectivities of the individual speakers who produce the flow of utterances. Grammar is a virtual reality that is reproduced—and transformed—in and through the forms of communication by which the members of a speaking mass speak to each other.

Thus, a child who is born into a speaking mass acquires, through listening and inference, the usages of its parents and the others that it encounters. He or she acquires a sense of linguistic structure—a grammatical knowledge built on an underlying linguistic competence (Chomsky 1957, 1965)—that makes possible the organisation of its own speech and allows it to understand the speech of others. This linguistic ability is an *embodied* sense. It is a mental disposition programmed into the brain and is analogous to such motor dispositions and skills as the ability to walk or to ride a bicycle. It is, that is to say, an aspect of the habitus (Bourdieu, 1972). While it is possible to infer rules or norms of grammar and even to write them down in books of grammar—they exist only in embodied form, but speech nevertheless conforms to the rules. Grammar, as embodied in the habitus, produces also a *relational* structure: it organises the relations among the various lexical elements to form structured sentences. This clearly demonstrates what I have called the relational primacy in the idea of structure, as it is the sentence, as a structured set of words, that communicates the speaker's meaning.

This conception of language provides a clear model for how we can understand social structure more generally. Language is one aspect of social life, and by making possible the communicative interaction of individuals it is, as Spencer recognised, central to the structuring of all other aspects of social life. At the same time, the way in which linguistic communication operates provides a model—not, please note, a metaphor—for all forms of social interaction.

2   Culture, Social Structure, and Personality

The theorist who provided the best developed framework for articulating this view of social structure is the much misunderstood and maligned Talcott Parsons. In *The Social System* (Parsons, 1951), Parsons set out a view of social structure as being defined by a normative order of institutions that regulates social relations and is internalised in human minds and bodies. This view brings together the institutional, relational, and embodied aspects of social structure.

The structure of a 'social system', Parsons argued, comprises the value commitments and norms that define the roles through which social action is organised and the collectivities or groupings into which actors are formed. The social system, then, is a complex of norms and of collectively organised role relations. The personality systems of the various actors in a society comprise the internalised tendencies of action that are driven by energising motivational forces to produce the human agency through which social relations are formed. The relationship between these two systems—the social system and the personality system—defines what later writers would discuss as the relationship of agency to structure.

These two systems, so far as sociologists and social psychologists are concerned, are what Parsons called 'concrete' systems of action. Their structural patterns are the constructed objects of attention for these two sciences. A cultural system, on the other hand, he saw as an 'abstract' system. What he means by this is that culture does not exist separately from the social and personality systems but is inferred by the sociological analyst as a logical construct of the ideas held in common by the members of a society. Cultural objects include ideas of all kinds: for example, the ideas of the circle and the triangle, the aesthetic forms of the Dorian Arch, the sonata form, the novel, and so on. Cultural systems are religious doctrines, scientific theories, values, numerical systems, etc., that exist only in dispersed form in individual minds and social practices. Culture is the basis of the norms and institutions that are central as key aspects of social structure. Some social theorists (Archer, 1995; Martin, 2009) have tried to recognise this by seeing institutional structure as 'cultural structure', but it is important to keep the two separate. Cultural meanings are sustained and reproduced through the communication of meanings. A cultural system, then, is abstract or virtual in relation to the social and personality systems. The point may be further made, of course, that social and psychic structures must themselves be seen as virtual realities despite being the real, concrete objects of study for sociologists and social psychologists.

Parsons elaborated on this further in his argument that value patterns are 'latent' structuring elements within the structure of the social system. The internalisation and embodiment of value patterns in the personalities of actors enables them to be 'institutionalised' as social norms and so the values exist only in a state of latency. The key element in the structuring of social activity is to be found in the cultural formation of the normative expectations that regulate this activity and are clustered into institutions. It is norms and institutions that ensure that we do things in particular ways and that social activity happens predictably and 'normally' or 'as a rule'. The abstract value patterns are latent within the concrete norms towards which actors orientate their actions. In acting on the basis of their internalised value orientations, a plurality of actors will institutionalise them as expected patterns of action. In so far as individuals conform to these expectations, they will establish a corresponding system of social relations. This is Parsons's view of the 'fully institutionalised social relationship'.

Parsons's fundamental point, then, is that institutional and relational structures consist only of the embodied habits of action that result from individual subjectivity. The abstract cultural pattern is the latent shaping element, but only through its embodiment. This argument can be developed by exploring the Durkheimian view that a culturally formed social system can be seen as comprising a 'social consciousness' (a system of communication sustaining collective representations) and what may be called a 'social reticulation' (a system of interdependencies sustaining collective relationships), both of which correspond to a psycho-biological habitus (a system of dispositions that sustains practices and recurrent tendencies).

3   Social Consciousness, Culture, and Social Structure

Durkheim (1893) introduced the idea of the social consciousness in his *Division of Labour in Society*, exploring this alongside the rather narrower idea of the 'collective consciousness', which comprises the *moral* binding force in social life. The more general idea of a social consciousness, however, has much wider relevance to the ways in which actions give rise to social structures. Culture and normative structures, I wish to argue, are elements in a social consciousness that exists only in the minds of the individuals in which it is embodied and the cultural artefacts in which their ideas are recorded and stored as 'texts' (Smith, 1999: 78; Scott, 1990: Ch. 1).

The social consciousness, Durkheim argued, comprises 'representations' and 'affective elements'—thoughts and feelings—that form "a determinate system with a life of its own" (Durkheim, 1893: 39) and with properties that constrain individual thoughts, feelings, and actions. The examples of normative constraint given by Durkheim include the need to understand the rules of a particular language in order to be understood and to understand others and the need to use a particular currency if the buying and selling of goods and services is to be possible. Those socialised into Japanese culture and living in Japanese society, for example, must speak Japanese and use Japanese currency if they are to get by on a daily basis.

Durkheim's (1895) rather elliptical statement that social facts are realities *sui generis* left him open to the misunderstanding that he saw 'social consciousness' as a substantive entity separate from individual consciousness. This was the reason why Morris Ginsberg and Bronisław Malinowski warned the young Talcott Parsons during his visit to the London School of Economics that Durkheim had advocated an 'unsound' theory of the 'group mind'. This warning, however, was somewhat disingenuous as Ginsberg and his mentor

Leonard Hobhouse (1924) had themselves developed a remarkably similar view in their own work and had even referred to the idea of a 'social mind' (a terminology that Durkheim himself had never used).

Hobhouse was, in fact, one of a number of sociologists who explored the idea of social consciousness in a way that filled many of the gaps in Durkheim's argument. He drew on the quasi-Durkheimian view of the US sociologist Franklin Giddings (1896), of Columbia University, who had formulated a strong view of the 'social mind' (see Chriss, 2006). Hobhouse (1911) used precisely the same terminology in lectures that he delivered during a visit to Columbia in 1911.

In his later work, however, Hobhouse abandoned the phrase 'social mind' and referred, instead, to what he saw as the less metaphysical term 'collective mentality'. Hobhouse made clear that he saw this collective mentality, or social consciousness, as being dispersed in the minds of individuals but sustained and transformed through the constant flow of their communication (see Scott, 2016). This view that social consciousness is real but dispersed accorded precisely with Durkheim's own statement that the social consciousness is not a substantive entity but is "diffused over society as a whole". It is, he said, "totally different from the consciousness of individuals, although it is only realised in individuals" (Durkheim, 1893: 39). It is only methodologically that it can be treated 'as if' it were a thing.

Durkheim's failure to pursue his insight into the diffusion or dispersal of the social consciousness reflected his opposition to what he saw as the psychologistic arguments of his great rival Gabriel Tarde (1890). Giddings and Hobhouse had been far less reluctant to recognise that social structures had their foundations in the communicative interaction and interpersonal influences that are studied in social psychology. A parallel argument about the social mind and social psychology was especially well developed by Charles Cooley (1909). These writers exemplify precisely what Durkheim meant by social consciousness and the mental character of social phenomena.

The strongest formulation of this idea in the early twentieth century was, perhaps, the argument of William McDougall (1920), whose formulation of the Durkheimian argument it was that had incurred the wrath of Ginsberg. McDougall wrote of the 'group mind' and held that his critics rejected this concept only because they fundamentally misunderstood the nature of the individual mind and consciousness. Individual consciousness, he argued, is not a substantive entity but is a system of mental flows among the constituent elements of the mind. Consciousness is an emergent property of this system of mental flows. In precisely the same way, he argued, a system of communication among the members of a group produces forms of consciousness that would not arise in the absence of communication. There is, therefore, a true group mind: groups are able to think, decide, and act in precisely the same way as individuals. This view has been rediscovered, though in a bowdlerised form and without any recognition of prior sociological work, in popular writings on 'the wisdom of crowds' (Surowiecki, 2004).

The social consciousness comprises cultural objects, value orientations, and norms that are sustained in communication and stored in the texts of written documents. These external, material stores of meanings, 'written' by some individuals and 'read' by others, extend the reach of human communication. Electronic and digital means of communication and storage extend it further. The ideas of Durkheim, Giddings, Cooley, Hobhouse, and McDougall give a sophisticated and important basis to the more recent symbolic interactionist and phenomenological arguments on social construction. By contrast with many of these later writers, the pioneers were very clear that they were identifying real social facts with properties of their own and with the power to constrain individuals, but that are, nevertheless, virtually real. This is what Durkheim meant in saying that a social consciousness is a reality *sui generis* and so can be treated by sociologists 'as if' it was a thing.

4   Social Reticulation: Micro and Macro

The social consciousness carried by a communicating mass of individuals is complemented by what I have called a 'social reticulation' formed in relation to the latent values and norms of the social consciousness. This reticulation is a system of relations of various kinds formed in a 'lamination' or hierarchy of complexity (Elder-Vass, 2010: 49ff). At its base is a micro level of local interaction from which various macro levels of extra-local interdependencies arise. The micro-social level of relations comprises the episodic encounters in copresence of individuals as the occupants of roles and as the members of collectivities. The macro-social level of relations comprises the decontextualized interdependencies of roles and collectivities seen independently of their individual occupants and members. The micro level of everyday life comprises interactive responses of a man to his wife, a mother to her child, a shop assistant to his or her customers, and so on. Such relations involve varying degrees of alliance, cooperation, competition, and conflict that comprise a state of social order or disorder that Goffman (1983) called an interaction order. These relations are embedded in the more extended and indirect relations that transcend local situations and form structures of patriarchy, kinship, marketing, and so on. These are transcendent, extra-local relations of similarity, congruence, and contradiction among structural parts and comprise a state of overall social organisation or disorganisation. Each level of social reticulation is real, and it is not sensible to prioritise one over the other or to argue that either level should be disregarded as unreal. Thus, we must reject the argument of Althusser (1962) that macro structures are fundamental and that individuals and their interactions are their mere 'bearers'. Similarly, we cannot accept the view of Blumer (1962) that the face-to-face interactions of individuals are fundamental and that macro-structures are mere subjective 'frameworks'. The micro and macro levels are complementary to and imply each other.

The micro level of local and interpersonal relations is a network of interaction. It is the result of ongoing mutual constructions of the situation and of the attitudes and actions of its participants. It is the world of everyday life, the lifeworld of embodied living in particular locales. Knowledge of the everyday world is a sedimentation of our experiences, the sedimented elements that can be taken-for-granted as what 'everybody knows'. Each participant negotiates a shared understanding with others through constructing representations and accounts. Participants mutually—simultaneously and interdependently, but always imperfectly—legitimate their own actions and shape the actions of others by attempting to define limits to the options open to them. Each individual may understand the world differently—uniquely—but there will be a greater or lesser commonality or overlap in views. Each participant holds to an understanding of what he or she believes to be the case and what he or she believes others believe. Thomas Scheff (1967) has seen this reciprocal orientation as the basis of consensus. This consensus 'must be sufficient to justify their actions as appropriate and so to ensure that the actions of the various participants mesh or coordinate with each other. Whenever such a commonality exists, individuals will tend to act in such a way that their interactions mesh: the relations in which they engage are expressions of the common understanding and the definitions of situations that they inform. Interactionists stress that such a consensus and meshing of actions is a contingent accomplishment: there may always be failures of understanding and mutual ignorance, leading to deviance, conflict, and a lack of coordination. This is clear from the example of language. Actual speech will always involve errors and innovations despite the existence of shared grammatical rules. Many such errors are insignificant and are ignored: speakers may still understand each other while recognising and tolerating deviance from grammatical norms. Over time, however, recurrent errors and innovations may spread and accumulate to become the source of grammatical change.

When there is sufficient commonality in subjective orientations, whether in everyday or specialised activities, it is as if the actors are acting under an external normative structure that shapes their actions. For example, the usages acquired as embodied dispositions to organise speech in particular ways come to be represented in the minds of individuals and may be recorded in grammar books and manuals. Speech is thereby given a normative expression: 'correct' speech is expected, morally required, or sanctioned. It is experienced as if it were governed by an externally real linguistic structure, in terms of which utterances may be authoritatively judged to be grammatically correct or incorrect. This is particularly the case where documentary records and texts re-enter the flow of communication when read by actors and discursively employed in the regulation of speech. This is extended in conversation, where conversation analysts have shown that competent speakers acquire a sense of social structure that organises their conversations with others. They acquire norms of turn-taking, inclusion, persuasion, and so on. Similarly, discursive communication in stories and reports comes to be organised through institutional forms of argument and explanation, plot, and narrative.

The normative regulation of action always and necessarily occurs at the micro level. Norms operate only in so far as actors take account of them in their encounters with others, whether consciously or as embodied dispositions. The immediate norms regulating the interactions of everyday life include norms of interpersonal behaviour concerning queuing, conversational turn-taking, politeness, civility, and trust, together with specialised and situational norms concerning appropriate role behaviour in various specialised settings and locales: how to be a 'customer', how to be a 'student' or 'worker', what makes a good 'father', and so on. These specialised norms may be undergirded by more general norms such as those of commerce, marriage, neighbourliness, health, education, and democracy.

This micro level of everyday life is the backdrop to all our social activity and comprises the myriad locales and persons that are typically encountered in houses and shops, on roads and pavements, at workplaces, etc., and all the various objects that they typically contain. An individual's everyday world becomes broader and deeper as more aspects of specialised activities become routinised and sedimented. Locales of interaction that are newly encountered may be assimilated to an understanding of the everyday world as they become more familiar: the department stores where we do our shopping, the schools and colleges we attend, the factories and offices in which we work, the hotels in which we stay, and the hospitals we attend as patients or staff (Goffman, 1961; Strauss et al., 1963; Roth, 1963).

The various specialised activities in which we engage—going to work, lobbying parliament, going to church, etc.—all take place within a framework of shared and tacit understandings and help to form the social consciousness within which distinct points of view and situational definitions shape social actions. Thus, the everyday world is differentiated into a number of distinct—and perhaps mutually discrepant or contradictory—realities (Schütz, 1932). Each specialised activity depends upon a commonality and complementarity of understanding: there must be some common understandings that define the nature of the activity and some complementarity of understandings that ensure that the actions of those in different social positions will mesh. This complementarity may not form a perfect concordance between actors. All that is necessary is that there be sufficient congruence for their interaction to be mutually predictable. These specialised worlds are intersubjective realities that sustain a network of relations.

Interactions among individuals and collectivities (small groups, clubs, organisations, and such quasi-groups as social movements and classes) form a network of interactions, both face-to-face and mediated, involving family and friendship relations, neighbourly care and support, market transactions, political patronage, and a variety of other interconnections that form extensive chains of action and reaction that ramify through space and time and may stretch across the whole population of a territory and beyond. This network of interactions can be explored through the techniques of social network analysis (Scott, 2017a), which provides techniques for mapping the micro-level relations. The use of social network analysis to pursue a micro-level relational sociology has been advocated by Mustafa Emirbayer (1997) and Nick Crossley (2010; and see Powell and Depelteau, 2013).

In social network analysis, actions are represented mathematically and diagrammatically as 'points' and their relations can be represented by 'lines' to depict the network structure. The choices and preferences made by actors describe the direction and strength of the various lines and the structure of the various 'figurations' formed (Elias, 1969; Mouzelis, 1991) can be described numerically and qualitatively as showing the density, cohesion, and centralisation of an overall network, the cliques and clusters that it contains, and the centrality of various actors within them. A typical sociogram, showing interlocking directorships between business enterprises is shown in Figure 4.3.

Such a complex network of interactions is a virtual relational structure: Its properties are experienced as real by its participants but the meanings that sustain it exist only in the subjectivity of individuals, their textual records, and the communicative interaction flows among them. The commonality and complementarity underpinning the interaction order 'contains' the virtual relational structures that constrain individual and collective actions.

My argument is that in producing an interaction order the actors also produce the social relations that comprise the macro relations of their society. These are not different substances or things but different virtual

FIGURE 4.3 A network of micro relations: interlocking directorships

levels. Macro-level relations are contained within the micro-level interactions, appearing as enduring and persistent extra-local interdependencies that 'emerge' from interactions. An emergent property is one that results from the combining of two elements, each of which continues to operate in its own way. Rather than merely aggregating, the elements affect each other because of their arrangement or organisation and so alter the ways in which their individual powers are expressed (Elder-Vass, 2010: Ch. 2).

This argument departs from methodological individualism (Watkins, 1952), which holds that all explanations of social phenomena *must* refer to properties of individuals and their relations to each other. While it is the case that social phenomena are explained by the actions of individuals and the influences resulting from the actions of others, it is important also to recognise that these individuals act as the occupants of roles and members of collectivities (Mandelbaum, 1955) and that an explanation must also refer to the emergent extra-local relations. Relational structures have real powers by virtue of the integral forces and situational constraints through which they are constituted. Macro-structural phenomena are causally effective "conjunctions and developments" of micro-level phenomena (Kontopolos, 1993: 84) and we do not have to unpack them in detail in every particular explanation that we give: we can bracket them off and treat the macro-relations as if they were autonomous.

Such conjunctions and developments are very complex. The model of unintended consequences, as developed from Smith and Ferguson by a variety of writers (Merton, 1936; Giddens, 1976; Axelrod, 1997) and that has been developed into models of 'morphogenesis' and 'structuration' (Archer, 1995; Giddens, 1982) is the basis of this. People act on the basis of their definition of the situation and the particular conditions, but their actions have ramifying consequences for others that were neither intended nor foreseen. These concatenate across the system in chains of interaction and there is an entwining and entangling into altered situations and, correspondingly, altered actions. The emergent outcomes are opaque to the participants.

In interacting with a customer, a shop assistant must also, over time, interact with managers, warehouse staff, and delivery workers. These must, in turn, interact with higher-level managers, suppliers, shopfitters, postal staff, vehicle repairers, government tax officials, and so on. Similar considerations apply to each role and collectivity in the interweaving chain of interactions. It is the effect of what happens in one encounter on all other encounters that results in macro-level emergent relations from the interaction order. Micro relations join individuals as occupants of roles or members of collectivities; macro relations join the roles and collectivities themselves or categories of roles and collectivities. These deeper relations have properties and powers that are irreducible without loss to the interaction level within which they are nevertheless contained.

Thus, entering a shop to purchase groceries or clothing contributes to the reproduction of the relations of consumption and production: market relations, a division of labour, property relations, employment relations, monetary and credit relations, and so on. Similarly, making tax payments, drawing benefits, and engaging with polling station staff to cast a vote contribute to the production of political relations of governance: relations of citizenship, enforceable rights, relations of political representation. Other examples of macro-level structures include structures of educational and health inequality by class, gender, and ethnicity, migration chains, rural–urban divisions, and structures of power and influence that together constitute the 'ruling relations' of a society (Smith, 1990).

Thus, we may identify property, employment, and monetary relations and also see these, in their combination, as defining class relations. We may identify relations of schooling and examination, relations of parenting and socialisation, etc. And we may see all of these as involved in the movement of individuals from one occupation to another and so as comprising, in their combination, relations of social mobility. We can study the mobility structures through the statistical associations among occupational categories, as the

statistical rates that are the externally measurable reflection of the 'social facts'
of occupational structure and social mobility. These structures of relations are
real but not substantive, and it is in this sense that Karl Mannheim said that
"capitalism' can be seen as 'a system of patterns which govern the relevant
actions of the individual" and which "exists only in a fluid state of interlocking
actions" (Mannheim 1932–33).

Techniques of social network analysis can be used on many such structures, the most useful being those that employ mathematical techniques to
decompose interactions into the deeper, underlying relations that emerge
from them. Of particular importance are approaches to 'structural equiv-
alence' (White et al., 1976) that uncover blocks and clusters of actors that
have similar or equivalent relations to other such blocks. This might show,
for example, that the interactions between particular shop assistants, customers, delivery staff, etc., are formed into extra-local relations common to
all occupants of these 'roles', making possible a map of the role structure
of retailing. Such techniques can uncover the macro relations underlying
networks of interlocking directorships, as in Figure 4.4. In this simplified
example of the memberships of 6 persons sitting on 7 company boards, similar patterns of membership across the network are shown by a '1' and dis-
similar patterns by a 'o' (Scott, 2017a: Ch. 8). Blocks of 1s indicate the roles
or positions in the network. Similar techniques are latent class analysis
(McCutcheon, 1987) and the multiple correspondence analysis (Rouanet and
Le Roux, 2009) that Bourdieu (1979) used to map class and status relations of
cultural consumption.

Thus, the outcome of interaction is a social structure of 'macro' relations
that exist virtually, as, in this sense, the 'underlying' relations of the interaction
order. It was, again, Mannheim (1932–33) who said that:

persons: companies:	a	b	c	d	e	f
A	1	1	1	o	o	o
B	1	1	1	o	o	o
C	1	1	1	o	o	o
D	1	1	1	o	o	o
E	o	o	o	1	1	1
F	o	o	o	1	1	1
G	o	o	o	1	1	1

FIGURE 4.4   A structure of macro relations: a block model

The problems and alternatives which the single individual faces in his actions are presented to him in a given social framework. It is this framework which structures the role of the person and in which his actions and expressions take on a new sense.

MANNHEIM, 1932–33

5   Social Integration and System Integration

The micro level exhibits a particular state of integration, described by David Lockwood (1964) as 'social integration' (see the related views in Giddens, 1984; Habermas, 1981). The relational properties measured in social network analysis describe various degrees and forms of social integration. Norms always exist first at the micro level in the understandings of individuals formed in the social consciousness. Interacting individuals and collectivities establish shared understandings and a 'negotiated order' that makes possible a coordination of their actions and forms of joint action in cooperation, competition, and conflict. Where there are failures in mutual understanding and a resulting lack of coordination, there is social disorder, rather than social order and cohesion, and a consequent potential for social disintegration and schism. This was discussed further in David Lockwood's *Solidarity and Schism* (Lockwood, 1992).

Like the micro-structures, macro-structures are virtual structures. They can be identified, and their properties be described, through sociological analysis, but they have no substantive existence apart from the individuals whose subjectivity sustains them. Relations are sustained within the collective mentality as a product of the embodied dispositions of clusters of actors. The larger social structure that emerges from the interaction order exhibits a particular state of social organisation and disorganisation that Lockwood called 'system integration'.

System integration is a state of congruence or malintegration between the institutional structure of a society and its macro-level relations. The macro-level relations are the 'non-normative' factors that Lockwood sees as comprising a 'substratum' that delineates 'the factual distribution of means' and that set limits on the opportunities available to actors and implies specific interests for them. An institutional structure is a system of 'information' connections in which the degree of 'fit' between elements is a matter of their meaningful coherence. The information connections comprise what Pitirim Sorokin (1937–41) called 'logico-meaningful' integration and coherent clusters of these normative elements comprise social institutions. The integration characteristic of an institutional structure can be described, Sorokin argued, using terms such as consistency, complementarity, or logical contradiction. Thus, an element may be internally inconsistent or contradictory and may be inconsistently combined with other elements. A relational structure is a system of 'energy' pressures resulting from the limits imposed by the structural constraints. The connections among these relational elements are what Sorokin referred to as those of a 'causal-functional' connection. The "parts are related to one another, directly, or, if indirectly, by several internal 'centres'". These connections involve a systemic interdependence because the change or elimination of one part "perceptibly influences the rest of the synthesis" and a part when found in a different combination of parts cannot exist or undergoes profound modification to become a part of the combination. Sorokin added that "the degree of functional unity or functional interdependence is everywhere not the same". That is to say, the degree of integration is variable.

This point was taken up by Alvin Gouldner (1959), who argued that only in certain cases does the system interdependence of parts comprise a stable and enduring 'equilibrium'. The degree of 'functional reciprocity' between parts can vary and departures from full reciprocity result in varying degrees of instability. Disequilibrium occurs when interdependence is low, as the various parts then have much 'functional autonomy'. The greater the extent to which a part tends to maintain its autonomy, the greater is the 'tension' within the structure as a whole. Disequilibrium also occurs when interdependence is high but involves negative feedback. In this situation the parts operate in ways that undermine each other.

There is, of course, a definite relationship between the institutional structure and the relational structure, though this is not a simple one-to-one relationship. The social structure is a complex combination of institutional and relational structures and it is necessary to look at the integration of relational structures, the integration of institutional structures, and the integration between these two. Lockwood followed Marxian terminology and referred to this as a state of structural 'contradiction' between the institutional and relational parts. His example is Marx's claimed contradiction between the institutional 'relations of production' (legal norms of property ownership and wage labour) and the 'forces of production' (the non-normative, relational combination of labour with technical and financial resources) within the economic structure of a capitalist mode of production.

6   Conclusion

This state of system integration is an emergent property of the virtual structure and it is important to explore the specific connections between this and the state of social integration. The real limitation of Parsons's view was his focus on the fully institutionalised social structure in which he depicted a one-to-one correspondence between cultural patterns, normative expectations, and actual relations, and so a precise correspondence between social integration and system integration. He did, however, recognise that this is a limiting case that he was analysing for convenience and that was a yardstick for looking at the actual structures found in empirical societies. Thus, an analysis that takes account of cultural diversity, conflicting expectations, and contradictory relations would disclose the frequent lack of congruence between micro and macro, social and system integration, and the consequent complexity of social structure. As Karl Mannheim recognised, the social world is not "a single and completed structure, but an aggregation of partially structured orbits" (Mannheim, 1932–33: 75). The recognition of varying degrees of system integration is a way of placing this at the centre of attention.

Similarly, there is no one-to-one relationship between social integration and system integration. David Lockwood's paper highlighted this as a fundamental limitation of the Parsonian view, which assumed that one could be read off from the other. It is important to analyse separately the integration at each of these levels and then to trace out the mechanisms that link the two together and that are responsible for the variations and disjunctions between them—in short, the ways in which intentional actions have unintended and unanticipated consequences, which establish new conditions that constrain future actions. States of social and system integration are reproduced as social facts in and through the activities that the norms regulate.

References

Althusser, L. (1962). "Contradiction and Overdetermination", in L. Althusser (ed.). *For Marx*. Harmondsworth: Allen Lane.

Archer, M.S. (1995). "Realist Social Theory", *The Morphogenetic Approach*. Cambridge: Cambridge University Press.

Axelrod, R. (1997). *The Complexity of Cooperation: Agent-Based Models of Competition and Collaboration*. Princeton, New Jersey: Princeton University Press.

Blumer, H. (1969) [1962]. "Society as Symbolic Interaction", in H. Blumer (ed.). *Symbolic Interactionism*. Englewood Cliffs: Prentice-Hall.

Bourdieu, P. (1977) [1972]. *Outline of a Theory of Practice*. Cambridge: Cambridge University Press.

Bourdieu, P. (1984) [1979]. *Distinction: A Social Critique of the Judgment of Taste*. London: Routledge.

Chomsky, N. (1957). *Syntactic Structures*. The Hague: Mouton.

Chomsky, N. (1965). *Aspects of the Theory of Syntax*. Cambridge: M.I.T. Press.

Chriss, J. (2006). "Giddings and the Social Mind", *Journal of Classical Sociology* 6 (1): 123–144.

Cooley, C.H. (1909). *Social Organisation*. New York: Schocken.

Crossley, N. (2010). *Towards Relational Sociology*. London: Routledge.

Depelteau, F. and Powell, C. (eds.). (2013). *Applying Relational Sociology*. New York: Palgrave Macmillan.

Durkheim, E. (1984) [1893]. *The Division of Labour in Society*. London: Macmillan.

Durkheim, E. (1982) [1895]. *The Rules of the Sociological Method*. London: Macmillan.

Elder-Vass, D. (2010). *The Causal Power of Social Structures*. Cambridge: Cambridge University Press.

Elias, N. (1978) [1969]. *What is Sociology*. London: Hutchinson.

Emirbayer, M. (1997). "Manifesto For A Relational Sociology", *American Journal of Sociology* 103 (2): 281–317.

Giddens, A. (1976). "Functionalism: après la lutte" in A. Giddens (ed.). *Studies in Social and Political Theory*. London: Hutchinson.

Giddens, A. (1982). "Action, Structure, Power", in A. Giddens (ed.). *Profiles and Critiques in Social Theory*. London: Macmillabn.

Giddens, A. (1984). *The Constitution of Society*. Cambridge: Polity Press.

Giddings, F.H. (1970) [1896]. *Principles of Sociology*. New York: Johnson Reprint.

Goffman, E. (1961). *Asylums: Essays on the Social Situation of Mental Patients and Other Inmates*. New York: Doubleday.

Goffman, E. (1983). "The Interaction Order", *American Sociological Review* 48: 1–17.

Gouldner, A. W. (1959). "Reciprocity and Autonomy in Functional Theory", in A.W. Gouldner (ed.). *For Sociology*. Harmondsworth: Penguin.

Habermas, J. (1984) [1981]. *The Theory of Communicative Action,* Volume One: Reason and the Rationalisation of Society. London: Heinemann.

Hobhouse, L.T. (1911). *Social Evolution and Political Theory*. New York: Columbia University Press.

Hobhouse, L.T. (1966) [1924]. *Social Development: Its Nature and Conditions*. London: George Allen and Unwin.

Kontopolos, K. (1993). *The Logics of Social Structure*. Cambridge: Cambridge University Press.

Lockwood, D. (1964). "Social Integration and System Integration", in G.K. Zollschan and W. Hirsch (eds.). *Explorations in Social Change*. London: Routledge and Kegan Paul.

Lockwood, D. (1992). *Solidarity and Schism*. Oxford: Clarendon Press.

López, J. and Scott, J. (2000). *Social Structure*. Buckingham: Open University Press.

Mandelbaum, Maurice (1955). "Societal Facts", in J. O'Neill (ed.). *Modes of Individualism and Collectivism*. London: Heinemann.

Mannheim, K. (1956) [1932–33]. "Towards a Sociology of the Mind", in K. Mannheim (ed.). *Essays on the Sociology of Culture*. London: Routledge and Kegan Paul.

Martin, J.L. (2009). *Social Structures*. Princeton, NJ: Princeton University Press.

McCutcheon, A. (1987). *Latent Class Analysis*. London: Sage.

McDougall, W. (1939) [1920]. *The Group Mind*. Cambridge: Cambridge University Press.

Merton, R.K. (1936). "The Unanticipated Consequences of Purposive Social Action", *American Sociological Review* 1 (6): 894–904.

Mouzelis, N. (1991). *Back To Sociological Theory: The Construction of Social Orders*. London: Macmillan.

Parsons, T. (1951). *The Social System*. New York: The Free Press.

Powell, C. and Depelteau, F. (eds.). (2013). *Conceptualising Relational Sociology*. New York: Palgrave Macmillan.

Roth, J. (1963). *Timetables*. Indianapolis: Bobbs-Merrill.

Rouanet, H. and Le Roux, B. (2009). *Multiple Correspondence Analysis* London: Sage.

Saussure, F. (1966) [1916]. *Course in General Linguistics*. New York: McGraw-Hill.

Scheff, T.J. (1967). "Toward a Sociological Model of Consensus", *American Sociological Review* 32 (1): 32–46.

Schütz, A. (1972) [1932]. *The Phenomenology of The Social World*. London: Heinemann Educational Books.

Scott, J. (1990). *A Matter of Record: Documentary Sources in Social Research*. Cambridge: Polity Press.

Scott, J. (2001). "Where is Social Structure?", in. J. Lopez and G. Potter (eds.). *After Postmodernism*. London: Athlone Press.

Scott, J. (2016). "The social theory of Leonard Hobhouse", *Journal of Classical Sociology* 16 (4): 349–368.

Scott, J. (2017a). *Social Network Analysis*, 4th Edition. London: Sage.

Scott, J. (2017b). "Social Structure", in P. Sohlberg and H. Leiulfsrud (eds.). *Concepts in Action: Conceptual Constructionism*. Leiden: Brill.

Smith, D. (1990). *The Conceptual Practices of Power*. Toronto: University of Toronto Press.

Smith, D. (1999). *Writing The Social*. Toronto: University of Toronto Press.

Sorokin, P. (1937–41). *Social and Cultural Dynamics*, Four Volumes. London: G. Allen and Unwin.

Spencer, H. (1873) [1860]. "The Social Organism", in H. Spencer (ed.). *Illustrations of Universal Progress*. New York: D. Appleton and Co.

Spencer, H. (1873–93). *Principles of Sociology*, Three Volumes. London: Williams and Norgate.

Strauss, A., Schatzman, L., Ehrlich, D., Bucher, Rue, and Sabshin, M. (1963). "The Hospital and Its Negotiated Order", in E. Friedson (ed.). *The Hospital in Modern Society*. New York: Free Press.

Surowiecki, J. (2004). *The Wisdom of Crowds*. New York: Doubleday.

Tarde, G. (1903) [1890]. *The Laws of Imitation*. New York: H. Holt and Co.

Watkins, J.W.N. (1973) [1952]. "Ideal Types and Historical Explanation", in J. O'Neill (ed.). *Modes of Individualism and Collectivism*. London: Heinemann.

White, H.C., Boorman, S.A., and Breiger, R.L. (1976). "Social structure from multiple networks: I.", *American Journal of Sociology* 81.

CHAPTER 5

Constructing the Conceptual Tools for the Global South

David Fasenfest and Raju J. Das

1   Introduction[1]

The 20st Century closed with capitalism apparently victorious; the free market was generating profits in the context of globalisation, and everyone was certain that expansion and growth would continue without end. In Fukuyama's telling (1989), the fall of the Soviet Union put an end to Marxism's political plans and heralded an era of hegemonic liberal democracy, His frame of the end of history was in opposition to Marx's notion of social change and epochal transformation, and in his view this puts paid to the idea that capitalism will evolve.

> The twentieth century saw the developed world descend into a paroxysm of ideological violence, as liberalism contended first with absolutism, then bolshevism and fascism, and finally an updated Marxism that threatened it would lead to the ultimate apocalypse of nuclear war.
> FUKUYAMA, 1989: 1

Liberal democracy brings with it: "... economic calculation, the endless solving of technical problems, environmental concerns, and the satisfaction of sophisticated consumer demands" (Fukuyama, 1989: 17).[2] His focus on the developed world is a harbinger, and a reminder, that the rest of the world, the so-called Third World or the Global South, is to be viewed as being on the same path and should model itself on the Global North.

---

1   The authors would like to thank participants who provided feedback at the project workshop held in Trondheim, and useful comments by Håkon Leiulfsrud and Peter Sohlberg on earlier drafts.
2   More recently, Fukuyama modified his position (Fukuyama, 2018) and noted that "At this juncture, it seems to me that certain things Karl Marx said are turning out to be true" (see https://bit.ly/2IQaEpK).

Capitalism has experienced a steady shift from long-term concerns such as developing technology and making investments in product development as the source of wealth (i.e. surplus) creation to simply making money from money—in effect, the focus is now on short-term financial returns. As manufacturing declined (in part as a result in this shift), the financial industry has played an ever-larger role, facilitated by a steady erosion of regulatory constraints on what banks and other financial institutions could do. Two main consequences emerged: on one hand, there was a shift towards shareholder value, corporate restructuring favouring outsourcing and increasing compensation to senior officers; at the same time, it resulted in greater inequality, neoliberal policies that undermined social protections, and in general fostered broader global connectivity and potential for instability. This led to a financial crisis in 2007 and 2008 brought on by the unrestrained creation of private credit and money by a financial system that was out of control and short-sighted. As the capitalist world struggled with the fallout of the financial collapse, the financial press and investment firm reports asked whether Marx was right after all and warned against the ever-growing inequality and concentration of wealth.

Lost in all of this, at least from the perspective of the centres of capitalist power and wealth, is how to understand what is happening in the rest of the world. Capitalism's development transformed the nature of production and repurposed land to its requirements. This transformation consequently depended upon colonial expansion to provide both food that sustained the growing proletariat in the industrial centres of England and Northern Europe and the raw materials consumed by industrial productive forces (see Dobb, 1946 for a classic narrative of European capitalist development).

From the outset, social theorists reflected on the transition in Europe as a model of social, political and economic development which would bring the whole world into the so-called modern era (Weber, 1978 provides the blueprint for this modernist intellectual agenda). At each phase, events outside Europe were understood in relation to European development even when viewed with a critical lens. What follows is a brief digression concerning how non-European societies were viewed, focusing on developments during the 19th and 20th centuries and culminating with what we now understand as the Global South today. The aim of this chapter is to return attention to Marx's own views on the Global South, and to highlight the usefulness of core concepts in current efforts to understand contemporary developments in those regions.

2   The Non-European World

The period of colonial expansion that predates the transition to capitalism as the dominant mode of production in Europe can be characterised as a period of genocide, slavery, exploitation, and conquest, all in the service of European powers. European colonial expansion had a significant impact on the world, not the least of which was a constant state of conflict. Whilst the 20th century experienced World War I (1914–1918) and World War II (1939–1945), there was an earlier global conflict from 1702 to 1814 between England and France, the major colonial powers of the day.[3] These two powers were embroiled in conflicts over monarchical successions in Spain and Austria, in conflict in India and the Seven Year War fought in North America (1744–1763), involvement during the American Revolution (1778–1784), the revolutionary wars in France (1793–1802), followed by the Napoleonic wars (1803–1814).[4]

At the time Marx was writing, 90 per cent of the world's industrial production was situated in England, mainly around Manchester, and some parts of northern Europe. His contributions, broadly stated, dealt with the nature of production (with his explanations on the forces and relations of production, and how they shaped society) and the role of history in understanding the development of economies and societies. Whilst he focused on the economy, Marx was also actively seeking greater emancipation through political practices. Looking for the potential for political change in Europe, few of his writings dealt with non-European societies (Kalmring and Nowak, 2017: 331) beyond journalistic reflections on India, China, and the Ottoman Empire. Sperber (2013) notes that Marx was addressing the issues of his day, not ours, and thus has little relevance for the present, while Gareth Stedman Jones (2016) seeks to return Marx to the nineteenth century.

Efforts to understand countries that made up the colonial and later post-colonial world remained firmly entrenched in a Eurocentric world view. Theorists expounded on the so-called core versus periphery of the global economy, which became parsed as less-developed versus more-developed countries (LDC v MDC). 'Development' was necessarily to be accompanied by the rationalisation of colonial administrations and the transformation of the

---

3   This is not the first century of conflict between England and France: the 100 Years War was fought from 1337 to 1453 and set the tone of the wars to follow, drawing in most European countries. It was then that the battle of Agincourt (1415), memorialised by Shakespeare, was fought.

4   There were only 25 years of relative peace in a global conflict that embroiled all their colonies.

economy into a 'modern' industrial state, whether through export-led growth or import substitution industrialisation.

In the face of liberation movements and wars of colonial independence of the 20th Century, institutions such as the World Bank and the International Monetary Fund were set up to manage global capitalist development, and to promote policies and practices that would replicate the economies that flourished in Europe. By the 1960s, scholars like Cardoso (1977), Cardoso and Faletto (1979) and Frank (1969; 1978) pointed to dependent development. The countries in Latin America, Asia, and Africa were trapped by their relationships to advanced capitalism in Europe.[5] After World War II two large blocs of states emerged: the so-called capitalist First World centred around the United States and the socialist Second World of the Union of Soviet Socialist Republics with much of Eastern Europe, later joined by the People's Republic of China. The former colonial and other non-aligned nations were labelled as the Third World.

3   The Global South

As Dados and Connell (2012: 12) point out, the notion of the Global South first appeared in Gramsci's *The Southern Question* (1995), when he discusses how southern Italy had "been colonised by capitalists from northern Italy". This framed the development of regions outside capitalist Europe in terms of a binary North/South, an extension of the core/periphery framework of World Systems theorists. The Global South was initially a designation to identify economically disadvantaged nations and a replacement for the Third World. In this iteration, implicit reference was still based on a distinction from European nations and carried with it a post-colonial imagery. This binary meaning was increasingly challenged (see Prashad, 2007; 2012), raising the question of whether the political use of the term 'south' was meaningful. Prashad (2012) defines the Global South in terms of those transnational social movements emerging to resist policies of neoliberalism.

Connell (2007) raises the notion that one must consider new theoretical frameworks and non-Eurocentric intellectual orientations when thinking about something like the Global South. Rather, she posits that they reflect the theorising rooted in the world's multiple peripheries. After all, the 'south' is not simply geography—indeed, there are 'souths' in the north and 'norths' in the south. This leads to a deterritorialised conceptualisation of what is meant by

---

5   See Dietz (1980) for a useful summary of dependency theory.

Global South, one in which resistance to a capitalist political and social reality binds those with a shared experience of subjugation under global capitalism (consider the Zapatista movement in Mexico as an example of an anticapitalist rather than a nationalist struggle). Whereas 'post-colonialist' refers to a common oppositional reaction to Western capitalism and European cultural and economic domination, (as exemplified by the work of Fanon, 1961), the Global South emerges as networks of power and opposition to global capitalism itself.

Recently, de Sousa Santos (2014) takes the idea of the Global South to the next level, arguing against what he calls *epistemicide*. It is not enough to view the Global South in critical and oppositional terms which have a Western understanding of both social injustice and transformative movements—in other words, ideas rooted in a Eurocentric critical tradition. He argues instead for epistemologies of the South, asking for strong questions which can address "... the societal and epistemological paradigm options ..." (2014: 20). Essentially, he maintains Western understandings of the world ignore "decisive cultural and political experiences and initiatives in the countries of the global South" (2014: 21). Epistemologies of the south are derived from ecologies of knowledge and intercultural translation.

> At the core of ecologies of knowledge is the idea that different types of knowledge are incomplete in different ways and that raising the consciousness of such reciprocal incompleteness (rather than looking for completeness) will be a precondition for achieving cognitive justice. Intercultural translation is the alternative both to the abstract universalism that grounds Western-centric general theories and so the ideal of incommensurability between cultures.
>
> DE SOUSA SANTOS 2014: 212

At the end of the day, de Sousa Santos seeks a way towards a truly bottom-up rather than a top-down political aggregation leading to greater solidarity and social justice.

Given this framing of the Global South why, one might ask, should we engage with Marx at all? After all, recent scholarship argues for a separation from historically Western thinking and, quite clearly, Marx is a quintessential Western thinker. In response, we offer two perspectives that motivate our interest in applying Marx's concepts in developing an analysis of the Global South. First, we argue that Marx provides an analytical framework apart from a purely Euro-centric view of social processes and limited notions of social development and change. It is precisely because those regions that we have come to understand as the Global South are the products of, and are organised in opposition to, capitalist development that there is value in considering how Marx, as the single most incisive analyst of capitalism, can help to develop the conceptual frame for dealing with the challenges faced. Marx operates at the highest level of abstraction—the system of capitalism in its pure form. Scholars operating at intermediate levels of analysis seek to understand how capitalism operates over time and within some historically medicated context. Countries of the Global South differ, exhibiting aspects of late-development capitalism, and as such they pose special challenges when trying to understand their political economy. It is at the most basic level of analysis, exploring the singularity of any country's stage of development and specific social relations of production within the context of capitalist practices (internally and internationally) that we can begin to understand, utilising the insights of Marx's analysis of capitalism, variations in and potentials for true non-Eurocentric and counter-hegemonic outcomes in the Global South.

The second reason we need to develop ways to evaluate and understand what have traditionally been called countries of the Global South by applying concepts found in Marx is that globalisation and the increased interconnectedness of national economies have produced Global South regions in the Global North. Issues of sustainable development and climate change pose major challenges in many parts of the highly developed North, blurring the distinction between those advanced and established economies and those at various stages of development (Horner, 2019). Increasingly there are calls to "move beyond macro-scale, North-South spatial characterisations of development" (Horner, 2019: 8) because growing income inequality is reflected not just amongst individuals, or between the North and South countries, but also within countries of the Global North across regions that are differently affected by austerity and neoliberal policies.

4   Marx in Context

Post-colonial and post-modern theorists argue that regions of the South are very different from Europe, and so for them Marx's ideas have limited if any relevance in formulating research approaches to these societies. We must remember that, whilst capitalism developed first in Europe, little in what Marx wrote indicates that he believed there was anything inherently superior about European society (Gasper, 2002). Eagleton goes on to point out that while Marx was indeed a European, it was in "Asia that his ideas took root, and in the so-called Third World that they flourished most vigorously" (Eagleton, 2011a: 225).

It is in the periphery (Lenin's land, Mao's villages) that Marx's work had its greatest impact on social change. For example, the work of Marx informed an intense debate at the start of the 20th Century on the transition of Japanese society and the nature of emerging capitalism. Two schools of thought led this debate: *Kōzaha* referred to those who submitted articles to the *Lecture Series on the History of Development of the Japanese Capitalism* published in 1932–33, and their theoretical stance was close to that of the Japanese Communist Party (JCP). *Rōnōha* referred to those who, critical of the JCP and rejecting the guidance of the Comintern, submitted articles to the journal, *Workers and Farmers*, launched in 1927 (Aoki, 2020).

There is a need to avoid two dangers in assessing Marx's relevance to the Global South: on the one hand, world-regional exceptionalism that absolutises the specificity of the regions of the Global South, and on the other, Eurocentrist universalism that mechanically applies Marx's ideas as if regions of the Global South were merely tropical or warmer Europe, a late-Europe as it were. We can classify Marx's ideas based on both social relations and geography. In the first instance, his ideas explore all forms of society, all forms of class society, the capitalist form of class society, and finally advanced forms of capitalism. Whilst generally abstract, these ideas properly framed are applicable to the Global South. Whilst geographically some of his ideas may be specific to Europe (for example, his discussion of land enclosures that displace workers to increase wool production for the textile mills of England), others are specifically relevant to the Global South as former colonies of Europe (that is the locus of food production needed to replace lost agriculture in England). To the extent that capitalist relations increasingly develop in the Global South, those ideas specific to 19th Century European capitalism are relevant for the Global South (the displacement of people from the land, the growth of industry in cities, and an emerging class society based on ownership of and control over the means of production). This becomes evident in the emergence of African Marxism, Asian Marxism, Latin American Marxism, Indian Marxism, and Chinese Marxism (which is being promoted in China's various Schools of Marxism located in its major universities), as well as Marxist studies programs focusing on international development, imperialism, agrarian change, etc., in the Global South.

5 What Distinguishes Marx's Approach to the Study of Society?

Marx's intellectual work reflects, and seeks to promote, radical-democratic and anti-capitalist social change through a materialist-realist and dialectical ontology and epistemology and historical-materialist generalisations about all forms of class society to include its deeply held prejudices and material practices against oppressed groups such as women and racialised minorities. Marx undertakes a political economy of capitalist society; his analysis encompasses the economy, state, culture, and ecological transformation and he expounds on revolutionary political practice. Marx is, in essence, a dialectical materialist:

> My dialectic method is not only different from the Hegelian but is its direct opposite ... [in the sense that] the ideal is nothing else than the material world reflected by the human mind and translated into forms of thought ...
> MARX, preface to *Capital vol. 1*

Marx's materialism is about the production and reproduction of the means of life. It is about how humans produce/reproduce a) their bodies which have material needs, and b) the material conditions of production (e.g. produced spatial organisation, environment, technology, etc.), and c) the means of subsistence, through the interaction with nature, and through social relations of production, property, and domestic labour.

Marx emphasises four key philosophical principles: 1) the materiality of life/society; 2) social relations (the idea that an object or an individual is an ensemble of multiple social relations forming a totality); 3) the systemic and totalising character of society; and 4) that society changes through internal contradictions. Given that he sees society as an ensemble of relations, a site where all things are interrelated, and that some of the mechanisms are not easily observable, he makes use of the method of abstraction. He separates what is essential from what is accidental; he looks at things from certain vantage points, abstracting from other vantage-points, and adjusts the scope of a concept depending on his purpose. Marx looks at relationships on multiple levels of generality (all human society, class history, capitalism in the abstract, advanced capitalism, and capitalism in a given time and place, see Ollman, 2003).

Arguably, his philosophical ideas—especially, its stress on the materiality of life—are as relevant to the Global South, where the material needs of the clear majority remain unmet, as they are to the North. Marx's dialectical-materialist perspective allows one to see the Global South in terms of its stark *material* problems (the problems of lack of food, shelter, clothing, etc.), in terms of its various *contradictions* and in terms of *internal relations* to the imperialist system, and so on. This philosophical aspect of Marx's relevance to the Global

South has not been emphasised; to the extent that the study of the Global South has been shaped by post-colonialism/post-modernism, and to the extent that these perspectives are skeptical of Marx, a counter-critique of the post-colonial perception of the South can and must be based on Marx's own philosophical ideas. Given that post-colonialism stresses the perception of the Global South as constitutive of the Global South, Marx offers the following as a response: "... one cannot judge" either a time period or a place:

> by its consciousness, but, on the contrary, this consciousness must be explained from the contradictions of material life, from the conflict existing between the social forces of production and the relations of production.
>
> MARX, *Preface to the Critique of Political Economy*

Marx is against superficial generalisation or overgeneralisation. He emphasises that categories and hypotheses derived from Western Europe are not to be simply transferred to other social realities:

> Thus, events strikingly analogous but taking place in different historic surroundings led to totally different results. By studying each of these forms of evolution separately and then comparing them one can easily find the clue to this phenomenon, but one will never arrive there by the universal passport of a general historico-philosophical theory, the supreme virtue of which consists in being super-historical.
>
> MARX, 1970 [1859]: 21

However, that does not mean that one cannot make any scientific generalisation based on abstraction about underlying mechanisms that operate widely: if capitalism is to happen and become a dominant relation, separation of direct producers on a large scale is necessary. This is true in the USA as much as in China. As Marx writes:

> If Russia is tending to become a capitalist nation after the example of the Western European countries, and during the last years she has been taking a lot of trouble in this direction—she will not succeed without having first transformed a good part of her peasants into proletarians; and after that, once taken to the bosom of the capitalist regime, she will experience its pitiless laws like other profane peoples.
>
> MARX, 1970 [1859]: 21

What Marx had written about the Russia of his time, then a relatively less developed country, applies to all other countries, including all of the contemporary Global South. Of course, whether that separation happens in a politically enforced way or through class-differentiation amongst commodity producers (and this Lenin stressed in his own discussion of Russia) is a separate matter.

Marx applies his philosophical materialism to the study of society. Human beings, as a part of nature, have material needs (needs for food, shelter, clothing, etc.) as well as cultural needs, with the material needs having a degree of priority. To satisfy these needs, humans must interact with nature and with one another. They combine their labour with the means of production that are ultimately derived from nature, in the context of social relations of production, to produce things to satisfy their needs. When productive forces develop, a surplus is produced, and, with this, class inequality and class struggle over the surplus ensues. In a class society, whether of the Global South or of the North, society's means of production are controlled by a small minority; so, the great majority, free or unfree, have to perform surplus labour. As Marx writes in *Capital vol. 1*:

> Wherever a part of society possesses the monopoly of the means of production, the worker, free or unfree, must add to the labour time necessary for his own maintenance an extra quantity of labor-time in order to produce the means of subsistence for the owner of the means of production, whether this proprietor be ... a slave owner ... or a modern landlord or a capitalist.
>
> MARX, 1977: 344

The state arises to reinforce and support class inequality generally. Ideologies play a similar role. And this is true about the Global South as well as the North.

The economic, political, and cultural/ideological processes interact within a whole in which the economy is *ultimately*—though not immediately—dominant. Why? We must first eat, drink, have shelter, and clothing and medicine, etc., before we can pursue politics, science, art, religion, etc. The mode of production of material life, the way we produce our livelihood, conditions our social, political and intellectual life process in general. Once again, here is Marx in *Capital volume 1*:

> each particular mode of production and the social relations corresponding to it at each given moment, in short, 'the economic structure of society', is 'the real foundation on which arises the juridical and political superstructure and to which correspond definite forms of social

consciousness' ... '[T]he mode of production of material life conditions the general process of social, political, and intellectual life' ... [T]he middle ages could not live on Catholicism, nor the ancient world on politics.

MARX, 1977: 175–176

Human society has evolved through various forms of class society (slavery, feudalism, capitalism, etc.). In capitalism, most things are produced for sale, so they are commodities. In pre-capitalist societies commodities might circulate but mainly to satisfy needs. By contrast, investing money to produce commodities to make more money is a defining characteristic of capitalism.

When direct producers are subjected to primitive accumulation, i.e. when they are coercively dispossessed of their means of production (or means of livelihood/employment), then they must work for capitalists for a wage. This results in workers' exploitation which benefits capitalists, and in an expansion of wealth in its capitalist form. As Marx points out in *Capital*, the fact that half a day's labour is necessary to keep a labourer alive for 24 hours, does not in any way prevent him/her from working a whole day for the capitalist.

For Marx, commodity production under capitalist social relations results in first, the concentration and centralisation of productive forces in fewer hands (and fewer areas), and second, a more or less constant tendency towards investment in means of production relative to investment in wages, causing a long-term fall in the rate of profit (see Roberts, 2016). The results are: economic crisis; the expansion of a reserve army of unemployed and underemployed resulting in their immiseration in absolute and relative terms; rising inequality between workers and owners; the proletarianisation of independent commodity producers; and the concentration and centralisation of productive forces. These factors combine in advanced countries to create a drive for a spatial fix (the export of capital), setting up pressure towards inter-imperialist rivalry and imperialist control over relatively less developed parts of the world. Massive adverse impacts on nature and on human bodies (unsafe working conditions), as well as alienation, also result. The capitalist state's fundamental role is to protect the property rights of capitalists and to ensure general conditions for profit-making at home and abroad.

6   Marx's 'Global South-Specific' Ideas

Marx's general analysis of capitalist development—commodification, pre- and non-capitalist relations slowly and unevenly being supplanted by capitalist-market relations, dispossession, exploitation, periodic crises, the tendency of workers and peasants to rise in revolt, and so on—are generally applicable to the Global South as capitalism develops in that region.

Although Marx's empirical examples came from Britain, his approach to capitalism was basically global or internationalist. World commerce was the presupposition of capitalism, he wrote: "The production of commodities, their circulation, and that more developed form of their circulation called commerce [trade], these form the historical groundwork from which it rises" (Marx, 1977: 247). The modern history of capital dates from the creation in the 16th century of a world-embracing commerce and a world-embracing market. Thus, the world-geography of trade is a precondition for capitalism, which makes capitalism a global phenomenon.

And then, he argued, the development of capitalism in its heartland was crucially dependent on its interaction with the colonies. This meant an international division of labour imposed by imperialism, which is an on-going process:

> By ruining handicraft production in other countries, machinery forcibly converts them into fields for the supply of its raw material. In this way East India was compelled to produce cotton, wool, hemp, jute, and indigo for Great Britain. ... A new and international division of labor, a division suited to the requirements of the chief centers of modern industry springs up and converts one part of the globe into a chiefly agricultural field of production, for supplying the other part which remains a chiefly industrial field.
>
> MARX, cited in GHOSH, 1984: 45

Imperialism, therefore, imposes an international division of labour:

> competitive accumulation produces uneven and combined development as it tends to concentrate high-value added production and capital in the system's most competitive centres, determining a forced specialisation of dependent countries in low-value added sectors, repatriating profits extracted in these countries, and leading to forms of unequal exchange between nations with different productivity levels.
>
> PRADELLA, 2017: 156

Imperialism also meant a drain of surplus.

> The discovery of gold and silver in America, the extirpation, enslavement and entombment in mines of the aboriginal population, the beginning of the conquest and looting of the East Indies, the turning of Africa into

a warren for the commercial hunting of black-skins, signalised the rosy dawn of the era of capitalist production. These idyllic proceedings are the chief momenta of primitive accumulation. On their heels treads the commercial war of the European nations, with the globe for a theatre.

MARX, 1990 [1867]: 915

In other words, the development of European capitalism depended on conquest, genocide and slavery in the Global South. The relationship between the North and the Global South means that the surplus from colonies, in the context of already-existing capital–labour relations, was converted into capital, and that this capital was invested not only in industry as in England but also in agriculture as in Scotland (Byres, 2007). And this also means that imperialism by depriving the colonies of its surplus, blocks economic development in the Global South of the type that occurred in Europe. Marx thus points to the exploitation of colonised nations by imperialist nations, a process that was responsible for the under-development of the Global South and the development of the North, a process that has not ceased. As compared to his earlier analysis, in his later writings Marx seems to recognise that the destruction of the old order by colonialism and free trade does not necessarily lay the material foundation of a new order (Kalmring and Nowak, 2017: 335). Here Marx identifies external rather than internal causes of a blockage of industrial–capitalist development in these countries.

Most anti-colonial movements in the Global South were inspired by Marxism (Eagleton, 2011a). Marx supported freedom of movement in colonies, including in India and Ireland. Yet, the relevance of Marx's ideas for the communist revolution in the Global South is heavily debated. Marx writes in his famous *Preface to A Contribution to the Critique of Political Economy*, that:

At a certain stage of development, the material productive forces of society come into conflict with the existing relations of production or—this merely expresses the same thing in legal terms—with the property relations within the framework of which they have operated hitherto. From forms of development of the productive forces these relations turn into their fetters. Then begins an era of social revolution. The changes in the economic foundation lead sooner or later to the transformation of the whole immense superstructure. ...

No social order is ever destroyed before all the productive forces for which it is sufficient have been developed, and new superior relations

of production never replace older ones before the material conditions for their existence have matured within the framework of the old society.
MARX, 1970 [1859]: 21

So, what relevance does Marx's theory of revolution and social transformation have for the Global South? In many Third World countries, productive forces are not developed to the same extent as in advanced countries. Democratic and anti-imperialist revolutions in many countries remain incomplete. Does it mean that productive forces under capitalism should be first allowed to be developed to produce a conflict within capitalist social relations before a communist revolution can take place in the Global South?

It is implausible that Marx would argue for a two-stage theory of revolution, one where a bourgeois-democratic revolution of the type that took place in Europe, is necessary to create conditions for capitalism which, in turn, will be followed by a socialist revolution in the Global South. Lenin and Trotsky argued that the bourgeoisie in the late capitalist countries were incapable of finishing the democratic revolution, and therefore that task fell on the workers and semi-proletarians, who, while fighting for a democratic revolution would be compelled to go on uninterruptedly to convert the democratic revolution into a socialist revolution. This idea of permanent revolution is originally in Marx:

> While the democratic petty bourgeois want to bring the revolution to an end as quickly as possible, achieving at most the aims already mentioned, it is our interest and our task to make the revolution permanent until all the more or less propertied classes have been driven from their ruling positions, until the proletariat has conquered state power and until the association of the proletarians has progressed sufficiently far—not only in one country but in all the leading countries of the world—that competition between the proletarians of these countries ceases and at least the decisive forces of production are concentrated in the hands of the workers. Our concern cannot simply be to modify private property, but to abolish it, not to hush up class antagonisms but to abolish classes, not to improve the existing society but to found a new one.
> MARX AND ENGELS, 1850

It is also implausible that, given his internationalist approach, Marx would want to think about the relation between productive forces and social relations on a country-by-country basis: there is no reason why a country should have to await a high level of economic development before it launches a political movement for socialism. That relation must be seen at the international scale, where there is clearly a contradiction between existing capitalist social relations and the development of productive forces. Capitalism is past its due date. It is quite possible that workers in the Global South can succeed in taking state power before workers in the developed countries.

7   Concepts for the Global South

Marx's relevance to the global South can be better appreciated if he is seen as a theorist of both capitalism and class relations *sui generis*, and not just as a theorist of capitalism. Once one emphasises the class character of society, one can see that a given country will have multiple forms of class relations, including capitalism and pre- and non-capitalist relations, and multiple forms of capitalism itself as a class society. In this light, one can make several claims about the way to apply Marx's conceptual framing to examine the Global South:

Multiple class relations: Countries of the Global South are not to be seen merely as having less income and more absolute poverty. Instead, they must be seen fundamentally in terms of class: as countries that have suffered from aborted—or incomplete—revolutions against the propertied classes, aborted democratic revolutions, including agrarian revolutions against feudal relations, aborted national (or anti-imperialist) revolutions, and aborted or failed anti-capitalist revolutions. The capitalism of the Global South is deeply impacted by imperialism and coexists in a social formation which may contain remnants of feudalism and commodity production based in relations other than wage-labour as well as indigenous-collective traditions. The capitalism that exists in the Global South is not exactly like that of advanced countries. As Patnaik says, Marx's *Tribune* articles on India offer "a hint of a broader perspective within which *Capital*, and the perspective surrounding *Capital*, has got to be located" (p. lvi), and these articles offer "a perception of capitalism, as existing not in isolation but in the midst of pre-capitalist formations which it dominates and molds to its own requirements" (p. lviii, quoted in Byres, 2007).

Primitive accumulation: Marx may have paid more attention to politically enforced dispossession (primitive accumulation) separating workers from the means of production than class differentiation in a commodity-producing society, something Lenin emphasised in what can be called his version of *Capital* (*Development of Capitalism in Russia*). Marx draws attention to commodity owners going out of business in his discussion, in *Capital vol. 1,* of concentration and centralisation. Some anti-Marxists believe that class differentiation does not exist to the extent that Marx and Marxists say it does. In the Global South, small-scale farmers are subjected to class differentiation, even if that process is mediated by government policies providing some help to peasants, etc. But class differentiation is also slowed down because peasants under-feed

themselves and their animals. And in many cases, the value of property peasants own is only nominal, given their enormous debt. For Marx, primitive
accumulation is an international process. It occurred both within each country undergoing capitalist transition and in the colonies. The presence of direct
producers with access to means of production was a barrier to capitalism and
had to be broken not only in Europe but also in the colonies.

> in the colonies. ... the capitalist regime everywhere comes into collision
> with the resistance of the producer, who, as owner of his own conditions
> of labour, employs that labour to enrich himself, instead of the capitalist.
> The contradiction of these two diametrically opposed economic systems,
> manifests itself here practically in a struggle between them. Where the
> capitalist has at his back the power of the mother-country, he tries to
> clear out of his way by force the modes of production and appropriation
> based on the independent labour of the producer.
>
> MARX, 1977

As noted above, Marx conceptualised colonialism and imperialism as constitutive elements of the development of capitalism (Pradella, 2017: 156). For capitalism to exist, direct producers must not have direct access to means of production and subsistence (Marx, 1977). The very idea of primitive accumulation
has great contemporary relevance for the Global South, where small-scale producers are in the process of being dispossessed. Marx's idea of dispossession
has been revived recently by Harvey (2007; 2003) amongst others, although his
theorisation is not un-problematic (Das, 2017).

Economic and extra-economic coercion: For Marx, capitalism is based on a
combination of economic and extra-economic coercion of direct producers.
Once direct producers have been separated from the means of production,
economic mechanisms of exploitation are more or less sufficient, although
extra-economic mechanisms are used from time to time. At the dawn of capitalism, extra-economic coercion played a crucial role. This included slavery.

> *Slavery* is an economic category like any other. Thus, it also has its two
> sides. Let us leave alone the bad side and talk about the good side of slav-
> ery. Needless to say, we are dealing only with direct slavery, with Negro
> slavery in Surinam, in Brazil, in the Southern States of North America.

> Direct slavery is just as much the pivot of bourgeois industry as machin-
> ery, credits, etc. Without slavery you have no cotton; without cotton you
> have no modern industry. It is slavery that gave the colonies their value;

> it is the colonies that created world trade, and it is world trade that is the precondition of large-scale industry. Thus, slavery is an economic category of the greatest importance.
>
> MARX, 1847

But slavery did not just happen then. It continues, including in the Global South. Capital can make currently free labour unfree in order to discipline labour, and therefore the imposition of unfreedom is a form of class struggle from above (Brass, 2011; Das, 2016).

The global character of capital–labour relations: Marx appears to give the impression that his theory of capital–labour relations operates in a closed system, that it is perhaps more about Europe or England and about industrial capitalism than about capitalism as such and so on. His is a theory of capitalism that can be viewed as existing globally. The capitalist class and the working class are increasingly world-classes, and the law of competition or the law of value ultimately and freely operate at the global scale, although it is mediated by national and regional level processes. Marx conceptualises the antagonism between wage-labour and capital as a global tendency, encompassing and reproducing relations of colonial and imperialist exploitation and oppression (Pradella, 2015: 159). His ideas about capital–labour relations and mechanisms underlying what he calls general law of capitalist accumulation (chapter 25 of *Capital vol. 1*) are applicable to the world-stage now more than during his time and can be used to understand the Global South more than during his time. The *Communist Manifesto* which Marx wrote together with Friedrich Engels makes the point that capital must nestle everywhere, settle everywhere, establish connections everywhere, which reflects our current reality, with consequences for the Global South and its relationship with the North. Capitalists from advanced countries increasingly shift production to selected regions of the Global South to take advantage of the global immobility of labour, and the subsistence (or below-subsistence) wages and despotic/authoritarian working conditions that exist in the Global South. This produces a super-exploited working class and super-profit for businesses of the North, at times at the expense of profits of capitalists in the Global South. Low-cost imports from Asia and other parts of the Global South protect the value of the US Dollar as the hegemonic currency, and thus the financial assets of the capitalist class (Patnaik and Patnaik, 2015). Marx's reserve army has become truly a global reserve army. This forces income deflation on the world's workers, beginning in the Global South, also affecting the workers of the North who are increasingly subjected to neoliberal 'labor market flexibility' (Foster et al., 2011). Indeed, because of the possibility and actuality of super-exploitation of workers in the Global South, their brothers and sisters in North are facing low wages and precarity; the threat of movement of jobs to the Global South has disciplinary effects on workers in the North.

Marx's idea of the latent reserve army is relevant here. The army of migrant labour from poor countries generates conflict within the working class nationally and internationally (Jonna and Foster, 2016). For Marx, the reserve army or the "surplus population becomes ... the lever of capitalistic accumulation, nay, a condition of existence of the capitalist mode of production", and it "belongs to capital quite as absolutely as if the latter had bred it at its own cost" (Marx, in *Capital vol. 1*). Some scholars from Latin America say that a segment of the reserve army is not going to be employed by capital, foreign or domestic, so they call this segment the marginal mass living a precarious life. Note, there are racialised people with no skills under these same conditions also in the North (Wright, 1995).

When the *Communist Manifesto* was written in the late 1840s, most of the world's population consisted of small-scale agrarian producers. Today, with the spread of capitalist market relations, the vast majority of people live by selling their labour power in almost every region of the world, including in the Global South. With the rise in total global investment (expansion in accumulation), there is an increase in capital at one pole and increase in the proletariat at another pole. The Global South demonstrates this, thereby completing the picture of capitalism that Marx painted.

The slogan, 'workers of the world, unite', based on objectively existing common grounds amongst workers of both the Global South and the North, makes more sense now than during Marx's own times. Marx's idea that workers would be driven to resist capitalist exploitation enabled by improvement in transport and communication will be proven to be true when workers launch massive revolts in India, Brazil, South Africa, Egypt, etc. In 2016, 180 million Indian workers participated in what was perhaps the largest strike in human history. The working class is a far larger sector of the population with far more power partly because of the expansion of the working class in the Global South. This is true whether or not they are always conscious of their power, and of the fact that their interests and those of capitalists are not reconcilable.

Instability and inequality: Marx outlines "the tendency of capitalist society to expand, polarise, destabilise, and destroy. These words seem to be drawn from current world experience", says Laibman (2013). Capitalism is not only crisis-prone; increasingly and at an accelerating pace it is also creating inequality.

> With the crisis of 2007–08, for the first time in recent experience, the two understandings—of capitalism's effects on economic stability, and of its shaping of the distribution of wealth and power—came together.
>
> LAIBMAN, 2013: 451

Now the current world experience includes that of the Global South: economic crisis emanating in the North affects the Global South (including opportunities for exports from the Global South to the North). When there is a crisis of profitability, advanced capitalism seeks to make use of cheap labour and resources in the Global South to counter such a crisis.

Not only is inequality increasing between poorest and richest countries, but it is also increasing within fast-growing lower-income countries (the so-called emerging economies as well as ex-socialist countries). The inequality between countries of the North and those of the Global South—for example inequalities between businesses of North and workers and peasants of the Global South—reflects Marx when he states: "Wealth in one pole and misery in another". We now have an integrated world capitalist system, with a global rich and global poor—as Marx predicted. The proliferation of sweatshops and export processing zones are all very much in keeping with Marx's anticipation of global inequality.

Super-exploitation: Marx's view of capitalism as generalised commodity production assumes that all labour is wage labour, although he makes a distinction between forms of circulation and different forms of property (property based on one's own labour, and property based on the appropriation of surplus labour from workers). But in the Global South, peasant labour is widely prevalent and coexists with wage labour, and is integrated into capitalist exchange, financial relations (usury) and mercantile relations. Some peasants produce for the market and provide cheap wage-labour. Other peasants are paid only for the product of their labour; their products enter the world market at very low prices for the benefit of trans-national corporations (TNCs) in the Global North—either to provide cheap raw materials or to be processed and then resold at much higher prices. These products from the Global South sell at much lower prices relative to the labour involved than high end products from the North. Marx assumes that wages cover the costs of reproduction of labour power (value of labour power) but he says that for millions of people, wages fall below the value of labour power:

> Thus, the cost of production of simple labour-power amounts to the cost of the existence and propagation of the worker. The price of this cost of existence and propagation constitutes wages. The wages thus determined are called the minimum of wages. This minimum wage, like the determination of the price of commodities in general by cost of production, does not hold good for the single individual, but only for the race. Individual workers, indeed, millions of workers, do not receive enough to be able to exist and to propagate themselves; but the wages of the whole

> working class adjust themselves, within the limits of their fluctuations, to
> this minimum.
>
> MARX, 1976: 27

This happens due to the over-supply of labour relative to demand, including the over-supply of labour caused by the reserve army of labour produced
through technical change. Given the massive reserve army of labour in the
Global South, one that has been expanding since the colonial period, millions
of people work in absolute poverty, and millions more are working poor. Partly
because of the difference in the relative supply of labour in poor and rich
countries, wages for a given kind of work in poor countries are much less than
those in richer countries, leading to the super-exploitation (appropriation of
above-average rate of profit) of workers in the Global South, something Marini
from Latin America, among others has pointed out. A study of autoworkers
showed that those in the US are 18% more productive than their counterparts
in Mexico but are paid 14 times as much (Gilbert, 2017).

Imperialism and Underdevelopment: For Marx, capitalism is a class relation
and exists at multiple scales (city, region, nation, globally). Capitalism seen
globally is imperialism, which signifies exploitation of workers and peasants
in the colonised countries by the businesses of advanced countries, reinforced
by national (and racial) oppression. Low-cost access to their land/resources
and to workers, just like the use of advanced technologies, becomes a means of
competitive advantage for capitalists of advanced nations supported by their
more powerful states. Colonised countries also become dumping grounds for
surplus products and over-accumulated capital (not to speak of pollutants
and wastes) from imperialist countries and are subjected to exploitation in
sphere of financial capital (e.g. trade, debt, speculative capital). Imperialism
indeed produces a distinct stamp on the periphery of the capitalist system, a
system of global uneven development. In the *Communist Manifesto*, Marx and
Engels write:

> The bourgeoisie cannot exist without constantly revolutionising the
> instruments of production, and thereby the relations of production, and
> with them the whole relations of society. ... Constant revolutionising of
> production, uninterrupted disturbance of all social conditions, everlast-
> ing uncertainty and agitation distinguish the bourgeois epoch from all
> earlier ones.

If this is the case, how would Marx explain the relative economic backward-
ness of the Global South, where per capita income, labour productivity and the

general level of living are all rather low, relative to those in advanced capitalist countries? Does the thesis of constant revolutionisation of productive forces apply to Europe and outposts of Europeans only?

We argue that it is in Marx's ideas that we can find some of the explanations for the Global South's under-development. Marx writes about the destructive impact of colonialism. In many ways, imperialism continues to block economic development in the Global South as it drains the surplus in that region. Operating in tandem is a process that is rooted in the structure of class relations within the countries of the Global South. Following primitive accumulation, capitalism evolves in two stages, as Marx discusses in *Capital vol. 1*. In the first stage (formal subsumption of labour), capital appropriates surplus value in its absolute form, based on long hours (and one may add, low real wages). During this stage, technical change does not quite happen. In response to the struggle against long hours, capital resorts to labour-saving technical change, making workers produce more value for every unit of time, thus appropriating surplus value in its relative form (Marx calls this the real subsumption of labour). The transition from formal to real subsumption does not take place spontaneously. England took almost 200 years for the transition to take place, a transition that was mediated by class struggle. Given the massive reserve army in the Global South, partly created by imperialism, struggle against formal subsumption is not effective enough to force capital to deploy real subsumption. The on-going drain of surplus (via unequal exchange) deprives the Global South of the capital needed for investment in machinery and improved raw materials. In other words, and in terms of Marx's own theory in *Capital*, the South is a site of blocked transition from formal to real subsumption. The result is a backward form of capitalism (for further details, see Das, 2012; Das, 2017: chapter 8). The Global South consequently suffers not only from capitalism but also from its incomplete development.

This does not mean that no technical change in production occurs in the Global South. The assembly line and other techniques do not have to be invented in the Global South and can be easily adopted, thus allowing the countries to make a 'leap'. Given the low rate of profit in advanced countries and the over-accumulation of capital, the Global South with its cheap labour and resources is attractive to imperialist capital. Fractions of imperialist and 'national' capital operating in the Global South must use technology to remain globally competitive, for example in specific sectors where machines cannot be replaced by living labour (e.g. oil drilling). The results are that backward levels of economic development and lower forms of class relations (remnants of feudalism; peasant production and formal subsumption of labour by capital) coexist with islands of advanced capitalism (real subsumption) in the Global South. Or in the words of Trotsky:

A backward country assimilates the material and intellectual [achieve-
ments] ... of the advanced countries. But this does not mean that it follows them slavishly, reproduces all the stages of their past ... Although
compelled to follow after the advanced countries, a backward country
does not take things in the same order. The privilege of historic back-
wardness ... permits, or rather compels, the adoption of whatever is ready
in advance of any specified date, skipping a whole series of intermediate stages. ... The European colonists in America did not begin history all
over again from the beginning.

Unevenness, the most general law of the historic process, reveals itself
most sharply and complexly in the destiny of the backward countries. Under the whip of external necessity their backward culture
is compelled to make leaps. From the universal law of unevenness
thus derives another law which, for the lack of a better name, we may
call the law of *combined development*—by which we mean a drawing
together of the different stages of the journey, a combining of the separate steps, an amalgam of archaic with more contemporary forms.
Without this law ... it is impossible to understand the history of [the
periphery] ...

TROTSKY 2008 [1932]: 4–5

8   Conclusion

Marx's thinking helps us to understand the Global South in terms of its historical and on-going relationships to the North, and offers insights based on his
general concepts of class-exploitation, commodity, accumulation, and others
that account for the complexity and variation in social and political opposition to capitalist—and especially neoliberal—social relations found in the
Global South. We need to see Marx's ideas, and consider a Marxism of Marx,
in terms of:
a)   being relevant to the understanding of economy, politics, culture and
     nature in the abstract and at the level of the world-market, and
b)   as comprising bodies of work (various *Marxisms*) that i) critically capture
     the 'unique' ways in which capitalism develops in, and impacts, specific
     world-regions, including in the Global South, and ii) demonstrate how
     the different world-regions of the Global South are developing unevenly
     relative to one another and relative to the imperialist countries, within
     the framework capitalist imperialism.

In the end, Marx helps us to understand the development of capitalism, the way it will change, and its relationships globally regardless of whether it is an examination of advanced capitalism in the Global North, or the varied and complex nature of capitalist development in the Global South His work and ideas can help us understand the challenges countries of the Global South will face in a capitalist global economy. And perhaps they can be a guide to how to avoid the exploitation and harm created in seeking a new global economy not ruled by capitalist social and productive relations.

References

Aoki, H. (2020). "Marxism and the Debate on the Transition to Capitalism in Prewar Japan", *Critical Sociology*, https://doi.org/10.1177/0896920520914074.

Brass, T. (2011). *Labor Regime Change in the Twenty-First Century*. Leiden: Brill.

Byres, T. (2007). "Karl Marx on India", *Journal of Agrarian Change* 7 (1): 128–132.

Cardoso, F.H. (1977). "The Consumption of Dependency Theory in the United States", *Latin American Research Review* 12: 7–24.

Cardoso, F.H. and Faletto, E. (1979). *Dependency and Development in Latin America*. Berkeley and Los Angeles: University of California Press.

Connell, R. (2007). *Southern Theory*. Cambridge: Polity Press.

Dados, N. and Connell, R. (2012). "The Global South", *Contexts* 11 (1): 12–13.

Das, R. (2017). *Marxist class theory for a skeptical world*. Leiden: Brill.

Das, R.J. (2016). "David Harvey's Theory of Accumulation by Dispossession: A Marxist Critique", *World Review of Political Economy* 8 (4).

Das, R. (2012). "Forms of Subsumption of labor under capital, class struggle and uneven development", *Review of Radical Political Economics* 44 (2): 178–200.

De Sousa Santos, B. (2014). *Epistemologies of the South: Justice Against Epistemicide*. London: Routledge.

Deitz, J.L. (1980). "Dependency Theory: A Review Article", *Journal of Economic Issues* 14 (3): 751–758.

Dobb, M. (1946). *Studies in the Development of Capitalism*. London: Routledge & Kegan Paul, Ltd.

Eagleton, T. (2011a). *Why Marx was right*. New Haven, Conn.: Yale University Press.

Eagleton, T. (2011b). "In praise of Marx", *The Chronicle of higher education*. Available at: https://www.chronicle.com/article/In-Praise-of-Marx/127027.

Fanon, F. (1961). *The Wretched of the Earth*. New York, NY: Grove Press.

Foster, J., McChesney, R., and Jonna, R. (2011). "The Global Reserve Army of Labor and the New Imperialism", *Monthly Review* 63: 06. Available at: https://monthlyreview.org/2011/11/01/the-global-reserve-army-of-labor-and-the-new-imperialism/.

Frank, A.G. (1978). "Development of Underdevelopment or Underdevelopment of Development in China", *Modern China*, 4 (3): 341–350.

Frank, A.G. (1969). *Latin America: Underdevelopment or Revolution*. New York, NY: Monthly Review Press.

Fukuyama, F. (1989). "The End of History?", *The National Interest*, Summer: 3–18. Available at: https://www.embl.de/aboutus/science_society/discussion/discussion_2006/refi-22june06.pdf.

Fukuyama, F. (2018). *Identity: The Demand for Dignity and the Politics of Resentment*. New York, NY: Farrar, Straus and Giroux.

Gasper, P. (2002). "Is Marxism relevant in the Third World?". Available at: http://socialistworker.org/2002-1/405/405_08_MarxismRelevant.shtml.

Gilbert, D. (2017). "Is Marxism Relevant? Some Uses and Misuses". Available at: https://abolitionjournal.org/is-marxism-relevant-some-uses-and-misuses-by-david-gilbert-political-prisoner/.

Ghosh, S. (1984). "Marx on India", *Monthly Review* 35 (8): 39–53.

Gramsci, A. (1995) [1926]. *The Southern Question*. New York, NY: Bordighera Press.

Harvey, D. (2007). "Neoliberalism as creative destruction", *The Annals of the American Academy of Political and Social Science* 610: 22–44.

Harvey, D. (2003). *New imperialism*. Oxford: Oxford University Press.

Horner, R. (2019). "Towards a new paradigm of global development? Beyond the limits of international development", *Progress in Human Geography*, March. Available at https://doi.org/10.1177/0309132519836158.

Jones, G. (2016). *Karl Marx: Greatness and Illusion*. Cambridge, MA: Harvard University Press.

Jonna, R. and Foster, J. (2016). "Marx's Theory of Working-Class Precariousness: Its relevance today", *Monthly Review*. Available at: https://monthlyreview.org/2016/04/01/marxs-theory-of-working-class-precariousness/.

Kalmring, S. and Nowak, A. (2017). "Viewing Africa with Marx: Remarks on Marx's Fragmented engagement with the African continent", *Science and Society* 81 (3): 331–347.

Laibman, D. (2013). "On the 130th anniversary of the death of Karl Marx: Answers to questions from China's People's Daily", *Science and Society* 77 (4): 451–458.

Marx, K. (1847). *Poverty of philosophy*. Available at: https://www.marxists.org/archive/marx/works/1847/poverty-philosophy/ch02.htm.

Marx, K. (1877). *Letter to Editor of the Otecestvenniye Zapisky*. Available at: https://www.marxists.org/archive/marx/works/1877/11/russia.htm.

Marx, K. (1970) [1859]. *A Contribution to the Critique of Political Economy*. Moscow: Progress Publishers.

Marx, K. (1976) [1847]. *Wage, Labor and Capital*. Moscow: International Publishers.

Marx, K. (1990) [1867]. *Capital*, Volume 1. London: Penguin.

Marx, K. and Engels, F. (1850). "Address of the Central Committee to the Communist League". Available at: https://www.marxists.org/archive/marx/works/1847/communist-league/1850-ad1.htm.

Marx, K. and Engels, F. (1948) [1848]. *Communist Manifesto*. Moscow: International Publishers.

Nimtz A. (2002). "The Eurocentric Marx and other related myths", in C. Bartolovich and L. Lazarus (eds.). *Marxism, Modernity and Post-colonial Studies*. Cambridge: Cambridge University Press.

Ollman, B. (2003). *Dance of the Dialectic*. Urbana-Champaign: University of Illinois Press.

Patnaik, U. and Patnaik, P. (2015). "Imperialism in the Era of Globalization". Available at: https://monthlyreview.org/2015/07/01/imperialism-in-the-era-of-globalization.

Pradella, L. (2015). Globalisation and the Critique of Political Economy: New insights from Marx's writings. New York: Routledge.

Pradella, L. (2017). "Marx and the Global South: connecting history and value theory", *Sociology: the Journal of the British Sociological Association* 51 (1): 146–161.

Prashad, V. (2007). *The Darker Nations: A People's History of the Third World*. New York: The New Press.

Prashad, V. (2012). *The Poorer Nations: A Possible History of the Global South*. London: Verso.

Roberts, M. (2016). *The long depression*. Chicago: Haymarket Books.

Smith, J. (2016). *Imperialism in the 21st century*. New York: Monthly Review Press.

Sperber, J. (2013). *Karl Marx: A Nineteenth-Century Life*. New York: Liveright Publishing.

Steinmetz, G. (2014). "On the articulation of Marxist and non-Marxist theory in Colonial Historiography. Vivek Chibber's Postcolonial Theory and the Spectre of Capital", *Journal of World Systems* 20 (2): 282–288.

Trotsky, L. (2008) [1939]. *The history of the Russian Revolution*. London and Atlanta: Pathfinder Press.

Weber, M. (1978) [1922]. *Economy and Society*. Trans. Guenther Roth and Claus Wittich. Berkeley and Los Angeles, CA: University of California Press.

Wood, E. (1998). *Retreat from Class*. London: Verso: London.

Wright, E. (1995). "The class analysis of poverty", *International journal of health services* 25 (1): 85–100.

CHAPTER 6

The Significance of Social Bonds

Göran Ahrne

1 The Banner of Bonds

In the first chapter of his book, *Durable Inequality*, Charles Tilly writes about the possibility of finding an alternative to the deadlock that exists in the social sciences around the question of individual and society, action and structure, or micro–macro. With the notion of social bonds, he argues, the pitfalls of both an individualistic and a holistic perspective may be avoided: "In the choice between essence and bonds, nevertheless, I want to hold high the banner of bonds" (Tilly, 1998: 21). In so doing, Tilly refers to classical sociologists such as Marx, Weber, and Simmel, and calls this tradition a relational realism, that is, "the doctrine that transactions, interactions, social ties, and conversations constitute the central stuff of social life" (2002: 72). Tilly argues that this perspective opens up new avenues to "allow for partly autonomous individual processes as well as strong effects on interaction by such collectively created structures as social categories and centralized organizations" (2002: 73). What, then, is a social bond? To make use of this concept as a theoretical alternative, as Tilly suggests, it must be analysed in greater detail to define what it implies and which functions and consequences it has. In comparison with other concepts with similar aims, such as social structure or culture (see the chapter by John Scott in this volume), the social bond is a relatively underdeveloped concept. It is a typically homeless idea without a clear anchorage in any specific sociological tradition or paradigm. This chapter aims to define how we can go about investigating social bonds, that is, how to make social bonds into research objects in themselves. How are they established? What are they composed of?

Bonds are generally defined as something that binds, fastens, or holds together. To hold or bind physical objects together may require ropes, nuts and bolts,[1] or even chains, depending on the size and form of the objects and for how long the bond is supposed to hold. The same goes for social bonds;

---

[1] Elster's book *Nuts and bolts for the social sciences* is, however, not about social bonds but about social mechanisms in general, and the author is not interested in bonds. For him, 'the elementary events are individual human actions' (Elster, 1989: 3).

different types of relationships require different kinds of bonds depending on which people are involved, what they are supposed to do, and for how long the relationship is expected to continue. Calling it a bond signals that it fills the same functions as physical bonds; social bonds can, in fact, at least partly, also have a physical design, for example, keys to a common home or an access card to a place of work (cf. Papakostas, 2012).

In sociology, there is much talk about interaction. Interaction typically happens face to face: people meet and interact in public places, in streets and squares, cafes or restaurants, or other similar locations (Goffman, 1972). Interaction implies that the people interacting can observe and perhaps talk to each other and that they adjust their behaviour according to each other's moves and wishes or try to persuade the other to do things in a different way.[2] Such interaction is often assumed to take place among people who do not know each other and do not expect to meet again.

Interaction with unknown people is occasional and presupposes a conjunction of time and space. It has a beginning and an end, and it does not require any social bonds. The interaction is facilitated if those who interact have a common notion of an interaction order (Goffman, 1983) or if they can follow rules about how to behave. People move around freely and come and go without seeming to be bound by any social bonds, until someone with whom you have started a conversation exclaims, 'Oh, I have to leave. It was nice talking to you but now I have to go back to work', or, 'I am going to meet my friends now'.

2   The Significance of Bonds

To be able to interact with the same people on multiple occasions, a relationship has to be created (cf. Crossley, 2011: 35) and, for that purpose, social bonds are required. There can be many reasons that people want to meet again and do things together. Perhaps they have strong feelings for each other, like each other, and want to see each other more often; they may have common interests that they want to develop; they may depend on each other for other reasons, or they may just be involved in economic transactions.

In his discussion of social relationships, Max Weber notes that these bonds may be "of the most varied nature", containing conflict and hostility as well as sexual attraction, friendship, loyalty, or economic exchange (1968: 27). These many motives may overlap, but motives alone are not enough to create a

---

2   Mutual adjustment (Lindblom, 2001).

relationship. Something more is needed, some measures that make the sticking together achievable: social bonds.

Social bonds transcend time and space. They are not for the present but for the future: what will happen next? How will we meet again? Social bonds provide connections to other people who are waiting for you or expecting you to return. Though many relationships may persist without or with very rare instances of interaction, they are still kept together by social bonds.

People involved in clusters of social bonds are still individuals, and social bonds do not make us less human. That people are bound by social bonds does not cause them to cease to be private individuals with a free will and possibilities to decide on their own actions. Nevertheless, this is precisely the reason why social bonds are required: bonds make individuals into social beings. To investigate social bonds between individuals is to transcend an individualistic perspective without losing sight of the individuals themselves. It is not individuals that are the constituent elements of society but the bonds between them; 'we' is not a plural form of 'I', something more is added: a social bond that makes 'I' into 'we'.

Nor do social bonds connect individuals with society in a general sense, so that different individuals would have stronger or weaker bonds with society, making them more or less integrated. No, social bonds exist between individuals and connect them with each other. Society is not somewhere else; it is here, between us.

Since people are involved in many different social bonds, the patterns of bonds between inhabitants in a certain country do not add up nicely into an independent cluster of bonds that could be regarded as an autonomous society. In every state or country in the world, there are many people who are connected through social bonds with people in other countries or states stretching far beyond their boundaries.

When we encounter people in public places, their social bonds are rarely visible, yet most people carry pieces of their bonds with them in their wallets or telephones; a bank card, access cards, an ID card, telephone numbers, a list of addresses. If someone wears a uniform, however, a social bond is disclosed.

It is difficult to imagine an individual without any social bonds. Someone without any bonds would be stateless, homeless, unemployed, and without friends or relatives. As social beings, people are bound by several social bonds that shape their everyday lives, and, according to Alfred Schutz (1962: 224), an individual's social bonds constitute an essential part of how much of the world is within one's reach. At the same time, individuals are often likely to experience a strain between different bonds with competing demands; each individual can only maintain a limited number of social bonds.

We live constantly with our social bonds and are well aware of them. Moreover, we keep track of the social bonds of others; who their friends or colleagues are, whom they live with, who their relatives are. Their social bonds are decisive for how we relate to them, what we tell them, and what we ask them to do. Others also expect us to be part of social bonds, to be bonded. People are frequently asked about both their present and previous bonds; they are often more important to others than an individual's personal traits or characteristics.

A social bond keeps people together but also puts something between them. Even if it unites them, a bond may cause friction and tensions. Through its very nature, a social bond becomes a third party that comes between those who are united and shapes their relationship; at the same time keeping them together and apart.

All individuals are involved in several bonds, but rarely with the same people. A social bond is not a complete fusion between the parties involved; they are not welded together. People involved in social bonds are not a chain gang. Social bonds are often long-lasting, but at the same time, they must allow for people to occasionally free themselves from a bond to be able to join other bonds. This does not mean that the original bond has to be dissolved.

People can be more or less dependent on their social bonds during different life phases, but some bonds always remain, and, in their struggle to deliberate themselves from their bonds, people constantly find themselves in new bonds. Bonds may be more or less adaptable and flexible; within the frames of many bonds there is also room for varying degrees of independence.

Most of the things people do can at least partly be explained by their social bonds. It is hardly the case that people nowadays are bound by fewer social bonds than before; it is rather the opposite. Therefore, we cannot talk about increasing individualism. In pre-modern social constellations, people were probably bound by fewer but stronger and tighter bonds than today: in late modernity, most individuals have more bonds, but many of them may be somewhat narrower and more flexible.

Though social bonds are not as visible and obvious as physical bonds, like physical bonds, they are first of all regarded as uniting certain people for certain purposes. However, they not only unite people; they also separate people from each other. When people form social bonds, they seal themselves off from others.[3] If social bonds connect people around a certain common issue, they also exclude others from what is common for those involved in the bond.

---

3 Bonds constitute a closed relationship in which 'participation of certain persons is excluded limited or subjected to conditions' (Weber, 1968: 43).

One reason for excluding people can be that they are already involved in other social bonds of the same kind, for instance, membership in a political party or a marriage. Many social bonds are exclusive in this sense. Individuals are, however, also excluded from social bonds even if they could in principle have been eligible. Those who try to be involved may be rejected for many reasons by those who are already involved; perhaps they do not want to increase the number of people within the group or perhaps they have found other individuals who they have judged as better qualified or more desirable.

3   How Are Social Bonds Established?

No one can choose or create their own social bonds unless the other party or parties have agreed to it. In general, it is reasonable to think of most social bonds as mutual agreements, where both parties have participated in and agreed to the establishment of a bond. Bonds in this sense are voluntary. Nevertheless, that they are voluntary does not mean that a bond is a free choice; even if people make choices, it is up to the other party or parties involved to accept them.

In exceptional cases, however, it can be possible for a person to pay to be included in a social bond, for instance, as a member of an association or as an owner of a stock company. Social bonds can also be established through the use of force or violence when people are imprisoned and watched. Since social bonds not only concern those who are involved but also those who are on the outside, other parties may take an interest in certain social bonds being established and maintained.

Even if a social bond has been established voluntarily, it is not necessarily a symmetric relationship. On the contrary, in many voluntary social bonds, there are differences between the parties involved in terms of the power that affects the relationship. It goes too far to say that such relationships have been established by force; however, it is reasonable to assume that bonds in an unequal relationship must be formed differently than those where the distribution of power is relatively equal.

All in all, we can distinguish three ways in which social bonds emerge and are established:

First, a social bond can be established beforehand. In other words, it may be given (Spencer and Pahl, 2006: 41), which usually means that there has never been a choice by any of the parties to establish a bond or not. This is typically the case for the bonds into which an individual is born; a child's bonds to its parents and siblings. A child, however, is also born into bonds of kinship and citizenship, that is, a bond with a state (cf. Ahrne, 2019). These bonds are often the strongest and most long-lasting of every individual. Though such bonds cannot be seen as voluntary, they are not directly established by force either; they are, rather, taken for granted.

Second, social bonds can evolve gradually. People meet in different situations and may slowly become acquainted when they meet again. After some time, they learn more about each other and start to do things together. Networks are often seen to emerge in this way.

Third, social bonds can be established when people decide that they belong together in some respect. Some people start a football club or another association, while others may start a business together. New social bonds are established when the football club recruits new players, or the business employs more workers. A bond is also established in this way when two people make a common decision to become a couple and live together and perhaps to get married. Bonds that are decided are communicated as such to the environment, in contrast to bonds that emerge gradually without any definite decisions between the parties.

4   What Are the Qualities and Functions of Social Bonds?

A social bond holds people together: it has to fit and embrace individuals into patterns of bonds that will enable them to act jointly for common purposes. How a social bond is formed and how strong or elastic it must be depend, to a large extent, on what the relationship is about and how much tension exists between those who will be involved.

We can distinguish five aspects of the quality of a social bond, which are similar to the five design principles that Elinor Ostrom (1990) found to be essential preconditions for collective action (cf. Ahrne and Brunsson, 2011; 2019):[4]

1.   How the reach of the bond and who is involved is determined, and how visible this is.
2.   The bond's ability to specify what those involved can expect of each other, that is, the purpose and fitness of the bond.

---

4   These five principles are 1) clear boundaries and membership, 2) congruent rules, 3) collective choice arenas, 4) monitoring, and 5) graduated sanctions (Ostrom, 1990: 90, 185–186). Arthur Stinchcombe made similar distinctions regarding organisations in general when he discussed 'an extended definition of hierarchy'. He mentioned labour contracts, the exercised right to measure and reward performances, standard operating procedures, decision-making, and dispute-resolving meetings (Stinchcombe, 1990: 199).

3.   The possibilities to test and control the strength of the bond.

4.   How the bond is maintained, strengthened, or repaired with different types of sanctions.

5.   How strings are pulled in order to activate, resume, or change the bonds. Regarding these aspects, first of all, individuals who are joined in a social bond have to recognise the existence of such a bond and that both parties are aware of each other and their relationship. This is the most important aspect of any social bond; without such a recognition there is no bond. In order for the bond to transcend time and space, those who are included also require ways to keep in touch. It is not enough that they recognise each other if they happen to run into each other in the street; to be able to form a bond they need more information about each other, perhaps an address, a telephone number, or some other information on how each can be reached. Most social bonds, however, comprise more than two individuals. Those who are brought together by social bonds should be able to know who the others are; to be aware of the reach of the bond as well as knowing who is excluded.

Secondly, social bonds connect individuals with each other but are rarely absolute in the sense that the bond covers everything that a particular individual does; it usually involves certain aspects of their life and has a specific purpose.[5] Therefore, bonds have to fit exactly that which they are meant for. They need to communicate and be expressions of some type of expectations regarding what they are meant for and what the parties involved can do together, as well as when, where, and how. Bonds have to be adjusted to each individual, give indications about the position of each individual, and enable and allow each individual to do certain things but not others. At the same time, such bonds have to be constructed in a way that allows the actions of the different parties to fit together to generate common results; something that each individual could not have achieved on their own. Moreover, a social bond often also requires a certain flexibility and elasticity.

Thirdly, for a social relationship to persist during a longer period, the bonds that keep it together have to be maintained intact and their strength and sustainability must be controlled and tested. To engage themselves, those who are involved need to know that the others are still there, ready to resume the connections. Alternatively, those who are involved must simply trust each other and hope that they all do what is expected of them. When the bonds are fastened (again), there is not necessarily direct interaction among those who are involved, and therefore they require some information about what the

---

5   Compare this with the concept of the 'zone of indifference' (Barnard, 1968; Stinchcombe, 1990).

others are doing, that is, how well they are performing their tasks and fulfilling expectations.

Fourth, it is not enough to check and test the bonds; they also have to be maintained and improved. Cracks or other deficiencies in the bond need to be attended to, and those who are perceived to cause such problems have to be addressed and asked to change so that the bond can be adjusted. If they do not, they can be threatened with exclusion. To repair or strengthen a bond, its firmness and fitness can be improved through all kinds of feedback between those involved, who can praise and encourage each other in many ways.

Fifth, since people are involved in a number of different bonds, some are occasionally dormant but far from dissolved. For the relationship to continue, the bonds need to be in good shape and ready to be reconnected. We can think of social bonds as links and connections that people continuously carry around and can easily be connected with corresponding links with certain others when required. However, the bond must also contain some information on when to reconnect or some notion about who shall pull the strings, how that can be done, and how new initiatives or changes can be communicated, otherwise it will remain dormant.

These functions do not have to be satisfied at once: some social bonds are established gradually, while others may be established with all these functions, even if, from the beginning, they are planned to be rather short-lived. The primary function is the recognition of who is involved. If a social bond is going to last for a longer period, however, most of these functions must be present, although social bonds can vary in strength and other qualities, and many bonds are dissolved after just a short time.

5   What Are Social Bonds Made Of?

Besides their different functions, social bonds are constructed with various types of raw material, comprising differing forms of interpersonal communication. The content of this communication varies widely depending on what function it has, while the form of communication varies according to what the bond is about.

First of all, there are two forms of communication that we can distinguish: institutional and organisational. An institution is a stable, routine-reproduced pattern of behaviour, combined with norms and conceptions that are taken for granted by larger or smaller groups of people (Jepperson, 1991). Institutions emerge from long processes of mutual adaptation among people (Berger and Luckmann, 1991: 75); they develop slowly (Czarniawska,

2009) and are difficult to change (North, 1998: 498). Thus, institutions emerge in a historical process of interaction and habitualisation, "which precede any institutionalization" (Berger and Luckmann, 1991: 71). Such a process begins when two or more individuals interact repeatedly and begin to develop a common understanding of what they are doing and how to do it; their interaction becomes predictable, and they note, "There we go again". Berger and Luckmann summarised it as: "Their life together is now defined by a widening sphere of taken-for-granted routines" (1991: 75). Nonetheless, this is only the first step in a process towards institutionalisation and a long time is necessary before, "There we go again" becomes, "This is how these things are done" (1991: 77). In this stage of the process, its origin becomes forgotten.

In institutional communication, there is no sender. The origin of the content is unknown; it has emerged gradually and becomes taken-for-granted as something that is undoubtedly true and correct. In this form of communication, the message is: "This is how things should be done; this is how it should be". It is stories about traditions, norms, rumours. Fashion and trends are also forms of institutional communication about what is the 'right' thing to do during a certain period.

When social bonds are constructed, institutional elements can be used for various purposes; they are ready-made and easy to use. Institutional components can be expected to produce stronger and tougher bonds that will be more reliable and work in many contexts. At the same time, however, they are coarse, rough, and hard to change or adapt.

Organisation, on the other hand, is a form of communication that emanates from decisions for others (Schoeneborn et al., 2014: 309). A decision always has a sender: a message about a certain decision refers to a decision-maker, who also has the responsibility for the decision (Brunsson, 2007). Anyone who is not satisfied with a decision, therefore, knows to whom they can direct their complaints or protests. A decision-maker can be a single person but also a board or a larger democratic assembly. Individuals too can make common decisions, which they communicate to other people and organisations, for instance, that they have decided to become a couple and get married.

Contrary to institutions, organisational decisions are not taken for granted. In many ways, a decision is a surprise, and those who will be affected by the decision wonder what it will be. Decisions are choices between alternatives— the decision-maker could have chosen another alternative—and, thus, are often contested: Why was another alternative not chosen?

At the beginning of their book, *Organizations*, James March and Herbert Simon emphasise that, in comparison with other influence processes in society, the most salient quality of organisation is its specificity; organisational instructions contain great detail (March and Simon, 1958: 3).

If organisational components are to be used in the construction of social bonds, they have to be designed and decided for each new bond. They are, therefore, more variable and can be better adjusted to each case than institutional elements. At the same time, however, they are probably harder to arrange; they are not taken for granted and can be contested. Neither are they as stable as institutional components as they can be changed with new decisions.

Besides institutional and organisational, other types of communication can become components of social bonds. Gossip, for instance, is a form of interpersonal communication comprising information about what people are saying about each other; what someone has seen or heard about someone else. Gossip often contains an evaluation of specific persons and their achievements (Burt, 2005: 105), evaluations that can be both negative and positive (Grosser et al., 2010). Gossip is a central feature in many networks, and opportunities to exchange gossip are often central to network cohesion (Elias and Scotson, 1999: 80).

Reciprocity is another form of communication that implies turn-taking in an exchange that can be used in the construction of social bonds. The norm of reciprocity is able to fulfil several functions in a social bond: it is "a plastic filter, capable of being poured into the shifting crevices of social structures and serving as a kind of all-purpose moral cement" (Gouldner, 1959: 249–250).

The model for an understanding of reciprocity is gift-giving, as analysed in the classical essay by Marcel Mauss (2002). Giving a gift, inviting someone to a party, or offering a service to someone can be interpreted as an attempt to form a bond. Though there is no agreement between the person who gives a gift and the one who receives it, there is an expectation that the gift (or invitation or service) should be returned. Gifts are not always immediately returned, however: there is a period of indeterminacy, and one cannot take for granted that the gift (or invitation) will ever be returned (Gouldner, 1959)—perhaps the receiver is not able to return the gift or does not want to. Moreover, reciprocity is also about power; an invitation or a gift is, at the same time, a challenge to the receiver to return the invitation or gift in an appropriate manner. Even if gifts or invitations have been returned many times the indeterminacy remains. Nevertheless, every time a gift or invitation is returned, it is a recognition of the continuation of a bond.

Some social bonds contain institutional or organisational communication through and through, but it is more common that bonds are shaped through combinations of various forms of communication pertaining to their different functions and qualities. A bond can be a blend of institution, organisation, and reciprocity to varying degrees, depending on purposes and circumstances, and different qualities are handled with different forms of communication. Bonds are often partially organised (Ahrne and Brunsson, 2011, 2019) and may change shape and quality over time.

A recognition of who is involved in a social bond can be based on a division between people according to a taken-for-granted notion of 'categorical pairs' (cf. Tilly, 1998) or to some other way of thinking of themselves as equivalent and similar to, or compatible with, others (Lamont and Molnár, 2002: 188). Alternatively, the recognition of a bond may rely on decisions about membership, which implies a more specific and transparent form of communication. Recognition of a bond can also happen in a process resting on reciprocity, in which invitations are given and returned. The purpose of a social bond and the expectations that come with it can further be based on common social norms and traditions. If those involved want to break with such traditions, they can use organisation to decide on new rules and goals for what they expect of each other.

When it comes to the control of the condition of the bond, if it is still in good shape or not, one possibility is to rely on rumours and prejudices. Ceremonies or rituals in which all involved are supposed to participate are good occasions for testing the strength of bonds (Hechter, 1987). Gossip can also provide information about the present strengths and weaknesses of a bond.

The maintenance of a social bond can rely on the people involved (who are regarded as living up to expectations) achieving a good reputation and a high status and being respected. Conversely, people who are not seen as fulfilling their duties or as misbehaving can be held in disdain and made to feel ashamed or even be regarded as sinners or traitors. They may also be exposed to bullying. Organisation can be used to strengthen a bond via decisions on rewards for good performance in the form of prizes, wage rises, or promotions. Further, repairing a bond can be achieved through decisions on negative sanctions in the form of warnings, fines, or threats of exclusion. In many bonds, status is a decisive factor for who is both able and expected to pull the strings, but it is also possible to decide on a hierarchy or constitution for making different kinds of decisions or to decide who shall convene.

6   The Aggregation of Social Bonds

Social bonds are established between individuals but often unite more than two people and sometimes many more. When many people are involved, the bonds between them produce a cluster that makes up a bounded collectivity with a common purpose and practice of some kind. A collectivity's bonds can have different qualities and can vary in strength and flexibility. In a nuclear family, for instance, the quality of the bond that unites the adults differs from the bonds between a child and the parents as well as the bonds between siblings. Bonds in a collectivity that is seen as a network can, to different degrees, consist of combinations of organisation, institution, and reciprocity (see Ahrne, 2019).

It is, therefore, necessary to distinguish between social bonds and the collectivities that they form. At the same time, however, they can be integrated into the analysis. An understanding of the qualities of the social bonds that form a certain collectivity gives clues to its possibilities to act, its strengths, and its weaknesses.

There is a plethora of terms to denote different types of collectivities: alliance, association, band, brotherhood, circle, clique, club, company, corporation, congregation, family, fellowship, gang, guild, league, movement, party, state, team, or troop. Many of these allude to the type of activity which is performed. There are also more abstract concepts for collectivities, such as network,[6] organisation, relationship, or figuration.[7]

All collectivities can be described and analysed in terms of the social bonds between those that are involved; one cannot understand the coherence or strength of any collectivity without considering the quality of the social bonds that hold it together. In much social science, however, collectivities are either seen as consisting of a gathering of individuals or as a structure devoid of individuals. Yet a group does not consist only of individuals but also of the bonds that keep them together. In the study of organisations, on the other hand, the main topic is usually internal positions within.

An analysis of what comprises social bonds concomitantly provides an image of the conditions for individual actors and how various collectivities are constructed. When we know how a specific social bond is fastened to each individual, and, at the same time, how it is bound together with others within the same collectivity, we can achieve an understanding of its relations to parts of its environment and a picture of its internal structure. This goes for all types of collectivities: from families and kinship to formal organisations, such as voluntary associations, corporations, and even states.

---

6   The social bonds that connect people in networks are usually called 'ties'. In networks, researchers seek patterns of ties but rarely examine how they are constructed and their quality (Azarian, 2010). Even if network scholars consider strong and weak ties (cf. Granovetter, 1973), they are rarely interested in what bonds are made of.

7   Norbert Elias, 1978.

Each collectivity, regardless of whether it comprises only a few individuals or millions, consists of a cluster of social bonds linking into each other constituting its structure. Holding the banner of bonds high therefore opens a way to explore how, through their bonded actions, individual actors reproduce and build the structural properties of both smaller and larger collectivities. Through social bonds, individual actions are transformed into social processes and structures: they are coordinated, complemented, and strengthened, and their results can be accumulated.[8]

This investigation of how we can think about social bonds also suggests that social bonds are multidimensional; they can have several functions and be constituted in a number of different ways. Focusing on social bonds does not mean introducing a new level of analysis in the debate about agency and structure. On the contrary, such a focus offers a more detailed way of understanding connections between individuals and social structures, uncovering a great many variations in the strength and scope of how individuals are involved in establishing and maintaining these structures.

References

Ahrne, G. (2019). "Organizing intimacy", in G. Ahrne and N. Brunsson (eds.). *Organization outside organizations: The abundance of partial organization in social life.* Cambridge: Cambridge University Press.

Ahrne, G. and Brunsson, N. (2011). "Organization outside organizations: The significance of partial organization", *Organization* 18 (1): 83–104.

Ahrne, G. and Brunsson, N. (2019). "Organization unbound", in G. Ahrne and N. Brunsson (eds.). *Organization outside organizations: The abundance of partial organization in social life.* Cambridge: Cambridge University Press.

Azarian, R. (2010). "Social ties: elements of a substantial conceptualization", *Acta Sociologica* 53 (4): 323–338.

Barnard, C.I. (1968). *The Functions of the executive.* Thirtieth Anniversary Edition. Cambridge, MA: Harvard University Press.

Berger, P.L. and Luckmann, T. (1991). *The social construction of reality: A treatise in the sociology of knowledge.* Harmondsworth: Penguin Books.

---

8   These arguments can be understood as an alternative answer to the question posed by Anthony Giddens in his book, *The Constitution of Society:* 'In what manner can it be said that the conduct of individual actors reproduces the structural properties of larger collectivities?' (Giddens, 1984: 24). It represents a 'duality of structure'.

Brunsson, N. (2007). *The consequences of decision-making*. Oxford: Oxford University Press.

Burt, R.S. (2005). *Brokerage and closure: An introduction to social capital*. Oxford: Oxford University Press.

Crossley, N. (2011). *Towards relational sociology*. Abingdon, UK; New York: Routledge.

Czarniawska, B. (2009). "Emerging institutions: pyramids or anthills?", *Organization Studies* 30 (4): 423–441.

Elias, N. (1978). *What is sociology?* London: Hutchinson & Co.

Elias, N. and Scotson, J.L. (1999). *Etablerade och outsiders*. Lund: Arkiv förlag.

Elster, J. (1989). *Nuts and bolts for the social sciences*. Cambridge: Cambridge University Press.

Giddens, A. (1984). *The constitution of society*. Cambridge: Polity Press.

Goffman, E. (1972). *Encounters: Two studies in the sociology of interaction*. Harmondsworth: Penguin Books.

Goffman, E. (1983). "The interaction order: American Sociological Association 1982 presidential address", *American Sociological Review* 48(1): 1–17.

Gouldner, A.W. (1959). *For Sociology: renewal and critique in sociology today*. Harmondsworth: Penguin Books.

Granovetter, M. (1973). "The strength of weak ties", *American Journal of Sociology* 78 (6): 1360–1380.

Grosser, T.J., Lopez-Kidwell, V., and Labianca, G. (2010). "A social network analysis of positive and negative gossip in organizational life", *Group & Organization Management* 35 (2): 177–212.

Hechter, M. (1987). *Principles of group solidarity*. Berkeley: University of California Press.

Jepperson, R.L. (1991). "Institutions, institutional effects, and institutionalism", in W. Powell and P. Di Maggio (eds.). *The new institutionalism in organizational analysis*. Chicago: The University of Chicago Press.

Lamont, M. and Molnar, V. (2002). "The study of boundaries in the social sciences", *Annual Review of Sociology* 28: 167–195.

Lindblom C.E. (2001). *The market system: what it is, how it works, and what to make of it*. New Haven; London: Yale University Press.

March, J.G. and Simon, H.A. (1958). *Organizations*. New York: John Wiley.

Mauss, M. (2002). *The Gift: The form and reason for exchange in archaic societies*. London: Routledge.

North, D.C. (1998). "Where have we been and where are we going?", in A. Ben-Ner and L. Putterman (eds.). *Economics, values and organization*. Cambridge: Cambridge University Press.

Ostrom, E. (1990). *Governing the commons: The evolution of institutions for collective action*. Cambridge: Cambridge University Press.

Papakostas, A. (2012). *Civilizing the public sphere: distrust, trust and corruption.* Houndsmills; New York: Palgrave Macmillan.

Schoeneborn, D., Blaschke, S., Cooren, F., McPhee, R.D., Seidl, D., and Taylor, J.R. (2014). "The three schools of CCO thinking: interactive dialogue and systematic comparison", *Management Communication Quarterly* 28 (2): 285–316.

Schutz, A. (1962). "On multiple realities", *Collected Papers I: The Problem of Social Reality.* Eds. M. Natanson. The Hague: Martinus Nijhoff.

Stinchcombe, A.L. (1990). *Information and organizations.* Berkeley: University of California Press.

Spencer, L. and Pahl, R. (2006). *Rethinking friendship: hidden solidarities today.* Princeton; Oxford: Princeton University Press.

Tilly, C. (1998). *Durable inequality.* Berkeley: University of California Press.

Tilly, C. (2002). *Stories, identities, and political change.* Berkeley: University of California Press.

Weber, M. (1968). *Economy and society. Volume one.* Berkeley: University of California Press.

CHAPTER 7

Organisations as a Sociological Research Object

How Schools Reproduce Inequality

Raimund Hasse

1   Whose Side—and of What—Are We On?

The 20th century experienced an enormous growth of science (De Solla Price, 1974), when, likewise, the impact of science and technology on society increased dramatically. Literally everything became a reasonable research object and all kinds of decision-making were expected to be based on scientific evidence, for example, in medicine, education, management, technology, and politics (Jasanoff, 1990). Against this background, the notion of constructivism, which attracted some attention in the philosophy of the sciences in the 1960s (Lorenzen, 1969), developed a critical undertone: if science is about constructions, and not focused on the discovery of the only truth, there may be alternatives to these constructions—and if there can be alternatives, scientific authority may erode. Thus, the 1970s witnessed a shortcut from constructivism to 'anything goes' (Feyerabend, 1975), and the sociology of sciences embarked on a programme of research that empirically described how such constructions are created (Knorr-Cetina and Mulkay, 1983).

Reflexivity has been an integral part of this sociology of the sciences, particular in its 'strong programme' variant (Bloor, 1976). One key question is this: what are sociological constructions? To tackle this question, it may be wise to go back to its foundation. When sociology emerged as an academic enterprise, several lines of demarcation were utilised in order to develop an identity. Against the backdrop of mass suffering in the early years of industrialisation, social turmoil, and the political threat of revolutionary movements, some intellectuals had the idea that society as a whole, and the living conditions of specific groups, deserved particular attention. Sociology in this context was viewed as a camera: it promised to create portraits of social groups or of society as a whole including norms and values, interests, habits, living conditions, and so on. Sociology also promised to provide 'videos' about human development from the ancient world, or even tribal societies, to modern capitalism and, in this context, attempted to identify ongoing master-trends, such as the specialisation and division of labour or rationalisation.

Regarding standpoints, the metaphor of a camera suggests a distinction between two sides: behind the camera and in front of it. Of course, behind the camera was the place for sociologists who—like any other scientists—could make observations and draw conclusions. In front of the camera were the objects under investigation: society, or excerpts of it, and people inhabiting various social domains. Based on such understanding, one could, albeit somewhat naively, believe that sociological observation has no impact on society, regardless of the claim that sociology contributes to enlightenment and improves the capacity for reflexivity and reforms.[1]

Sociology also developed criteria that determined towards what the sociological camera should be directed and what could be seen through its lens. In particular, social problems became a main target for sociological research (Burgess, 1953). The sociological camera, thus, focused on deviance and anomia, shedding light on various forms of suffering and phenomena with negative consequences—intentional or side effects, familiar or so far unknown—which were constructed as main research objects (Merton, 1938). In this regard, one may argue, sociology became a machine, rather than a camera, that contributed to the ongoing construction of social problems, and that these constructions became a major research object in sociology.

A huge amount of sociological research on social problems has aimed to identify various forms of inequality, particularly if such inequality does not result from the rigorous application of meritocratic ideals but from the ascription of social categories such as class, ethnicity, age, or gender. To take the camera metaphor, many sociologists, in mission-oriented as well as basic research, have aimed to take photos or videos of deviations from norms of equality and

---

1 Note that the foundation of sociology was also based on rather influential distinctions. Emile Durkheim (1980) developed the concept of social facts, claiming both that social facts can become objects of scientific research, just as facts in natural science, and that the discovery of social facts can be distinguished from other research objects that were the domain of medical, psychological, or other disciplines. Durkheim's 'rules of the sociological method' thus dealt with unique research strategies that seemed appropriate for identifying social facts. In a similar vein, Max Weber (1978) also drew lines of demarcation to develop a sociological identity. He particularly emphasised its difference from natural science by arguing that the social action of groups and individuals is based on sense-making and meaning that must and can be understood by the researcher. Weberian sociology is, thus, not only based on explanatory claims; instead, it also includes the aspiration to understand why people act the way they do, and, in that respect, sociology was more ambitious than economists who simply described and sought to identify causal laws. In sum, the institutionalisation of sociology as an academic discipline was based on normative ideals: neutral scientific observation as opposed to 'catheter socialism', in the case of Weber; more empathic and reform-oriented in the case of Durkheim.

fairness, just as other social sciences have committed themselves to other concerns, such as democracy and deliberation (political science) or efficiency (economics). As the sociological camera has also addressed and contributed to rationalisation processes (not only due to the knowledge it generates and provides but also because its concerns about the actor capacities of disprivileged groups), agency in social-work contexts and in applied research often has a normative connotation. Its improvement is a major concern for professional helpers who seek to set-up or maintain such agency for their clients (Hasse, 2019).

From the perspective developed thus far, the programmatic question, "Whose side are we on?", originally raised by H.S. Becker (1967) to argue against the seemingly 'neutral research' he considered impossible in the examination of social problems, can be answered quite easily and differently from Becker's genuine meaning: if a camera constitutes two sides, sociology stands behind it and research objects are in front of the camera. A further major question, then, is to which research objects do we direct our sociological attention, and how do we construct these objects?

2   Constructing Research Objects in an 'Asymmetric Society'

Many sociologists have emphasised the significance of organisations for modern societies. Max Weber focused on bureaucracies, which he described as an efficient and highly legitimate form of organisation; he expected the spread of this organisational form from public administration to many other social domains, including business (Weber, 1978). Émile Durkheim identified associations and corporations as the remaining islands of mechanic solidarity and viewed organisations as preconditions for negotiating interests between antagonistic groups, considering this an appropriate mode of governance (Durkheim, 1933). Michel Foucault shed light on the role of the specific organisations of prisons and hospitals; his main interest was the relation of these organisations to issues of power and knowledge (Foucault, 1994; 1996). Meanwhile, Goffman (1995) was mainly concerned with those organisations that have profound effects on the identity of their members and inhabitants and was, thus, particularly interested in total institutions, that is, organisations from which there seems to be no escape. And Luhmann (1975) further viewed societal developments and the expansion of formal organisations as co-evolutionary processes, a view that was based on the emergence and spread of specific organisations, such as business firms (economy), parties (politics), and schools (education). Thus, he could hardly imagine alternatives to formal organisations.

These authors, although not organisational sociologists, provide ample evidence for what may be labelled 'organisation society'. The concept of organisation society refers to a social formation whose structure is substantially determined by its organisational forms (Stinchcombe, 1965), which was proposed most convincingly by Charles Perrow (2002). According to Perrow's perspective, economies are characterised by the structure of firms and inter-firm relations, the organisation of workers in unions and working councils, and associations who represent economic interests. Consequently, he argued that organisational structures determine the system of work and the distribution of wages and salaries, but they are not only important with respect to the economy. Instead, in a similar vein, politics is both based on the organisation of governments and on the formation of political interests in parties, lobby groups, and social movements; education and science are based on schools and universities and their internal organisation in faculties and departments; media are dominated by publishing houses, TV stations, broadcasting services, and the few giants who rule new media; and even incarceration rates or surgeries correlate with the spread of specific organisations, that is, prisons and hospitals.

Finally, globalisation processes and what has been labelled 'world society' or 'world polity' are based on organisations, particularly in the form of inter-governmental organisations, multinational corporations, and a broad spectrum of international non-governmental organisations, ranging from social movements to standard setters and evaluation agencies (Boli and Thomas, 2000; Meyer et al., 1997). In this light, it has been argued that, at least at the global level, inter-organisational 'soft regulation' has compensated for, if not replaced, traditional forms of regulation by political authorities at the level of nation states (Sahlin and Wedlin, 2008). Deregulation of the latter has been compensated for by new forms of governance, which often are based on formal voluntary compliance. Such soft regulation, however, requires organisations to act both as regulators and as objects of regulation in what easily could be illustrated by reference to standard setting as the paradigmatic case for such soft regulation (Brunsson and Jacobson, 2000; Arnold and Hasse, 2015).

One of the most forceful arguments for drawing attention to organisations as driving forces of modern societies was presented by James Coleman (1982). Coleman restricted his analysis to the 20th century US as he described how business firms grew and expanded their markets, how government became centralised and founded powerful administrations, and how these two types of large organisation have contributed to the erosion of local communities. As a consequence, social cohesion was reduced and contemporary societies became divided into two spheres: on the one side are organisations and their agents (members and employees) who are expected to act on behalf of their principals, and on the other side, dis-embedded individuals who are expected to have preferences and attitudes. According to Coleman (1982), interaction between organisational agents and individuals is characterised by striking power imbalances in favour of organisations since organisations are equipped with better resources and their representatives can claim higher status in interactions with individuals. The notion of an asymmetric society refers to these imbalances, and Coleman assumed that this asymmetry would further increase.

Coleman's diagnosis is based on a scheme that is familiar to cultural theory: the distinction between communitarian and individual cultures, on the one hand, and hierarchies on the other (Douglas, 1982). His thesis about dominating hierarchies can be applied quite easily to the situation of the 21st century: international governmental organisations in New York or Brussels have supplemented, if not replaced, federal agencies in Washington and in other capitals, and large national corporations have transformed themselves into, or have been replaced by, multinational giants such as Apple, Alphabet, and IBM. The global expansion of organisations and the increase of international association can, therefore, be viewed as a characteristic feature of the 21st century (Bromley and Meyer, 2015).

Coleman provides an explanation for the increased power of large organisations that also includes knowledge asymmetries, arguing that contemporary society mainly generates knowledge about individuals' choices, attitudes, and opinions, whereas knowledge of organisations and their decision-making has remained weak. A further advantage possessed by organisations is that they find it easier to utilise this knowledge as they are able to hire professional experts and, subsequently, have better capacities to gather, store, and process relevant information. Finally, large organisations have the financial resources to initiate funded research that targets what they consider to be problematic and worthy of investigation, whereas individuals, apart from very few exceptions, do not have these resources.

In Coleman's view, the social sciences actively contribute to, rather than counteract, this knowledge asymmetry because there is much more research on individuals than on organisations. While the growth of psychology and the increased significance of psychological findings have contributed to this imbalance, major trends of sociology have exacerbated it. In particular, shifts towards survey research and evaluating mass data on opinions and other individual characteristics have pushed sociology further towards the exploration of individuals. Conversely, participatory observations of communities in the tradition of the Chicago school are no longer a typical object of investigation, and organisational research has remained comparatively rare. Mission-oriented research, mainly funded by federal agencies and large corporations, prefers individuals as research objects, and research problems are typically related only to issues that funders consider problematic.

Coleman's observation is remarkable since he has been among the most successful followers of Paul Lazarsfeld's research program, which established the shift in sociology from communities to individuals as preferred research objects. The famous 1966 Coleman report, *Equality of Educational Opportunity*, was based on mass data about students and teachers. The results of this research informed governmental agencies and initiated various reforms that, according to the argument developed by Coleman (1982), aimed to reduce or even compensate for educational inequality since that was a main concern of politics and the US administration in the 1960s and 1970s. Although less successful than expected—and although Coleman considered these reforms as still insufficient—they perfectly illustrate the research impacts on asymmetric societies: constructing individuals as research objects and providing knowledge about these research objects that can be utilised by organisations to initiate adaptations.

We can easily transfer this part of Coleman's reflection to the beginning of the 21st century. As methodological standards have risen, survey research about individuals has become more dominant than ever. At the same time, new research frontiers have developed in the context of big data. While academically speaking, these research strands pose challenges for the social sciences (Mohr et al., 2015), in practice they are used to improve social engineering and marketing. In fact, data about individuals have become the backbone of economic giants such as Amazon and Alphabet. These giants generate, store, and process data about individuals that may even be unknown to the individuals themselves. Knowledge about individuals has also become increasingly important in the insurance industry and in public services, all of which are represented by large organisations. One may thus conclude that the trend described by Coleman in the 1980s remains ongoing.

As sociology contributes to this trend, one—normative—implication of Coleman's analysis of asymmetric societies is to counter this imbalance by shifting the focus of attention from individuals and their preferences, attitudes, and habits to organisations. In the remainder of this chapter, we will illustrate what such a construction of research objects could look like. The case under investigation provides an organisational perspective on inequality in education (Hasse and Schmidt, 2012; Schmidt and Hasse, 2010) and aims to illustrate that organisational analyses need not be restricted to investigations

in organisational forms, issues of governance, and inter-organisational relations. Instead, organisational sociology can address the core issues of social
research.

3   Case Construction: School Assignment as an Empirical Example

Based on the thesis of an organisation society, one may assume that educational achievement is significantly determined by organisational structures
and by the decision-making of schools and other educational institutions. For
example, the institutionalisation of mass education requires sufficient schools
and universities. Another organisational factor is that schools often decide on
the selection and promotion of students or, at least, heavily influence it, providing their students with competences and signals. In so doing, educational
organisations profoundly affect the educational careers of students and their
entry into the labour market and are, thus, heavily involved in the reproduction of inequality.

In this sense, one may be surprised that inequality researchers often tend to
neglect the organisational basis for the (re-)production of inequality in education. Instead, they have mainly focused their sociological camera on students
and their family background and milieux. Accordingly, a great bulk of research
has concentrated on either individual characteristics (e.g. language competencies and socialisation prior to schooling) or impacts of the family context (particularly the educational background of parents, material living conditions,
and the appreciation of educational achievement). It has been argued in this
context that such characteristics and contextual features have a twofold consequence: they result in unequal learning conditions and dispositions while also
leading to the problematic decision-making of students and parents, which is
in line with socio-economic status and the corresponding educational aspirations but sub-optimal with respect to what could be achieved. The school
system, then, may be criticised for not actively compensating for the effects
of such inequalities, but it is not usually considered as a genuine cause of
inequality.

Compared to this mainstream research, there have been few scholars who
have argued that educational systems are actively involved in and reproduce
the inequality structures of contemporary societies (Chubb and Moe, 1988;
Lucas, 1999). These lines of research have redirected attention from students, their backgrounds, and their decision-making to teachers and school
authorities (Cicourel and Kitsuse, 1963; Oakes, 1985). Following these avenues

of enquiry, the question arises of how one can explain the robustness of the effects of these practices. This question seems worthy of investigation since these effects are not at all in line with the institutionalised ideals and policies of fairness and equal opportunity, and, furthermore, they appear to be a rather irrational allocation of talent as a scarce resource.

In the search for possible answers to this question, attention can be directed towards the methods teachers use to evaluate students, make decisions, and give recommendations. Typically, teachers' evaluations, decisions, and recommendations are based on grading and results in tracking. While grading is an integral part of almost any school practice, tracking, and therein inscribed status hierarchies, differs substantially—certainly across national systems of education, but also across regions and districts. Economically strong communities typically provide better opportunities to attend schools which qualify for higher education as compared with poorer communities.

A second difference regards the allocation to tracks. Sometimes, tracking results from a student's choice, which then has profound impacts on further options and choices. In other cases, tracking is heavily influenced or even determined by teachers and (other) school authorities, who more or less rigorously refer to grades or other test scores. Referring to arrangements that are in line with the latter case, German sociologists Gomolla and Radtke (2002) focused on discrimination effects that result from the decision-making of teachers and school authorities. Based on a broad range of organisation theories, the authors argued that these decision-making processes systematically discriminate students with a migration background. Though the developed argument is more complex, it can be summarised as follows: decision-making by teachers and school authorities is based on school-related functional requirements, taking organisational interests into consideration and referring to environmental expectations, which simultaneously constrains decision-making and serves as a resource pool for legitimising decisions. In other words, it is an object of retrospective sense-making. Discrimination, thus, is viewed as a side effect. It is unintentional, but nonetheless the outcome of reasonable considerations and not stemming from prejudice or biased stereotyping by individual teachers.

Student-related decisions, such as selection, tracking, displacement, or exclusion sometimes result from conferences and are often made in collaboration with students and parents. This focused decision-making, thus, is to be seen as a social process that is based on communication, in which arguments are used to explain, justify, or problematise (Schmidt and Hasse, 2010). In a small empirical investigation in Switzerland, we tried to identify discriminatory mechanisms that characterise the tracking of students at the interface between elementary and secondary school. The construction of the research object and its background can be summarised as follows.

As in other European countries, the school system in Switzerland is characterised by different types of secondary schools. Some of these types make greater demands and offer more opportunities than others. For example, students of a 'Sekundarschule' (and, if available, a 'Gymnasium') qualify for higher education, while those of a 'Realschule' do not. At the end of their time in elementary school, which is most often after six years of schooling, students are assigned to a certain type of secondary school. Due to federalist principles, details of the assignment vary between and even within Swiss cantons, but often class teachers' evaluations and recommendations significantly determine this assignment. Since later mobility between types of secondary school is exceptional, this assignment decision has profound impacts on a student's entire educational and occupational life course (Buchmann et al., 1993).

As shown by empirical evaluations of decision outcomes, students with a migration background tend to be disadvantaged systematically in these decisions, in particular when they are male and have achieved more or less average results (Coradi Vellacott and Wolter, 2005). Discrimination effects with respect to social categories become evident when we take national test scores into consideration. For example, for those in the Swiss-German cantons who achieved average results in national tests in maths and German, the probabilities for being assigned to 'Realschule' (lower level secondary school) vary significantly. If we combine citizenship with gender, these differences are taken to an extreme: 83% of Swiss girls who achieve average results are assigned to a higher-level secondary school ('Gymnasium' or 'Sekundarschule A'), while the chances for their male, non-Swiss classmates with the same results are only 37% (Haeberlin et al., 2004: 14).

Against this background, the decision process that produces this outcome deserves a closer look. In our case, this examination was methodologically based on utilising documents and files, on the one hand, and in-depth and group interviews with teachers and principals, on the other. Based on this material, it could be shown that assignment decisions are founded on two loosely coupled pillars: a formal procedure that draws heavily on official and clearly defined criteria, and broader cultural accounts that are also used when teachers communicate their decisions to parents and students.[2]

---

2   For a description of accounts as a sociological key concept that highlights justification and sense-making as a basis for social action and decision-making, cf. Scott and Lyman (1968). For a more recent application of this concept in organisational research, cf. Zilber (2002).

4   Manufacturing Consent: The Formal Arrangement

The formal criteria are determined by cantonal rules for the promotion of students. In our case study, one paragraph of the cantonal rules states that after six years at elementary school students must be assigned to one out of three types of secondary schools. Besides 'Werkschule', assignment to which is very exceptional and intended for those with learning disabilities and behavioural problems, there are two more common types: 'Realschule' (basic level) and 'Sekundarschule' (advanced level). Other paragraphs within the rules refer to assignment criteria. According to these rules, assignment should be based on (a) the talents, interests, and career aspirations of a student; (b) an estimation of the further development with respect to educational achievement, and (c) parental consent. It is also regulated that grades in three subjects (maths, German, and science) and behavioural attitudes should be taken into consideration as a proxy. As the evaluation of a student's talent, interests, and career aspirations, as well as the estimation of the future potential and behavioural attitudes, are characterised by a high degree of interpretative flexibility, the informed consent of parents and achieved grades become very powerful factors in the decision-making process.

There are also further political objectives and administrative inputs. Among them is the expectation of the board of directors of education of 'Inner Switzerland' (a federation of small rural cantons in German Switzerland) that two-thirds of the pupils should be assigned to 'Sekundarschule' and one third should be sent to 'Realschule'. In combination, these requirements imply the need to gain acceptance of one-third of the parents that their children be assigned to a secondary school with only basic demands that do not qualify for higher education.

The assignment process is not only structured by these regulations. Instead, there are further institutionalised practices that contribute to the formalisation of the decision process. Some of these practices are school-specific, while others are procedures that class teachers routinely apply. In our case, the class teacher initiated the assignment process via a first meeting with a student and their parents at the beginning of the first semester of the 6th school year. The assignment decision must be made during this semester. In this first meeting, the class teacher relays the preliminary results the student has achieved in the first weeks of the school year and, thus, aims to find an agreement on the expected assignment, which is recorded and signed by both the teacher and parents. Though no formal decision is made at this time, this first meeting has profound anchoring effects on further processing. In order to convince parents, class teachers present a detailed portfolio of each student that has been infused with data in the prior weeks and is composed of test results, working behaviour, and social attitudes. Often, teachers also present a student self-evaluation that includes their estimation of their educational achievement and aspirations. This self-evaluation is written in the classroom during school time and may inform about the different perspectives and aspirations of both the students and their parents. Furthermore, parents have completed an observation form that provides information on the behaviour and attitudes of the student outside school, for example, regarding their motivation to do homework.

Often, teachers and parents agree on the expected assignment. In cases that are ambiguous or non-consensual, class teachers avoid a clear recommendation at this initial phase of the process. Instead, they suggest signing a letter of intent that addresses objectives for the student in the months to come. The fulfilment of these objectives then is expected in order to be allocated to the preferred secondary school (i.e., in most cases, 'Sekundarschule' instead of 'Realschule'). Class teachers may also suggest that other teachers provide further information about the student or even participate in subsequent meetings with parents and students. Finally, some teachers consult other experts (e.g. school psychologists) or conduct tests (e.g. in the case of immigrant students, competency assessments in the native language), but such incorporation of experts and the consideration of other test results in the assignment process are rather exceptional.

To sum up, class teachers are well prepared for the first meeting with the parents of their students and can refer to a rich body of information in order to argue in favour of the assignment they expect to be appropriate. Another characteristic feature of this meeting is that the preliminary character of any recommendation is emphasised, allowing class teachers to easily manage contrasting points of view. In ambiguous cases, they try to obtain consent on the further process and about criteria, which, at a later point in time, can help to determine the assignment. Parents are only expected to sign that they agree on this procedure.

The entire decision process is composed of several meetings and takes roughly three months. During this time, the teacher produces a broad range of documents including technical information about the student: grades, test results, benchmarks, portfolios, and even evaluations of surveys with students and parents. These documents have the character of formal accounts that inform about a student's abilities, competencies, achievements, and future perspectives. Some of them are obligatory. In cases of diverging expectations between teachers and parents, gathering further data and information is suggested. Later, these data and information will help to determine and legitimise the final assignment recommendation.

It should be noted that, in cases of persistent disagreement, parents (as well as teachers and school authorities) are required to invest a great bulk of time and energy in the process. They also need social skills and communicative competencies to discuss the issue convincingly. The decision process thus requires resources that are not equally distributed and particularly disadvantage parents who lack language competency. Teachers and school authorities, on the other hand, are well aware of such differences and are also able to make informed guesses about which parents or types thereof might not accept a recommendation for a lower-level secondary school.

In cases in which parents do not agree with the recommendation, the class teacher formally informs the principal about the non-agreement. Three steps then follow, although parents can end the process at any step by agreeing to the recommended assignment:

1. The principal invites the parents and explains the recommendation to them. The recommendation is mainly justified by technical information about the student's class performance, that is, no references are made to national or international tests or to intelligence tests. Instead, grades provided by the teachers are the most important information at this point.

2. If the dispute persists, the case is negotiated with the school council, who places a vote on the issue. The class teacher and principal may participate and give recommendations but have no distinct vote in this committee. If the result of this additional arbitration is accepted by the parents, the definitive assignment form is filled, and the affiliating secondary school is informed.

3. If the parents still do not agree, they can file a complaint, which is sent to the cantonal director of education who then makes the final decision. This step may expand the school year, so it is important to note that the student is sent provisionally to the secondary school that has been recommended by the school officials and not in accordance with the aspirations of the students or their parents.

Two effects should be emphasised here. Firstly, parents' persistent disagreement with an assignment decision was extremely uncommon in the investigated case; parents rarely filed a complaint and sent it to the cantonal director. Most often, they accepted the assignment decision of the school authorities. Secondly, the allocation of students had been very much in line with the expectations of the government and administration, that is, the assignment rate to advanced secondary school and to basic secondary school deviated less than 3% from the norm (two thirds to 'Sekundarschule', one third to 'Realschule'); and assignment to 'Werkschule' had been as exceptional as intended (less than 2%).

5   Material Considerations and Collectively Available Accounts

To achieve contention and reach an assignment decision both parents and teachers can agree on, teachers also employ arguments and narratives that are only loosely coupled with the technical criteria of class performance-related achievements. These arguments and narratives are based on accounts in which teachers believe and with which they try to convince parents. Although they appear to be highly legitimate, these accounts can have discriminatory effects, as will be shown below.

5.1   *Accordance with Aspirations and Long-Range Ambitions*

References to the ambitions of a student can be found in teachers' descriptions of observed attitudes. One teacher describes this situation as follows:

> And then there are children who say: "I actually don't want to go to Sekundarschule". But the parents want their child to attend that type of school ... We had a girl whose mother favoured Sekundarschule very much, and in the last meeting she finally told us, "I've talked to my child and she doesn't want to go there, she says she'd be in the wrong place there". So, we had to say to the mother, "Then it's even clearer now, isn't it?" ... If the child declares that they don't want to go there, then it's already lost, in these cases. Then it's obvious that it won't work.
>
> Teacher 1[3]

A child's supposed long-term aspirations are another aspect that teachers may refer to:

> I always try to get a feeling for the child's intention. Is it to own a Ferrari as soon as possible? Is it to build a house? I tend to assume now that happiness is the main intention ... Satisfaction. Satisfaction can be reached by small means ... , a high school diploma doesn't mean that you are a happy person ... A good education, a good job may help, but the feat is to find a way—that is what happiness means to me. Am I happy attending the Realschule? ... I try to explain this to the parents.
>
> Teacher 2

---

3 These quotations derive from individual or group interviews with teachers and principals that were conducted and analysed in the aforementioned project.

Teachers in this investigation often referred to their experiences with the aspirations of students from a migrant background. Sometimes, they emphasised a lack of ambition, which they attributed particularly to boys from former Yugoslavia. One of the clear-cut statements was:

> I think it's a pity that children with a migration background, even if born in Switzerland so they should be integrated, are influenced by a special mentality ... In all these years, I've seen very few students with a migration background and a healthy ambition ... I'd say that most of them are predisposed by their peer group, by the group they belong to. They are not willing to achieve. I don't think it's a problem of intelligence, it's just a lack of interest.
>
> Teacher 2

5.2   *Protection against Unrealistic Demands*

According to most teachers, school grades are an important indicator, but underlying competencies and learning habits often make a difference, which has to be taken into consideration for the child's benefit. In a group interview, one teacher explained:

> It may well be that someone achieves a 5.0 while going to private lessons five times a week ... But when the speed of learning gets faster and there are higher demands, then they cannot maintain these efforts ... It's always ... prognosis ..., how will the child react when confronted with higher demands in a short time and from different sides?
>
> Teacher 5

By referring to child wellbeing, teachers may also propose an interim solution, as happened in the case of a student with grades around 4.5 and a work ethic that was deemed to be good, though, as the teachers described it, exhausting for the child:

> He had a work habit that would have enabled us to say "OK, he's engaging and could possibly make it", but he's already too much under pressure from our point of view ... We felt that it would be good for him to attend Realschule for just one year ... so we proposed, "Let the boy attend Realschule at first for a year, just to catch his breath. Learning matters are not that difficult there; there is more repetition ...". It's only one year later that he'd change to Sekundarschule, but it's not a year that's lost.
>
> Teacher 1

5.3 *Protection against Excessive Parental Demands*

According to many teachers, parents who do not agree with a recommendation tend to have unrealistic ideas and over-ambitious visions of what their child is able to achieve. As noted in the group discussion by several teachers, though parents might know their own children quite well in other respects, they do not have an appropriate picture of their scholastic profile and academic potential. The challenge of the class teacher, then, is—as described by the principal— to enlighten the parents, often simply by comparing the achievements of the child with the achievements of other students in the class. As a further problem, teachers mentioned that parents sometimes try to practice a form of self-fulfilment at the expense of their child, where a child is expected to reach for aims and achieve a standard of living that the parents may have wanted for themselves but could not achieve. One teacher spelled out:

> One big difficulty lies in the fact that many parents are in that specific age when you look back and think about what you have achieved in life … The most problematic case is when parents want to realise some form of late self-fulfilment at the expense of their children.
>
> Teacher 6

The teacher then reported a discussion with a mother who had complained about the teacher's recommendation for Realschule, in which he put forward both the argument of the overestimated importance of the assignment decision (cf. below) and the argument of excessive demands:

> I said, "But you yourself attended Realschule, and you made it in life [the family operates a business]—so leave it as it is. You can't confer your ambitions on your child. That's dangerous".
>
> Teacher 6

5.4 *Devaluating the Significance of the Assignment*

With respect to future options, many teachers argue that assignment decisions tend to be overrated. In such cases, they emphasise that they do not, in fact, profoundly impact the life course. One teacher claimed:

> It's always nice to hear from a weak student you once had to discuss with his parents … then he went into Realschule and today he's a manager in a big insurance company. School is not as important for life as many teachers think. Fortunately, in our country, you always have the opportunity to get ahead. You'll go to evening courses or something else, if you get

the feeling, "Now I'm at that point. Now I really want it" or "Now I'm so together and self-assured, I think I can make it and I'll really try ...
> Teacher 6

The citing of dramatic singular cases that show that nothing is determined by school careers seemed to be a common account here, as teachers' comments in group discussions and individual interviews suggest. Among the prominent examples known and told by nearly all participating teachers is that of V, who was characterised as '... not very pretty and really dumb, the weakest student I've ever had' (Teacher 6). In reference to this example, teachers recounted that she worked as a service maid after school and was able to communicate in French and in English with her guests. Later, she married a restaurant owner and became a businesswoman. One of the interviewed teachers explained:

> But it was v. She changed in such a positive way. Life decides much later, and we shouldn't overestimate ourselves and our function. I'm convinced of this.
> Teacher 6

Regarding this individual case, another teacher added:

> And that is actually quite comforting. All these examples—and there are several—reduce the pressure for us ... Fortunately, there are all these examples that give us confidence that the options are still open. For me, it's very comforting. Otherwise, I'd feel like a judge who puts down a guillotine.
> Teacher 5

The argument of this overrated importance on assignment, as illustrated by singular cases, is also used to calm and convince parents who are discontent with a teacher's recommendation. In the group interview, one teacher said:

> When you meet with the parents face to face, it's extremely important for many parents how we teachers look at it. By using examples of my former students ... I always try to show parents that school assignment is not a life decision. In a one-to-one situation, it's always difficult, especially for us, the teachers in the 6th grade. ... When you have to decide, you are the judge for a certain kind of parents. In this stressful situation, you refer to such examples as V or A, to show this (that school assignment is not that

important) and to exonerate the parents and ourselves and, in the end, also the child.

Teacher 2

6   Case Discussion

In most educational arrangements, assignment decisions have profound impacts on educational careers, and, as a result, they contribute to the reproduction of inequality. The investigation of the decision processes that determine student assignment has shed light on two types of account on which these decisions are based. Both types are used by teachers and principals as collectively available resources to make decisions and to communicate with parents and students to achieve consent. One type of account aims at legitimating assignment decisions by formal criteria, in particular grades. Such formalisation can be viewed as a typical means for organisations to legitimise their decision-making. In the presented case study, this type of account is not restricted to grades and test results. Instead, it also included the evaluation of a student's performance and their behavioural attitudes, which are documented in a technical format in order to strengthen procedural rationality. Quasi-grades in the form of emoticons are even applied to characterise emotional competencies (Hasse and Wyss, 2016).

In addition to these formalised criteria, we also found another type of account, which is based on broader cultural considerations and refers to reflections of the material decision effects on individual cases. The holistic estimation of a student's future potential, the need to protect them against excessive demands, and accordance with a student's supposed long-range aspirations are examples of this type of account. In combination, both types of account represent the highly institutionalised values of contemporary societies but are nonetheless the legitimation for decisions that significantly contribute to the reproduction of inequalities and are based on social categories such as gender and citizenship.

By relating educational achievement to the taken-for-granted accounts used by organisations—in our case, school authorities—a new explanation for an old, but not yet completely understood phenomenon can be provided. This research perspective may, thus, offer new insights into the organisation-based reproduction of inequality. Further, it is not only restricted to education; instead, this perspective may also stimulate research on inequality related to economic work organisations. Student assignment and issues of educational achievement may then be compared with the recruitment and promotion of employees, which also contribute to social inequality by providing unequal opportunities. The small case of decision-making in a Swiss elementary school may, thus, stimulate a much broader perspective on the causes and mechanisms that result in organisation-based forms of inequality reproduction and discrimination.

Regarding the course of argument that has been developed in this contribution, the presented case illustrates that a sociological focus on organisations does not need to be restricted to the analyses of organisational structures and formal procedures. Instead, we can also focus on world views and accounts on which the core activity of any organisation—decision-making—is based. These world views and accounts are collectively available to decision-makers; they are shared resources which can be, and are, utilised and that can, and do, have profound impacts on social structure.

7   Reflection on Organisation as a Research Object

The argument in this contribution was based on the very plain metaphor of sociological analysis as a camera. In so doing, a basic distinction could be made between those in front of the camera, that is, the research objects, and the researchers behind it. The metaphor of a camera also suggests that sociological analyses can be directed towards various objects, implying that it needs to be decided what shall become an object under investigation. In this context, and based on the self-critical reflection of Coleman (1982) regarding the impact of the social sciences on an 'asymmetric society', we argued in favour of focusing upon organisations as a relatively neglected research object.

Organisations as objects under investigation are in constant flux. Consequently, the notion of the organisation society requires continuous updating. Three examples may illustrate this point:
- Coleman's 'big players' of the 20th century: national corporations and centralised state authorities have transformed themselves into (or have been supplemented, if not replaced by) multi-national enterprises (MNEs) and international governmental organisations (IGOs). As business giants such as Amazon or Alphabet continuously generate data about individuals and can employ these data (to which politics and governments only have limited access), a new asymmetry is emerging, at least in the Western hemisphere, between powerful MNEs, on the one hand, and political and administrative organisations, on the other.
- Increasingly, various forms of *partial organisation* (inscribed, e.g. in networks, standards, rankings, and ratings) shape social behaviour (Ahrne and

Brunsson, 2011). In contrast to schools, hospitals, companies, and other *complete organisations*, partial organisations are not responsible actors to which expectations, such as compliance with norms of fairness and non-discrimination, can be directed. As partial organisations, nonetheless, have profound impacts on social behaviour and social structure, we need to know more about societal effects, for example, with respect to inscribing status differences and establishing new forms of exclusion.

– Finally, the idea of membership, typically implying employment of the workforce in most organisations, changes profoundly, not only with respect to the various forms of flexible work arrangements, including part-time work, work-life balance, and home offices but also regarding the basic idea of work. Platform providers such as Uber and Airbnb offer work opportunities that are not just incompatible with the traditional notion of employment and occupation (including the idea of upward mobility) but that also put stress on the established notions of welfare states and social insurance.

After having examined examples highlighting current organisational changes as research objects, it finally must be emphasised that the metaphor of a camera is certainly naïve because it suggests that research processes and results have hardly any impact on the object under investigation. This may not be true. With respect to financial economics, Donald MacKenzie convincingly demonstrated that research in this field has been far from a neutral process (MacKenzie, 2006). Instead, economic models and methods heavily influence decision-makers in the finance sector, since the latter tend to apply what researchers have developed. Consequently, researchers in financial economics investigate the effects of the application of their own knowledge and not an external reality, untouched by scientific results and research methods.

For several reasons, such construction of a research object is less advanced in sociology. Regarding the case presented in this chapter, teachers and principals are not as familiar with sociological findings and methods as decision-makers in the finance sector are familiar with tools and models of economics. Nonetheless, sociology contributes to the knowledge base of modern societies, and this knowledge base has an impact on social action and political reforms. In general, sociology certainly has added to what, according to Weber, are the master trends of modern society: disenchantment and rationalisation. This rationalisation not only affects any organisation but also modern states and individuals, all of which are increasingly embedded in a rationalised environment (Bromley and Meyer, 2015). Furthermore, a great bulk of sociological findings highlight various forms of inequality and discrimination. Consequently, for example, the teachers and principals we interviewed in our case study were well aware of the social problems that are inscribed into the assignment process.

Due to such input in society, sociology has profound effects on its research objects. The notion of construction, thus, cannot be reduced to cognitive constructions and research designs. Instead, it also regards interventions and manipulations of the research object—intentionally or not, and more often intermediated than directly, but certainly unavoidable. This matter of fact, finally, implies responsibilities that may explain why the plain notion of a value-free social science has become controversial when compared to the early days of Weber, and why Becker's (1967) fundamental question about the side on which we, as sociologists, are on requires ongoing reflection.

References

Ahrne, G., and Brunsson, N. (2011). "Organization outside organizations: The significance of partial organization", *Organization* 18 (1): 83–104.

Arnold, N., and Hasse, R. (2015). "Escalation of governance: Effects of voluntary standardization on organizations, markets and standards in Swiss fair trade", *Sociological Research Online* 20 (3). https://www.socresonline.org.uk/20/3/10.html.

Becker, H.S. (1967). "Whose side are we on?", *Social Problems* 14 (3): 239–247.

Best, J. (ed.). (1995). *Images of issues: Typifying contemporary social problems*. 2nd Edition. New York: Aldine de Gruyter.

Bloor, D. (1976). *Knowledge and social imagery*. London: Routledge.

Boli, J., and Thomas, G.M. (eds.). (2000). *World polity formation since 1875: World culture and international non-governmental organizations*. Stanford: Stanford University Press.

Bromley, P., and Meyer, J.W. (2015). *Hyper-organization: Global organizational expansion*. Oxford: Oxford University Press.

Brunsson, N., and Jacobson, B. (eds.). (2000). *A world of standards*. Oxford; New York: Oxford.

Buchmann, M., Charles, M., and Sacchi, S. (1993). "The lifelong shadow: Social origins and educational opportunity in Switzerland", in Y. Shavit and H.-P. Blossfeld (eds.). *Persistent inequality: Changing educational attainment in thirteen countries*. Boulder: Westview Press, 177–192.

Burgess, E.W. (1953). "The aims of the Society for the Study of Social Problems", *Social Problems* 1 (1): 2–3.

Chubb, J.E., and Moe, T.M. (1988). "Politics, markets, and the organization of schools", *The American Political Science Review* 82 (4): 1065–1085.

Cicourel, A.V., and Kitsuse, J.I. (1963). *The educational decision-makers*. Indianapolis, IN: Bobbs-Merrill.

Coleman, J.S. (1982). *The asymmetric society*. Syracuse, NY: Syracuse University Press.

Coradi Vellacott, M., and Wolter, S.C. (2005). *Chancengerechtigkeit im schweizerischen Bildungswesen*. Aarau: Schweizerische Koordinationsstelle für Bildungsforschung.

De Solla Price, D. (1974). *Little science, big science*. Frankfurt: Suhrkamp Verlag.

Douglas, M. (1982). "Cultural Bias", in M. Douglas (ed.). *In the active voice*. London: Routledge & Kegan Paul.

Durkheim, É. (1933). *The division of labor in society*. Glencoe, IL: Free Press.

Durkheim, É. (1980). *Die Regeln der soziologischen Methode* [The Rules of Sociological Method]. Ed. and trans. R. König. Darmstadt/Neuwied: Luchterhand.

Feyerabend, P. (1975). *Against method*. London: New Left Books.

Foucault, M. (1994). *Überwachen und Strafen: die Geburt des Gefängnisses* [Discipline and Punish: The Birth of the Prison]. Frankfurt am Main: Suhrkamp.

Foucault, M. (1996). *Die Geburt der Klinik: eine Archäologie des ärztlichen Blicks* [The Birth of the Clinic: An Archaeology of Medical Perception]. Frankfurt am Main: Fischer-Taschenbuch-Verlag (i.O.: Naissance de la clinique).

Goffman, E. (1995). *Asyle: über die soziale Situation psychiatrischer Patienten und anderer Insassen* [Asylums: Essays on the Condition of the Social Situation of Mental Patients and Other Inmates]. Frankfurt am Main: Suhrkamp.

Gomolla, M., and Radtke, F.-O. (2002). *Institutionelle Diskriminierung: Die Herstellung ethnischer Differenz in der Schule*. Opladen: Leske & Budrich.

Haeberlin, U., Imdorf, C., and Kronig, W. (2004). *Chancenungleichheit bei der Lehrstellensuche: Der Einfluss von Schule, Herkunft und Geschlect*. Aarau: SKBF.

Hasse, R. (2019). "What Difference Does it Make? An Institutional Perspective on Actors and Types thereof", *Research in the Sociology of Organizations* 58: 23–41.

Hasse, R., and Schmidt, L. (2012). "Institutionelle Diskriminierung", in U. Bauer et al., (eds.). *Handbuch Bildungs- und Erziehungssoziologie*. Wiesbaden: VS, 881–900.

Hasse, R., and Wyss. S. (2016). "Emotionalität als Mythos und Zeremonie? Zur Bedeutung emotionaler Ausdrucksfähigkeit und Selbstthematisierung im Kontext schulischer Beurteilungen.", in M.S. Maier (ed.). *Organisation und Bildung. Theoretische und empirische Zugänge*. Wiesbaden: Springer.

Jasanoff, S. (1990). *The fifth branch: Science advisers as policymakers*. Cambridge, MA: Harvard University Press.

Knorr-Cetina, K., and Mulkay, M. (eds.). (1983). *Science observed: Perspectives on the social study of science*. London: Sage.

Lorenzen, P. (1969). *Methodisches Denken*. Frankfurt: Suhrkamp.

Lucas, S.R. (1999). *Tracking inequality: Stratification and mobility in American high schools*. New York: Teachers College Press.

Luhmann, N. (1975). "Interaktion, Organisation, Gesellschaft.", in N. Luhmann (ed.). *Soziologische Aufklärung 2: Aufsätze zur Theorie der Gesellschaft*. Opladen: Westdeutscher Verlag.

MacKenzie, D.A. (2006). *An engine, not a camera: How financial models shape markets*. Cambridge, MA: MIT Press.

Merton, R.K. (1938). "Social structure and anomie", *American Sociological Review* 3 (5): 672–682.

Meyer, J.W., Boli, J., Thomas, G.M., and Ramirez, F.O. (1997). "World society and the nation-state", *American Journal of Sociology* 103 (1): 144–181.

Mohr, J., et al. (eds.). (2015). "Assumptions of sociality: A colloquium of social and cultural scientists", *Big Data & Society* 2 (2). https://journals.sagepub.com/page/bds/collections/colloquium-assumption-sociality.

Oakes, J. (1985). *Keeping track: How schools structure inequality*. New Haven, CT: Yale University Press.

Perrow, C. (2002). *Organizing America: Wealth, power, and the origins of corporate capitalism*. Princeton: Princeton University Press.

Sahlin, K., and Wedlin, L. (2008). "Circulating ideas: Imitation, translation and editing", in R. Greenwood, C. Oliver, K. Sahlin, and R. Suddaby (eds.). *The SAGE Handbook of Organizational Institutionalism*. Thousand Oaks: SAGE Publications.

Schmidt, L., and Hasse, R. (2010). "Kulturelle Zurechnungen und Vokabulare der Problemkonstruktion", *Soziale Probleme* 21(2): 141–166.

Scott, M.B., and Lyman, S.M. (1968). "Accounts", *American Sociological Review* 33 (1): 46–62.

Stinchcombe, A.L. (1965). "Social structure and organizations", in J. G. March (ed.). *Handbook of Organizations*. Chicago: Rand McNally.

Weber, M. (1978). *Economy and society: An outline of interpretive sociology*. Berkeley, CA: University of California Press.

Zilber, T.B. (2002). "Institutionalization as an interplay between actions, meanings, and actors: The case of a rape crisis center in Israel", *Academy of Management Journal* 45 (1): 234–254.

CHAPTER 8

Broken Promises and Lost Qualities
Constructing Management as a Research Object in Sociology and Anthropology

Emil André Røyrvik

Since disciplines can be understood as a specialised forms of rhetorical object construction practices (Larsen, 2006), this chapter aims to discuss and illustrate how these practices inform sociology and anthropology's preparation of their objects and problems. I focus the analysis by framing it in terms of how two different theoretical concepts, institutional logics and cultural logic, respectively construct management, positing that cultural logic represents anthropology's dominant rhetorical object construction practice, while the concept of institutional logics is illustrative of sociology. This way of constructing the research object has been deliberately simplified into 'ideal typical descriptions' in order to facilitate comparisons. The chapter applies the two theoretical concepts in constructing management as a research object and uses 'management by objectives' (MBO) as a case due to its emergence as the dominant mode of management during the last decades.

1   Rhetorical Object Construction in Anthropology and Sociology

Rhetorical practices are here framed within the broadly interpretative and semiotic research traditions that focus on meaning construction, which underscore how reality is understood through the languages that form it, including both tacit conceptualisations and the explicit vocabularies of language. A varied set of tropes and rhetorical figures shape our ways of understanding and conceptualising the world and organise our perception of reality and experiences into perspectives that guide thought and action (e.g. Lakoff and Johnson, 1980; Heradstveit and Bjørgo, 1992). This applies to scientific disciplines as well as sub-disciplines, as found in phrases such as 'the language of anthropology' (Larsen, 2006). Historical writing is, for example, underpinned by the narrative rhetorical plot structures identified by White (1973) as metaphor, metonymy, synecdoche, and irony. Similarly, Thornton (1988) argued that the central trope underlying ethnography is 'classification'. Rumsey (2004), meanwhile, labelled these types of underlying figures that form ethnography and analysis as 'macro-tropes'.

Based on this, I perceive a difference between *rhetorical* and *argumentative* practices in the social sciences. Although rhetorical practices can be consciously invoked in any argumentative practice, for example, in the explicit use of metaphors as empirical data or as an analytical strategy or narrative technique of presentation, rhetorical practices also more or less *tacitly* underlie and inform any discipline's figures of thought, that is, its lenses or 'eye'. These more or less implicit rhetorical practices and macro-tropes of a discipline create shared perspectives that enable its discourses and help to shape its research objects. The idea of disciplinary (macro)tropes is, thus, different from Bourdieu et al.'s (1991) argument related to the need for an epistemological break with everyday notions and folk theories but, in a similar way, calls for more reflexivity in social research projects.

According to Tord Larsen (2006), anthropology may be described through four distinct historical phases, all with 'the primitive' as the anthropological object par excellence. In the first historical phase, 'the primitive' is constructed 'as nature' (both the savage and the noble savage), in the second, it is constructed as 'pre-rational', in the third as 'authentic', and in our current phase, the primitive is constructed as the 'the lost primitive re-primitivised'. Each of the four phases emerges, according to Larsen, out of a rhetorical situation, which brings forth its own classification mechanism. The scientific revolution de-animated nature and established the dominant categorical dichotomy of subject and object (or mind and nature); the enlightenment added the opposition between rationality and irrationality or pre-rationality, and the industrial revolution institutionalised the contrast between the authentic and the alienated (and between the rural organic and urban mechanic). At a fundamental level, these dichotomies constitute the relationship between the knower and the known.

The prototypical and most legitimate of anthropological objects are, therefore, those phenomena that ethnographers as modern people have evolved 'away' from, such as "ontological hierarchies, the analogue relationship between micro and macro-cosmos, magic, sacrificing, totemism, clan organization, animism, ancestor worship" (ibid.: 6, author's translation), etc. In short, these rhetorical situations produce a set of classifications that distinguishes 'the primitive' or pre-modern from 'the modern'. According to Larsen (ibid.), three generalised figures or tropes, in particular, have been formative for anthropology: *exchange* constructs social life as the circulation of value, *language* constructs culture as the formation and play of signs, and the *body* constructs society as an organism.

Sociology has focused more on the categories on the other side of the dichotomies described above. The sociological object par excellence is, thus, arguably 'the modern', 'modern society', or simply 'modernity'. I argue that along with constructing this problem of modernity, the process brings along more or less undetected conceptual hitchhikers: underlying and implicit notions and (macro)tropes about the modern that shape the construction of the sociological research object.

The focus on institutions, exemplified by the institutional logics approach that I take in this chapter, is a rhetorical practice of sociological object construction that places it firmly within what I would argue to be the primary sociological object or problem, that of 'modernity'. Sociology typically prepares its objects of study rhetorically through an explicit or implicit reference to the ideas of modernity, with its underlying assumptions and tropes of progress, promises, rationality, efficiency, emancipation, justice, future orientation, and the like. Perspectives and analysis in specific sociological studies are often critical and 'disappointing', exemplified by key theoretical concepts such as disenchantment, alienation, the iron cage, exploitation, repression, colonisation of the lifeworld, etc. Such findings and explanations are arguably part of a rhetorical argument that hinges upon the 'gaze' and vocabulary of sociology in preparing a 'modern object' or problem.

From Auguste Comte, the founder of both positivism and sociology, to Jürgen Habermas (1996) and beyond, tropes of modernity underlie dominant currents of rhetorical sociological problem construction practices. Significantly, Comte appears in the very first sentence of *The Craft of Sociology* (Bourdieu et al., 1991: 1). I argue that the underlying tropes of modernity produce a deep ambivalence, or doubleness, particularly towards the broken promises of modernity, in much sociological analysis. This ambivalence is pronounced, for example, in Weber's rendering of the rationalisation of society and bureaucracy; in other words, the rational spirit's organisational manifestation from the emergence of the legitimate legal-rational authority and its securing of the citizenry's equal protection under the law, to a view that bureaucratisation was so powerful and irreversible (Weber, 1968) that it had become an iron cage imprisoning humanity "perhaps until the last ton of fossilized coal is burnt" (Weber, 1952: 181–182). In an interview with Hartmut Rosa, it appears that he, much like the earlier generations of the Frankfurt school:

> considers modernity in terms of *a broken promise*: the very technology
> and social revolutions that were supposed to lead to an increase in autonomy are now becoming increasingly oppressive
>
> LIJSTER, CELIKASTES, and ROSA, 2019: 64, my emphasis

In a similar way, Habermas' perspective of modernity as an 'unfinished' and 'incomplete' project exemplifies the ambivalent rhetorical practices of sociological object construction (Habermas, 1996; d'Entrèves and Benhabib, 1996). Both Habermas' perspective and its framing by sociologist Steven Seidman are illustrative: according to Seidman, in his critical analysis:

> ... Habermas continues to insist on the *utopian potential* of modernity. In a social context in which faith in the Enlightenment project of a good society promoted by reason seems to be a fading hope and spurned idol, Habermas remains one of its strongest defenders.
>
> SEIDMAN, 1989: 2, my emphasis

Another illustrative example is Wright's (2010) notion of 'real utopias'.

The rhetorical strategies of anthropology and sociology partially overlap, but generally speaking, anthropology as rhetorical object construction practice prepares its object in the various figures of the primitive. In so doing, it also brings forth *that which is lost* (the primitive [life] is lost, 'everyone' has become modern) as an underlying or implicit object, in an ethos or rhetorical feeling of *melancholia* (Larsen, 2006). I argue that sociology as a rhetorical object construction practice prepares its object through various figures of the modern, and, thus, brings forth ambivalent notions of broken promises that we might describe as *that which could have been realised* (a utopian trope) or *that which was realised in the negative* (a dismal trope) as an underlying or implicit object. Such 'dismal tropes' are the kinds of negative results and consequences actually realised, despite the positive potentials inherent in assumptions of modernity. Figures related to social problems have, in particular, directed the attention of the 'sociological lens', moving the focus to phenomena with perceived negative consequences (see Hasse in this volume). The ethos or feeling that encircles this modernist rhetoric of sociological object construction might, therefore, be described in terms of *ambivalence, disappointment,* and even disillusionment and betrayal on account of the broken promises, lost possibilities, and fading hopes for modernity. Thus, we find notions of the 'modern utopia' to be implicit (and sometimes explicit) in sociological object construction rhetoric.

I argue that critique, as a fundamental mode of representation, follows quite logically from sociology's rhetorical tropes and preparation of its problems and objects of study, not least grounded in its ambivalent doubleness towards modernity, as will be illustrated by the competing different institutional logics of management below. It also contributes to explaining the power and continuation of the critical stance in sociology; as Karin Widerberg notes in this volume, all sociologists are or are expected to be critical, including towards the foundations of the discipline and the craft of sociologists (although, of course, there are also other modes of sociological analysis).

2 Institutional Patterns: Management as Institutional Logics in Sociology

Building on a more than three-decades-long discussion on the 'new' approach to institutions (e.g. Meyer and Rowan, 1977; Zucker, 1977; DiMaggio and Powell, 1983; 1991), the notion of institutional logics shares with these authors a concern with how cultural and cognitive factors shape organisations, while it also differs in several respects, most notably by not focusing on isomorphism. Alford and Friedland (1985) introduced the term to account for the *contradictory* beliefs and practices found in modern institutions, highlighting the contending institutional orders of capitalism, state bureaucracy, and political democracy. Later, Friedland and Alford (1991) emphasised the relationships between society, organisations, and individuals, focusing on how the varying logics of institutional orders make available vocabularies of motive, a sense of identity, and organisational principles through practices and symbols. They argued that the major institutions of society are characterised by their separate 'logic', which is understood as a set of material practices and symbolic constructs constituting their organising principles and representing their worldview or way of thinking.

Building on several earlier definitions, Thornton and Ocasio defined in 1999 institutional logics as:

> the socially constructed, historical patterns of material practices, assumptions, values, beliefs, and rules by which individuals produce and reproduce their material subsistence, organize time and space, and provide meaning to their social reality.
>
> Quoted in THORNTON AND OCASIO, 2008: 101

In the institutional logics approach, the focus is on how differentiated and often contradictory institutional logics affect individuals and organisations in a variety of contexts and levels (Thornton and Ocasio, 2008).

3   The Institutional World of Management by Objectives

An institutional logics approach, in simplified terms, constructs and analyses
its research object through uncovering and examining the particular world-
view(s) of the institution. In this illustration, we will focus on the historical
emergence of MBO and the patterns of practices, concepts, and beliefs pertaining to it, exemplified by its instantiation in the Norwegian context. An institutional lens would argue that management emerged as a distinct modern social
institution at the turn of the 19th century (Shenhav, 1992). Peter Drucker, probably the most influential thinker on management theory and practice, wrote in
The Practice of Management:

> The emergence of management as an essential, a distinct and a leading
> institution is a pivotal event in social history. Rarely, if ever, has a new
> basic institution, a new leading group, emerged as fast as has manage-
> ment since the turn of the century. Rarely in human history has a new
> institution proven indispensable so quickly; and even less often has a
> new institution arrived with so little opposition, so little disturbance, so
> little controversy.
>
> DRUCKNER, 1954: 3

This same book also popularised the term 'management by objectives' (MBO)
and inaugurated the age of management *as* MBO. Drucker stated in the introduction that 'to manage a business means, therefore, to *manage by objectives*'
(1954: 12, italics in original) and provided six core messages for management
thinking and practice, with 'manage by objectives' at the top of the list.
According to Drucker:

> [The manager] determines what the objective should be. He determines
> what the goals in each area of objectives should be. He decides what has
> to be done to reach these objectives. He makes the objectives effective
> by communicating them to the people whose performance is needed to
> attain them
>
> DRUCKNER, 1954: 344

and "objectives are needed in every area where performance and results directly
and vitally affect the survival and prosperity of the business" (ibid.: 63). Drucker
emphasised that objectives must be set for both the short and long-term time at
all levels of the organisation, and both tangible and intangible objectives must
be included. He further argued that the greatest advantage of MBO is that it

enables the manager to control himself, and such self-control results in stronger motivation, and higher performance goals, and a broader vision. In essence, MBO makes management by self-control possible. Drucker found in this a separate legitimation for MBO and ended the chapter by labelling management by objectives and self-control as a philosophy of management. It is the only philosophy of management capable of uniting individual potential, responsibility, and strength, with common direction, vision, and the harmonising of not only the organisation and individual's goals but also connecting those to the commonweal (ibid.: 135–136), highlighting MBO as an important social institution.

The popularity of the concept accelerated when it was endorsed by and attributed to the success of large American high-tech companies such as Hewlett-Packard. Interestingly, Drucker later distanced himself from the concept of MBO, stating, for example, "MBO is just another tool. It is not a great cure for management inefficiency ... Management by objective works if you know the objectives: 90 % of the time you don't".[1] It was the United States, the United Kingdom, and France, in particular, that propelled the translation of MBO into public administration practices and institutions. Initially, during the first wave of public management reform in the late 1960s and '70s (Pollitt and Bouckaert, 2011) and the second wave of institutionalising MBO in the 1980s and '90s, reforms emerged into what has come to be called New Public Management (NPM) (Hood, 1991). Although MBO is largely associated with NPM in the public discourse, a host of other MBO-adapted and related concepts have flourished and now support the management institution, such as 'result-based management', 'value-based management', 'performance management', 'balanced scorecard', 'performance administration', and not to forget the currently widely popular concept of 'objectives and key results' (OKR), which is allegedly responsible for Google's success (Doerr, 2018). However, this arguably indicates that, although the labelling shifts, the core idea of MBO is deeply institutionalised across sectors and, furthermore, proves to be surprisingly resistant towards the incessant fads and fashions of management theory and practice (Brunsson, 2002).

4   MBO as Institutional Logics in Norway

Since the 1980s, a strong institutionalisation of MBO has ensued in both the public and private sectors of Norwegian society (e.g. Christensen et al., 2010;

---

1 Hindle, Tim. 'Management by Objectives'. *The Economist*. https://www.economist.com/node/14299761 (accessed April 15, 2018). See also Pugh and Hickson (2007).

Askim et al., 2014; Røyrvik, 2018). It has been implemented in the name of efficiency, simplicity and transparency, advocating autonomy and professionalism, accountability, and contributing to focusing on the most important goals, in addition to arguably contributing to increased motivation in the workplace.

In Norway's public sector, the implementation of the New Public Management 'version' of MBO has been a gradual process over the last 30 years (Askim et al., 2014). One key event was the budget reform of 1986, giving state agencies increased freedom to allocate their own budgets to specific tasks and activities, in exchange for the systematic measuring and reporting of results to the government and parliament. In 1989, a milestone government report titled *Towards a Better Organised State* (Mot en bedre organisert stat) was published and paved the way for a host of market-liberalisation policies and the 'marketisation' of the public sector. It marked a shift in the Norwegian mode of governance that was led by the coming to power of a new 'market-technocratic steering elite' (Slagstad, 2001: 503–524, my translation), which imposed markets, management, and measurement on Norwegian society.

From 1990, MBO was required in all state organisations, and, in 1996, it was inscribed as the basic principle of rule for the economic management of the state, when it was strongly emphasised that MBO was to structure the governing of public organisations (Askim et al., 2014). Several studies have documented that, in the Norwegian state system, MBO is to a great extent framed in the vernacular of various versions of 'performance management' (Lægreid, Roness og Rubecksen, 2008; Breivik, 2010). Relatedly, Helgesen (2001) showed how MBO has found its strongest position in Norway as a management philosophy, and Ramslien (2005) added to this conclusion while simultaneously arguing that, in some areas, MBO has developed towards a management technique with increasingly more differentiated and specified objectives comprising quantified goals for specific activities or services.

5   Critique and Two Different Ways of Approaching the
       Research Object

To understand the institutional worldview and patterns of practices and beliefs pertaining to MBO, institutional analysis provides a necessary *critique* of the concept. The scope of this critique relates, first, to the danger of having too many objectives and goals and how this might lead to an inflation of management (Askim et al., 2014). This relates to the many complaints about MBO as a 'time thief', consuming increasingly more time and displacing what people are supposed to and want to be doing to perform their work in satisfactory ways

(Muller, 2018). Further related to this and other problems with MBO is the issue of goal displacement and the gaming of the system (ibid.); when the focus is on visible, measurable results, a logical consequence is to modify behaviour and activities to satisfy the evaluation system, to the possible detriment of the actual work tasks and important overall objectives of the organisation. This 'perversion' of objectives can arguably be seen as lower-level, 'technical' (and ultimately economic) objectives drowning out the higher-level, overall normative objectives (e.g. Askim et al., 2014; Wathne, 2015). Johnsen (2015), for example, argued that with the implementation of MBO in the public sector, the traditional forms of detailed steering have continued, but in the vernacular of MBO, have created a mixed institutional system of governance.

Based on a sociological modernist institutional logics-based perspective, we can outline the construction of MBO as a research object in the mode of sociological institutional logics. Table 8.1 highlights the ambivalence, or doubleness, of its modernist rhetorical practices.

Through sociology's dominant rhetorical object construction practices of modernisation, we can recognise its deep ambivalence, or doubleness, distinguishing between one hopeful, utopian modernist institutional logic that forms practices in the field and another institutional logic of disappointment

TABLE 8.1   Two contradictory institutional logics of management by objectives, emerging through a focus on institutional logics' more or less implicit rhetorical 'perspective'

Contradictory institutional logics of management by objectives

Positive promises and the success of MBO ('hopeful, utopian, modernist logic')	Critical assessment of MBO ('disappointing, dismal, modernist logic')
Efficiency, simplicity, and transparency	Over-bureaucratisation, inflation of management, and time-thievery
Autonomy and professionalism	Institutionalised 'accountability' with detailed documentation, evaluation, and regimes of control
More motivation and engagement at work	De-motivation, apathy, disengagement
Focus on the most important human and social objectives in work-life	Goal displacement, gaming of the system, 'perversion' of objectives

and betrayal that forms the critique of the field. Each logic has a set of characteristics, and the second can rhetorically be seen as a kind of 'negation' of the first, illustrating the 'negative consequences' and social problems that have shaped much sociological attention. Taken together, both logics form the deeply ambivalent doubleness in the rhetorical gaze of the modernisation characteristic of sociological object construction, comprising the broken promises, betrayals, and (utopian) hopes of modernity.

6   Premises of Culture: Management as Cultural Logic in Anthropology

The concept of a cultural logic can be perceived to emerge from the general anthropological concern with 'cultural premises'. Simply stated, the cultural premises of dominant social practices collectively define a cultural logic. A cultural logic does not so much refer to a class of representations or practices as it points to their foundational function(s) in social life. These functions are, furthermore, conceptualised not as the numerous more instrumental or utilitarian functions but rather as the cultural horizon within which we think (and, arguably, feel) as part of some cultural collective when we go about our daily lives and envisage our common future. Harking back to the founders of North American cultural anthropology, such as Ruth Benedict and her classic 'Patterns of Culture' (1934), which is part of a tradition that conceptualises culture as a holistic unity comprising 'a more or less consistent pattern of thought and action' (p. 46), the notion of cultural logic has gained more contemporary and common currency, not least through the work of Frederic Jameson (1991). The concept broadly implies that there are cultural 'codes' implicit in all social practices and that the work of cultural analysis consists of identifying these codes, rhetorical figures, underlying epistemological premises, and implicit ontologies that inform and shape these practices.

Constructed through the anthropological perspective of cultural logic, MBO may be considered as part of a long western tradition that emerged during the Renaissance, premised upon the development of a cultural logic of objectivation through quantification, measurement, and standardisation (Larsen and Røyrvik, 2017). With the rise of neoliberalism and its organisational and institutional manifestations in management (by objectives), this cultural logic has taken on a particular form. A cultural logic analysis, that here only serves as an illustration, will trace and outline the constitution of the horizon of thinking pertaining to MBO and its co-contribution to the cultural logic.

As Alfred Crosby demonstrated in *The Measure of Reality* (1997), Europeans became obsessed with quantification from the period around 1300 AD, building the first mechanical clock and the cannon, and abstracting time and space into divided and discrete units disembedded from human action. A host of other inventions emerged: Portolano marine charts, perspective painting, and double-entry bookkeeping. Quite symbolically, around the critical time of 1300, Roger Bacon measured the angle of the rainbow. Crosby discussed the emergence of a *quantitative perception* that made modern science, technology, business practice, and bureaucracy possible, presenting a striking example of the shift towards quantification:

> When in the fourteenth century the scholars of Oxford's Merton College began to think about the benefits of measuring not only size, but also qualities as slippery as motion, light, heat, and color, they forged right on, jumped the fence, and talked about quantifying *certitude, virtue, and grace*. Indeed, if you can manage to think of measuring heat before the invention of the thermometer, then why should you presumptively exclude certitude, virtue and grace?
>
> CROSBY, 1997: 14

These ideas of measuring certitude, virtue, and grace might today seem absurd, but present society remains preoccupied with numerous new fields of quantification and quality standardisation and control. The measuring, objectification, and evaluation of newer and larger domains of social life proceed, for example, with the rise of new quality control regimes such as countless ISO standards, corporate social responsibility, corporate ranking in terms of ethics, country happiness measures and comparisons, self-tracking technologies, and so on. Anthropologist Ulf Hannerz (2007) has described as our contemporary 'neoliberal culture complex' by catchphrases such as *accountability, transparency, quality control, branding, auditing, excellence,* and *ranking,* and they signal the cultural logic of quantification. While possibly having given up on measuring grace, since it is of little importance in profane societies, we continue to measure morality and emotions and seek to control all kinds of intangible qualities.

In the neoliberal culture complex, MBO and its correlates have co-evolved with a governing logic of 'rule by numbers' (Shore and Wright, 2015), in particular where this rule is tied in with a privileged reference to 'the economy'. The economy, with its leadership/management and ownership (shareholders, investors, and financial markets), is the ultimate context of reference and concern (Røyrvik, 2021). The major organisational trends of 'radical economism'

(Røvik, 2016) and 'managerialism' (Clegg, 2014) have emerged as an important horizon of thinking within (and outside) of organisations. New Public
Management (NPM) can be concisely defined as the introduction of the
'three Ms' into public services: markets, managers, and measurement (Ferlie
et al., 1996).

A cultural logic analysis constructs MBO as both a part of and co-creation of
'the cultural logic of facts and figures',[2] which, in the contemporary, is constituted by a strong will and massive investment in objectifying the social world
through quantification, measurement, and standardisation. This cultural logic
of objectivation is not only descriptive or symbolic but also performative in
its shaping and co-creation of social reality. This generative capacity of our
current dominating forms of objectification serves, to a large extent, various
functions of power and control. In our case, it fits perfectly with contemporary
ideas of management, where, during the last decades, we can identify a broad
shift towards both top-down control and a movement from leadership to
'steering', involving the centralisation of power, re-hierarchisation, formalised
management systems, and 'hard HR', focusing on incentives and reward- and
information-systems (Røvik, 2016).

This managerialism of top-down steering through numbers, measurements,
standardisation, evaluations, etc., with economic goals as its ultimate concern,
has contributed to transforming MBO from its original conception and function in the middle of the 20th century (that is, as a recipe to displace detailed
control regimes in favour of greater autonomy and self-governance at work) to
its current function that enables the proletarianisation of professional work
and authoritarian work-life organisations and management regimes (Larsen
and Røyrvik, 2017).

The particular and dominant forms of objectivation in contemporary society are signalled by the coming of age of the culture of management, accountability, and transparency (e.g. Strathern, 2000); the audit society (Power,
1997); a world of standards (Brunsson and Jacobsson, 2000), and the rise of
widespread measurements, indicators (Merry, 2011), rankings, and ratings
(Espeland and Sauder, 2007). MBO and its numerous conceptual corollaries
are primary organisational vehicles in these cultural processes: according to
Shore and Wright (2015), who ask if we are witnessing the rise of a new type
of world order, these processes create both new kinds of subjectivity and new
forms of power and governance.

---

2 This is the title of the transdisciplinary research project from which the current work has
   emerged. See https://www.ntnu.edu/sosant/cuff.

As shown above, a cultural logic perspective constructs its research object, in this case, MBO, by placing it in the widest possible frame and context of the human condition and its predicament. A primary example of this approach is Frederic Jameson's influential book *Postmodernism, or, the Cultural Logic of Late Capitalism* (1991), in which he noted the apparent triumph of objectivation, in the form of commodification, over all spheres of life and society, which marks 'the cultural logic of late capitalism'. Jameson further identified several symptoms that indicate the cultural logic of our time. Some of the more significant of these symptoms include first, the weakening of historicity, a new 'historical deafness' which resembles a schizophrenic position that loses historicity to a series of unrelated 'presents' in time. A second of these symptoms relates to the emergence of a new 'depthlessness' akin to Baudrillard's (1994) simulacrum, which materialises in various forms of literal flatness, such as two-dimensional screens and skyscrapers with reflecting windows and qualitative superficiality. Another symptom is found in his description of the waning of affect and the emergence of a new type of emotional ground tone, which he labels 'intensities': Jameson argued that the general depthlessness and affectlessness of the current capitalist cultural logic are complemented by outrageous claims of intense emotional experiences—i.e. 'intensities'—that he relates to schizophrenia and addiction culture (1991: 28–29).

In several cultural logic analyses of work-life quantification, measurements, and management—in particular, various MBO and performance management concepts in the Norwegian context—Røyrvik (e.g. 2012; 2018) sought to link the emergence of the 'cultural logic of facts and figures' (or quantification and measurement) directly to ongoing transformations of sociality and subjectivity. This was inspired by Dufour's (2008) analysis of a 'total capitalism' in the 'postmodern neoliberal age', in which the modern critical and neurotic subject, with its social forms, is increasingly being transformed into a precarious and uncritical subject, finding itself in a kind of schizoid state of 'limit' or boundary-experience. Like Jameson, Dufour was also inspired by Baudrillard, and resembling Jameson's diagnosis in several ways, Dufour argued that the 'new' self is fashioned from commodified and fetishised things and relations, to the extent that it creates an internal distance between the subject and their own self, which co-constitutes the schizoid tendencies.

Røyrvik (2018) argued that MBO and its underpinning cultural logic of quantification, measurements, and standardisation of neoliberal financialised capitalism, with its ultimate concern of economy (managerialism and economism), is a key driving force in these transformations of subjectivity and the social. There is now a growing body of literature discussing the negative effects of various measures, including indicators and incentives, on different aspects of sociality and subjectivity, such as morality and identity. For example, several studies have empirically shown how 'motivational' measurement systems and incentives (economic, material, competitive, and ranking, etc.) can undermine not only the motivation and productivity of employees at work (e.g. Kohn, 1993) but also social values and the moral basis for pro-social behaviour (Bowles, 2016). Incentives may 'crowd out' ethical and generous motives (ibid.), which has broader implications for both subjectivity and sociality (Røyrvik, 2018).

By also including Jameson's analysis in this overall diagnosis, the argument would be that through the ubiquitous social practices of ultimately economic/ financial numbers and measurements, both subjectivity and the social are reified, commodified, flattened, 'superficialised', and diluted of qualitative depth, symbolic weight, and historical meaning, which contributes to the schizoid tendencies that Jameson, Dufour, Deleuze, and others have identified as symptoms of our current cultural condition.

7   Comparing the Perspectives

The concepts of institutional logics and the cultural logic both seek broad understandings of social phenomena by focusing on 'the cultural'. While institutional logics, with their focus on illuminating the practices, concepts, beliefs, worldview, and patterns that characterise institutions, to a large extent serve descriptive purposes, the concept of cultural logic has ambitions to unearth the widest and deepest cultural premises of social practice and thought. As such, institutional logics provide more practical and instrumental social critique (see Table 8.1), while cultural logic offers a broad diagnosis and a more fundamental cultural critique.

The concept of institutional logics is tied to predefined institutions, from the macro institutions of capitalism, democracy, and bureaucracy to institutions at various levels of organisation. The analysis of institutional logics is, thus, framed by particular and predefined social institutions, including architecture, higher education, public accounting, etc., or—as in our case—management, and typically a few competing logics can be uncovered within these institutions. The cultural logic framework, on the other hand, treats (combined) dominant social practices *as* cultural logic: social practice is performative in co-constituting the cultural logic of which it is an example. Institutional logics, at least in some dominating versions, clearly state that the logic does not emerge from organisational fields (Thornton and Ocasio, 2008: 119) but that local fields are instantiations of the logics, with their predefined categories of descriptive characteristics.

While both concepts address culture, the concept of cultural logic, with its ambitions of uncovering the cultural premises—or *codes*—that inform and shape social practice, aims at a broad diagnosis of contemporary culture and our time. In contrast, while institutional logics also aim at contextualisation, breadth of characterisation, and description, the concept of cultural logic seeks to uncover social functions perceived of as the 'horizon' and constitution of the imagination. It provides analyses with depth, levels, and the promise of a more substantial cultural critique than the more instrumental critique inherent in a modernist institutional logics approach. A cultural logic approach seeks to contextualise the case within the widest possible framework of the human condition and its premises and highlight the underlying epistemological premises and implicit ontologies that shape and inform social practice.

With regard to MBO and its corollaries, we can argue that, from a cultural logic perspective, MBO rests on a positivist epistemology that considers knowledge to consist of largely, 'hard facts' that can be counted, quantified, and represented as 'objective facts of reality'. In terms of implicit ontologies, MBO and its offspring rest on assumptions that perceive human nature as a rational 'utility-maximizing' economic man, which has clear objectives and goals, complete information about a given situation, and information about alternatives and consequences. This economic man is driven by external incentives (the proverbial stick and carrot) and can rate and rank alternatives on an unambiguous scale of preferences; furthermore, this economic man can also rationally choose the best alternative by doing the right thing and making the right decisions.

This way of being in the world can be seen to be rigidly modern, and the cultural logic approach provides a cultural diagnosis with an underlying rhetoric of that which is lost, in line with anthropological rhetorical object construction practices. It focuses on that which is lost in the quantification/measurements/audit culture that MBO and its corollaries are part of: in general, quality is lost to quantity, authenticity is lost to instrumentality and commodification, depth is lost to superficiality and shallowness, and true or adequate feelings or affect are lost to affectlessness, numbness, or 'intensities', to use Jameson's vernacular. Cultural logic further turns our attention to the transformations of ontologies or being in the world—that is, towards changes in the direction of the market-flexible, the commodified, and the simulated in the context of 'total capitalism'—with economic man as the sole model of human nature; although, in the postmodern phase, economic man is arguably turning out to be rather schizoid, if we are to believe authors like Deleuze, Dufour, and Jameson.

The cultural logic approach is, thus, in line with anthropology's object construction practices of rhetorical primitivisation, which is steeped in an ethos or feeling of melancholia and driven by a search and yearning for that which is lost. One main weakness of the cultural logic approach is the ease with which it slips into too broad strokes of generalisations and totalising diagnoses and how it might reify culture as total and unified systems of thought and action, in line with the tradition of American cultural anthropology dating back at least to Ruth Benedict's *Patterns of Culture* (1934) and her argument that 'culture is personality writ large'. In the rhetorical perspective of primitivisation, everything good is at risk of being, or already having been, lost in a modern world.

The strength of the institutional logics approach lies in empirical precision and empirically based analytical categorisations, which provide conceptual tools for understanding and explaining both institutional variance (within institutions) and wider institutional systems and their broad social underpinnings. Its main weakness, on the other hand, is found in how it is lynch-pinned to formally delineated institutions and how those are defined as more or less pre-given, for example, architecture, public accounting, etc. The conflicting ideal types of institutional logics that are constructed or found in the analysis are also described with a set of more or less given characteristics, such as the type of economic system, sources of identity and legitimacy, authority, etc. (e.g. Thornton and Ocasio, 2008: 128–129).

In line with the dominant forms of rhetorical object construction practices in sociology, with its primary problem of modernity, and the critical ethos of 'that which was not realised', and its rhetorical implicit feelings of disappointment—even betrayal—and broken promises related to possibilities and hopes of modernity, the institutional logics approach highlights a social critique related to the regrets of that which was realised in the negative and that which could have been realised (in the promises for the future) with the emergence of MBO and its corollaries.

In the modernist sociological object construction mode of institutional logics, we can see that, from the 1950s, management by objectives has promised emancipation, self-directedness, self-determination, and self-control, although what was realised historically and institutionally was, in fact, more authoritarian organisations with greater demands for loyalty and obedience. MBO and its corollaries promised efficiency, simplicity, and transparency, but what has been realised has to a large extent been over-bureaucratisation, inflation of management, and time-thievery. MBO promised autonomy and professionalism but delivered largely institutionalised 'accountability' with detailed documentation, evaluation, and regimes of control. It also promised more motivation and engagement in work, but due to its particular focus on external motivation factors (i.e. incentives) that drive out the more important internal motivation, it has, to a large extent, delivered demotivation, apathy, and disengagement. Finally, MBO promised the realisation of the most important human and social objectives in work-life but has instead delivered goal displacement and the gaming of the system, with the 'perversion' of objectives where lower-level, 'technical'—and, ultimately, economic—objectives displace the higher level, overall normative objectives (see Table 8.1).

In this light, we can see how the institutional logics frame is also in keeping with the rhetorical modernism of sociology's object construction practices, a deeply ambivalent sociological eye of disappointment, broken promises, and fading hopes, but still with yearnings and some anticipation for a better, even utopian, tomorrow and long-term future.

8   Final Remarks

In scrutinising the construction of management in sociology and anthropology, we see that although they are, superficially, quite similar concepts, institutional and cultural logic construct the object of management quite differently when we focus on their respective rhetorical object construction practices. These rhetorical practices form, more or less implicitly, the underlying assumptions and figures of thought that, in turn, shape the discipline's respective perspectives and their 'generalised' and 'preferred' objects, that is, 'the modern' and 'the primitive'. While anthropology's 'heroic rhetoric' of 'primitivisation' was described by Larsen (2006), the present chapter has compared this with the rhetorical practices arguably dominant within sociology. Through reflections on sociology's rhetorical tropes of 'modernisation', we can better understand its deep ambivalence towards modernity and the discipline's critical stance in its construction and analysis of its objects. Similar to other key notions in sociology, such as alienation and colonisation, some of the metaphors shaping the object of management from a sociological perspective are illuminating; for example, the *inflation* of management, MBO as a time-*thief*, the *gaming* of the system, and the *perversion* of objectives. All of these metaphors signal the main modes of rhetorical object construction practices in sociology, that is, those of a critical appraisal of social problems and negative consequences, encircled by feelings of disappointment, betrayal, and fading hopes in light of the (utopian) promises of modernity.

This chapter has attempted to openly display how it has rhetorically constructed the two disciplines of anthropology and sociology as both falsely homogeneous and also distinct from each other. The two disciplines share a long history and are formed by many of the same classics. Likewise, they are both radically diverse in approaches, methods, and perspectives. A more nuanced approach would have been possible, and could, for example, have focused on how the two theoretical constructs rather illustrate variations and similarities related to the degrees of qualities and emphasis in social analysis, and how they variously relate to different traditions within both anthropology and sociology. Both concepts are concerned with 'culture' and how it shapes society, organisations/institutions, and individuals and their thought and action, while both are also geared towards the broad analyses that account for multiple levels of the social (macro/micro) and wider cultural contexts of influence and constitution. Hence, there are obvious alternative routes of analysis, but that remains for another, future project.

The text has, thus, constructed its object in a comparative and somewhat 'dichotomous' way to make a general point and has sought to illustrate how more or less implicit rhetorical strategies and tropes of thought inform our ways of constructing and analysing research objects. It has also highlighted that there is no easy move from metaphors towards figureless and 'neutral' scientific concepts in the construction of objects in the social sciences (see also Scott's chapter in this volume). More or less implicit rhetorical tropes and practices are part of the constitution of any discipline or sub-discipline, and critical self-reflection of this should constitute an integral part of the craft of the disciplines.

References

Alford, R.R. and Friedland, R. (1985). *Powers of theory: Capitalism, the state, and democracy.* Cambridge: Cambridge University Press.

Askim, J., Eltun, R., and Fremstad, E. (2014). "Mål- og resultatstyring: Riktig oppskrift for styring av statsforvaltningen?" [Management by objectives and results: The right recipe for public administration?], in H. Baldersheim and Ø.Østerud (eds.). *Det norske demokratiet i det 21. århundre* [The Norwegian democracy in the 21st century]. Bergen: Fagbokforlaget.

Baudrillard, J. (1994). *Simulacra and simulation.* Ann Arbor: The University of Michigan Press.

Benedict, R. (2006) [1934]. *Patterns of culture.* Boston: Mariner Books.

Bourdieu, P., Chamboredon, J.-C., and Passeron, J.-C. (1991). *The craft of sociology: Epistemological preliminaries.* Berlin and New York: Walter de Gruyter.

Bowles, S. (2016). *The moral economy: Why good incentives are no substitute for good citizens.* Yale University Press.

Breivik, B. (2010). "Mål og resultatstyring i praksis" [Management by objectives and results in practice], *Notat* 9. Bergen: Uni Rokkansenteret.

Brunsson, N. (2002). *The organization of hypocrisy: Talk, decisions and actions in organizations.* Copenhagen: Copenhagen Business School Press.

Brunsson, N., Jacobsson, B., and associates (2000). *A world of standards.* Oxford: Oxford University Press.

Christensen, T. and Lægreid, P. (2002). *Reformer og lederskap. Omstilling i den utøvende makt* [Reforms and leadership. Restructuring in the executive power]. Oslo: Universitetsforlaget/Scandinavian University Press.

Christensen, T., Egeberg, M., Larsen, H.O., Lægreid, P., and Roness, P. G. (2010). Forvaltning og politikk [Public aministration and politics]. Oslo: Universitetsforlaget.

Clegg, S. (2014). "Managerialism: Born in the USA", *Academy of Management Review* 39 (4): 566–585.

Crosby, A.W. (1997). *The measure of reality: quantification and Western society.* Cambridge: Cambridge University Press.

D'Entrèves, M.P. and Benhabib, S. (eds.). (1996). *Habermas and the unfinished project of modernity: critical essays on the philosophical discourse of modernity.* Cambridge: Polity Press.

DiMaggio, P.J. and Powell, W.W. (1983). "The iron cage revisited: Institutional isomorphism and collective rationality in organizational fields", American Sociological Review 48 (2): 147–160.

Doerr, J. (2018). *Measure what matters. OKRs – The simple idea that drives 10x growth.* Portifolio Penguin.

Drucker, P. (1954). *The practice of management.* New York: Harper.

Dufour, D.-R. (2008). The art of shrinking heads. Cambridge: Polity Press.

Espeland, W.N. and Sauder, M. (2007). "Rankings and reactivity: How public measures recreate social worlds", *American Journal of Sociology* 113 (1): 1–40.

Ferlie, E., Ashburner, L., Fitzgerald, L., and Pettigrew, A. (1996). *The New Public Management in action.* Oxford: Oxford University Press.

Friedland, R. and Alford, R.R. (1991). "Bringing society back in: symbols, practices, and institutional contradictions", in W.W. Powell and P.J. DiMaggio (eds.). *The new institutionalism in organizational analysis.* Chicago, IL: University of Chicago Press.

Habermas, J. (1996). "Modernity: An unfinished project", in M.P. D'Entrèves, and S. Benhabib (eds.). *Habermas and the unfinished project of modernity: critical essays on the philosophical discourse of modernity.* Cambridge: Polity Press.

Hannerz, U. (2007). "The neo-liberal culture complex and universities: A case for urgent anthropology?" Anthropology Today 23 (5): 1–2.

Helgesen, S.B. (2001). *Aktivitetsmåling og atferdskontroll. En studie av mål- og resultatstyring gjennom Økonomiregelverket for staten* [Activity measurement and behavior control. A study of management by objectives and results through the state's economic rules and regulations]. LOS-center Report Ro102. Bergen: LOS-center.

Heradstveit, D. and Bjørgo, T. (1992). *Politisk kommunikasjon: Introduksjon til semiotikk og retorikk* [Political communication: Introduction to semiotic and rhetoric]. Oslo: Tano Aschehoug.

Hood, C. (1991). "A Public Management for All Seasons", Public Administration 69 (1): 3–19.

Jameson, F. (1991). *Postmodernism, or, the cultural logic of late capitalism.* Durham: Duke University Press.

Johnsen, Å. (2015). "For mye detaljstyring og for lite målstyring?" [Too much micromanagement and too little management by objectives?], *Stat & Styring* 25 (2): 36–40.

Kohn, A. (1993). *Punished by rewards: the trouble with gold stars, incentive plans, A's, praise, and other bribes.* Boston: Houghton Mifflin.

Lakoff, G. and Johnson, M. (1980). Metaphors we live by. Chicago and London: The University of Chicago Press.

Larsen, T. and Røyrvik, E.A. (eds.). (2017). *Trangen til å Telle. Objektifisering, måling og standardisering som samfunnspraksis* [The Imperative to Count. Objectification, measurement and standardization as social practice]. Oslo: Scandinavian Academic Press.

Larsen, T. (2006). "Melankoli og retorisk heroisme. Om former for antropologisk gjenstandsdannelse" [Melancholia and Rhetorical Heroism. The Forms of Anthropological Objectification], *Rhetorica Scandinavica* 40.

Lijster, T. and Celikates, R. (2019). "Beyond the Echo-chamber: An Interview with Hartmut Rosa on Resonance and Alienation", *KRISIS: Journal for contemporary philosophy* 1: 64–78.

Lægreid, P., Roness, P.G., and Rubecksen, K. (2006). "Performance management in practice: The Norwegian way", *Financial Accountability & Management* 22 (3): 251–270.

Lægreid, P., Roness, P.G., and Rubecksen, K. (2007). "Modern management tools in state agencies: The case of Norway", *International Public Management Journal* 10 (4):1–27.

Lægreid, P., Roness, P.G., and Rubecksen, K. (2008). "Performance Information and Performance Steering: Integrated Systems or Loose Coupling?", in S. van der Walle and W. van Dooren (eds.). *Performance Information in the Public Sector.* New York: Palgrave Macmillan.

Meyer, J.W. and Rowan, B. (1977). "Institutionalized organizations: Formal structure as myth and ceremony", American Journal of Sociology 83 (2): 340–363

Merry, S.E. (2011). "Measuring the world: Indicators, human rights and global governance", *Current Anthropology* 52 (3): 83–95.

Moynihan, D.P. (2008). *The Dynamics of Performance Management. Constructing Information and Reform.* Washington, DC: Georgetown University Press.

Muller, J.Z. (2018). *The Tyranny of Metrics.* Princeton: Princeton University Press.

Pollitt, C. and Bouckaert, G. (2011). *Public management reform. A comparative analysis – new public management, governance, and the neo-weberian state*, 3rd edition. Oxford: Oxford University Press.

Porter, T. (1995). *Trust in numbers: the pursuit of objectivity in science and public life.* Princeton, NJ: Princeton University Press.

Power, M. (1997). The audit society: Rituals of verification. Oxford: Oxford University Press.

Pugh, D.S. and Hickson, D.J. (2007). *Writers on organizations.* 6th edition. Thousand Oaks: Sage.

Ramslien, A.R. (2005). *Fra ritual til verktøy. Mål og resultatstyring av Utlendingsdirektoratet* [From ritual to tool. Management by objectives and results in the Norwegian Directorate of Immigration]. Report nr. 9. Bergen: Rokkansenteret.

Rumsey, A. (2004). "Ethnographic macro-tropes and anthropological theory", *Anthropological Theory* 4 (3): 267–298.

Røvik, K.A. (2016). *Trender og translasjoner. Ideer som former det 21. århundrets organisasjon* [Trends and translations. Ideas that forms the 21st century's organization]. Oslo: Universitetsforlaget/Scandinavian University Press.

Røyrvik, E.A. and Brodersen, M.B. (2012). "Real virtuality: Power and simulation in the age of neoliberal crisis", *Culture Unbound: Journal of Current Cultural Research* 4: 637–659.

Røyrvik, E.A. (2018). "The measure of sociality: Quantification, Control and Economic Deviance", in J.G. Carrier (ed.). *Economy, crime and wrong in a neoliberal era.* New York: Berghahn Books.

Røyrvik, E.A. (2021). "Sacralizing finance, sacrificing society", in T. Larsen, N., Rapport, K., Ram, K., Porter, T., and Blim, M. (eds.). *Objects and standards. On the limitations and effects of fixing and measuring life.* Durham: Carolina Academic Press.

Seidman, S. (ed.). (1989). "Introduction", *Jürgen Habermas on society and politics: A reader,* Boston: Beacon Press.

Shenhav, Y.A. (1999). Manufacturing rationality: The engineering foundations of the managerial revolution. New York: Oxford University Press.

Shore, C. and Wright, S. (2015). "Governing by numbers: audit culture, rankings and the new world order", *Social Anthropology* 23 (1): 22–28.

Slagstad, R. 2001. De nasjonale strateger [The national strategists]. Oslo: Pax Forlag.

Strathern, M. (ed.). (2000). Audit cultures: Anthropological studies in accountability, ethics and the academy. London: Routledge.

Thornton, R. (1988). "The rhetoric of ethnographic holism", *Cultural Anthropology* 3: 285–303.

Thornton, P.H. and Ocasio, W. (2008). "Institutional logics", in R. Greenwod, C. Oliver, K. Sahlin, and R. Suddaby (eds.). *The Sage Handbook of Organizational Institutionalism.* Los Angeles: Sage.

Wathne, C.T. (2015). *Som å bli fremmed i eget hus: Politiets opplevelse av mening og moti-vasjon i lys av nye styringssystemer* [Like becoming strangers in their own house: The Police's experiences of meaning an motivation in light of new management systems]. Doctoral thesis. Department of Criminology and Sociology of Law. The Faculty of Law. University of Oslo: Oslo.

Weber, M. (1952). *The protestant ethic and the spirit of capitalism.* New York: Scribner.

Weber, M. (1968). *Economy and society: An outline of interpretive sociology.* New York: Bedminister.

White, H. (1973). *Metahistory.* Baltimore, MD: Johns Hopkins University Press.

Wright, E.O. (2010). *Envisioning real utopias.* London and New York: Verso.

Zucker, L.G. (1977). "The role of institutionalization in cultural persistence", *American Sociological Review* 42: 726–743.

CHAPTER 9

On Thought Experiments in Sociology and the Power of Thinking

Michela Betta and Richard Swedberg

How is the research object constituted in sociology? There exist a number of different approaches, from the more positivistic ones to those based on hermeneutics and related approaches. All of these agree on one point, however, and that is that the object of study is basically empirical in nature. The idea that the object can be totally made up is not entertained. Neither is the idea that this way of proceeding can in some cases improve the understanding of a phenomenon.

To proceed in this manner is, however, what is done when a thought experiment is carried out. Two of the most famous thought experiments throughout history are the following. The first was carried out by Galileo Galilei in the late 1500s and challenged Aristotle's theory of motion (Galileo, 1954: 63). According to Aristotle, heavy objects fall faster than light objects. Assume, Galileo said, that we tie a small stone to a larger stone. The small stone would now prevent the large stone from falling as fast as it normally would. But it would also fall faster since the two are heavier than the large stone. Hence the theory cannot be correct.

The second thought experiment comes from modern philosophy and is known as the Trolley Problem. Assume you are driving a trolley and are about to kill five people who are working on the track unless you decide to switch to another track. On this other track, however, one person is working who will be killed if you choose this option. "Is it morally permissible for you to turn the trolley?" (Thompson, 1985: 1395). Regardless of how you answer this question, it shows the disturbing fact that you are ready to kill.

These and many other experiments of a similar type have led to a huge literature on thought experiments, especially in physics and philosophy (for overviews, see e.g. Sorensen, 1992; Häggqvist, 1996; Cohen, 2005; Brown and Fehige, 2017). An N-gram shows that, since the 1960s, the use of "thought experiments" has increased many times, and that today that term is more common than the term "critical experiment".[1] The idea of thought experiments has also entered

---

1 It has been pointed out that the current notion of a thought experiment is part of the same discourse as normal experiments, that is the type of experiments that became the

popular culture, as *The Left Hand of Darkness* (1969) by Ursula le Guin reminds one. This book, which is a classic in science fiction, is described by its author as a thought experiment. The question it tries to answer is the following: what would human societies look like if there were no gender?

There has been considerably less use of thought experiments in social science than in natural science, and in sociology next to none (but see e.g. Ellsberg, 1961; Ylikoski, 2003; Thoma, 2016; Brownlee and Stemplowska, 2017). Why is this the case; and more specifically, why has there been so little interest in thought experiments among sociologists? Is there something about sociology that makes it less suitable for thought experiments? Does sociology leave no room for thought experiments through its strong emphasis on empirical facts? Or do there maybe exist thought experiments in sociology; but little known or of low quality?

This chapter will try to answer these questions. Before doing so, however, something should be said about what constitutes a thought experiment. The consensus in the literature is that the term "thought experiment" stands for a fairly sprawling and not easily defined category (e.g. Häggqvist, 1996: 11; Brown, 1991: 1). According to Thomas Kuhn, for example, "the category 'thought experiment' is ... too broad and too vague for epitome" (Kuhn, 1977: 241).

Among the questions that have been asked about thought experiments and that have received different answers, are the following: Can you define a thought experiment as an experiment that is carried out exclusively in the mind of the researcher? Does conducting a thought experiment mean that the experiment cannot be carried out in reality; or alternatively, that it can be carried out in reality, but not just now? There is also the related argument by Ernst Mach that before any experiment is carried out, the researcher must run it through in his or her mind (Mach, 1972: 449).

Further diversity is introduced into the debate about the nature of the thought experiment by those who emphasise its element of narrative or suggest that it has the same structure as an argument (e.g. Brown and Fehige, 2017). Counterfactuals are sometimes seen as forms of thought experiments and sometimes not (e.g. Tetlock and Belkin, 1998; Florian, 2015).[2] The question has

norm after the 1500s and 1600s (Shapin and Shaffer 1985: 55). Before this time, there were "imaginary experiments" of the type that the alchemists conducted. Many of these were probably never carried out; they were also poorly described, with little thought of replication.

2   A compromise would be to argue that counterfactuals represent a special type of thought experiments. However, this question is solved, for an example of a counterfactual analysis by

also been raised if agent-based modelling, or simulation more generally, will not soon replace the thought experiment (e.g. Chandrasekharan, Nersessian and Subramanian, 2011). Some believe that the thought experiment is made possible by the inborn capacity of human beings to reason; others that it is best described as a form of mental modelling (e.g. Johnson-Laird, 1983; Nersessian 1992).

In this chapter, a sociological thought experiment will be given a stipulative definition that is broad in nature, reflecting the general state of the literature. This will also make it easier to discuss different types of thought experiments. The suggested definition of a sociological thought experiment reads as follows: *an experiment that is carried out in the mind of the researcher, in which imaginary data are used, and where the unfolding logic is sociological.*[3] It is possible to distinguish between different stages in such an experiment: the initial social state (I); the introduction of a specified change (II); the social process now set in motion and worked out in the mind of the analyst (III); and the end state (IV). The term unfolding logic refers to the fact that sociologists typically study patterns of social behavior, and that these follow their own logic as they come into being and change.

---

a sociologist that is called a thought experiment by its author, see Randall Collins' *Civil War Two* (2018). The author describes his work as follows: "In a way CW2 is the product of a great thought experiment, drawing on my understanding of history and human behavior, asking what would happen if another civil war happened in our near future [in the United States]." A synopsis of the volume reads as follows: "President Joshua Maccabee Jennings has just taken office, vowing to Make America Christian Again. When a Supreme Court Justice dies unexpectedly, the government falls into crisis, and secular states start seceding, soon forming the Coalition of Secular States of America."

3   By arguing that a thought experiment has to be carried out in the mind of the analyst and not by a machine, agent-based modelling and simulations more generally are by definition ruled out. There do exist reasons to argue the opposite, however, emphasizing the non-empirical nature of simulations and agent-based modelling (e.g. Macy and Willer, 2002: 146–150). Our reasons for *not* taking this position in this chapter are the following. First, simulation and agent-based modelling are already accepted methods in sociology; and to include and analyse them in this chapter would not entail anything new. More generally, it is hard for us to see what we add to our knowledge of simulation and agent-based modelling by simply calling them thought experiments. The empirical cases discussed by James March and co-authors in "Learning from Samples of One or Fewer" represent to our mind a more interesting case than simulation (March, Sproull and Tamuz, 1991). This chapter points out that organisations sometimes have to learn from only one or even no earlier experiences (e.g. "a military organisation has rarely fought in a battle. Yet it wants to learn from its history how to improve its ability to engage in warfare"). One could say that a hybrid kind of thought experiment is involved in this case, or one where imagination is mixed with a bit of experience.

1   Do Thought Experiments Exist in Sociology?

If you look at standard works in sociological theory or methods, you will not find any references to thought experiments. These are not even dismissed, say as a form of armchair sociology.[4] The closest you come to a discussion of thought experiments in sociology are a few articles in areas that look at the situation in fields that are close to sociology, such as organization studies and social studies of science (e.g., Folger and Turillo, 1999; Ylikoski, 2003).[5]

The lack of a discussion of thought experiments in sociology does not, however, mean that they have never been used by sociologists, be it in an embryonic form or in a more elaborate version. It is, for example, not uncommon for sociologists, as part of some general argument or analysis, to ask questions like, "If the facts were different, what would the outcome be?" (e.g., Hughes, 1945: 354–355; 1963: 888; Collins, 1981: 1007; Killewald, 2013: 110).[6]

---

4   Quite a bit of what belongs to theory in sociology has since World War II been labeled "armchair sociology" in mainstream US sociology (e.g. Sibley, 1971: 14; Rossi, 1986: 2; 1987: 370). By this term is meant a form of sociological analysis that is pre-empirical and pre-scientific. The situation is different, for example, in US economics, as exemplified by the positive response to Steven Landsburg's popular book from 1993, *Armchair Economist*. According to Landsburg, "Logic matters. It leads us from simple ideas to surprising conclusions ... Evidence matters too, but logic can be powerful all on its own" (Landsburg, 2012: viii).

5   Neither Latour (1998) nor Hill (2005) discuss what is usually seen as thought experiments, even if this term figures prominently in the titles of some of their articles (e.g. Hill, 1987, 2005; Latour, 1998). Instead they use the term "thought experiment" for such things as dystopias/utopias, novels and virtual societies. See also note 3. In a paper presented at the annual convention of the American Sociological Association in 2003, Gerald Markle and Frances MacCrea presented a paper entitled "What If? Thought Experiments in Sociology" (Markle and McCrea, 2003). Ideas similar to those expressed in this talk can also be found in Appendix B ("Thought Experiments") in their book *What if Medicine Disappeared?* (Markle and McCrea, 2008: 147–155). This book can itself be described as a thought experiment/counterfactual, which in some respects is similar to Nils Christie's *Hvis skolen ikke fantes* (1971) and Robert Fogel's *Railroads and Economic Growth* (1964).

6   The examples just cited in the text of this chapter have been located by going through sociological journals in JSTOR and typing in the word "imagine" in the column for "full-text." For some additional and also fuller thought experiments—by W.E.B. Du Bois, Jane Addams and Charlotte Perkins Gilman—see Hill (2005). One thought experiment by Gabriel Tarde has been summarised by Everett C. Hughes as follows: "He [Tarde] imagined a society in which men were all assured of plenty of food and other comforts with but a few minutes of labour each day; the economic friction was taken out of human interaction. He then gave his notions of what would happen to sex, music, the mind, and many other things. He even gave a gently satirical account, by members of that society, of a group called sociologists who had existed in some ancient time—Tarde's own time" (Hughes, 1963: 889). A more empirical and exploratory flavour characterises the thought experiment by Du Bois, which was located by Michael Hill (2005). In one of his articles Du Bois invites the white reader to make

Such questions, however, typically play a subordinate and marginal role in the overall analysis. Still, their existence does indicate that thinking in thought-experimental terms is part of the sociologist's repertoire, even if this is rarely acknowledged or mentioned.[7]

But there also exist some cases where sociologists have used thought experiments in a more conscious manner; and it is to these we now shall turn. The ones we have chosen can all be found in well-known sociological works. This feature makes them especially useful for the main purpose of this chapter, which is to introduce thought experiments into sociology.

The thought experiments that will be discussed come from the following works: Émile Durkheim's *Rules of Sociological Method* (1895), Max Weber's *Economy and Society* (1920–21), C. Wright Mills' *Sociological Imagination* (1959) and Robert K. Merton's *Social Theory and Social Structure* (1968).[8]

---

the thought experiment of imagining what it it would be like to live on the other side of the colour line: "Let me take you journeying across the mountains and meadows, threading the hills of Maryland, gliding over the broad fields of Virginia, climbing the blue ridge of Carolina and seating ourselves in the cotton kingdom. I would not like you to spend a day or a month here in this little town; I should much rather you would spend ten years, if you are really studying the problem; for casual visitors get casual ideas, and the problems here are the growth of centuries ... Were you here in person I could not easily take you across the line into the world I want to study. But in spirit let me lead you across ..." (Du Bois, 1904: 297–298; Hill, 2005: 9).

7   According to sociologists Gerald Markle and France MacCrea, who define a thought experiment as an answer to the question "what if?", "sociologists routinely pose this question, in teaching, in research, or in the privacy of their own thoughts" (Markle and MacCrea, 2008: 147). They continue, "In posing such questions, social scientists are really engaging in 'thought experiments', without the label and, as a consequence, *without theoretical or methodological rigor*" (Markle and MacCrea, 2008: 148; emphasis added).

8   To what has already been said about thought experiments by sociologists, the following can be added. There exists an interesting thought experiment that is based on the ideas of Tocqueville, known as "the spiral of silence." The basic argument is as follows: if all who are against some decision by the government do not speak out against this decision, the rest who oppose it will get the impression that the decision has a stronger support than it actually does—which in its turn will encourage even fewer people to oppose the decision openly, and so on (see e.g., Noelle-Neumann 1993 for discussion and empirical verification). One can also find a number of thought experiments in the work of Georg Simmel. The most famous of these is intended as a rebuttal of Nietzsche's argument about the eternal return (for a discussion, see e.g. Sorensen, 1992: 13–14). This thought experiment is however philosophical in nature, not sociological (similarly, see e.g. Simmel, 1895:40–41). The sociological thought experiments we have been able to locate in Simmel's work are, however, not accompanied by much of a discussion and hard to distinguish from non-empirical assertions of the armchair type. They are nonetheless numerous in number and often very interesting, as e.g. a reading of Simmel's work on the quantitative aspects of groups makes clear (Simmel, 1959). The affinity that exists between Simmel and thought experiments may be related to his focus

2   The Four Sociological Thought Experiments

We will begin the discussion of these four thought experiments by citing the original passages in which they can be found. Since several of them are quite difficult, we will then explicate these passages. This will be followed by a general discussion of their individual merits as well as some concluding remarks about the applicability of thought experiments in sociology.

In Ch. 3 of *The Rules of Sociological Method,* Durkheim discusses the function of crimes in society. As part of his argument, he presents a thought experiment about a society of saints. He begins his description with the word *imagine (imaginez).* The section reads as follows:

> Imagine a society of saints, a perfect cloister of exemplary individuals. Crimes, properly so called, will there be unknown; but faults which appear venial to the layman will create there the same scandal that the ordinary offense does in ordinary consciousnesses. If, then, this society has the power to judge and punish, it will define these acts as criminal and will treat them as such. For the same reason, the perfect and upright man judges his smallest failings with a severity that the majority reserve for acts more truly in the nature of an offense. Formerly, acts of violence against persons were more frequent than they are today, because respect for individual dignity was less strong. As this has increased, these crimes have become more rare; and also, many acts violating this sentiment have been introduced into the penal law which were not included there in primitive times.
>
> DURKHEIM, 1964: 68–69

Let us now proceed to the second case. Ch. 1 *Economy and Society* contains a section in which Max Weber explains how to go about verification in interpretive sociology. In some cases, he says, you do not know the motives of the actors and therefore have to conduct a "mental experiment" (*gedankliches Experiment*).[9] The full passage, which is hard to follow, since it is written in Weber's usual compressed style, reads as follows:

---

on formal sociology, in combination with a lack of interest in grounding his arguments in empirical data.

9   Weber also uses the same term in one more place in *Economy and Society* (but this time without the quotation marks he used to insert in order to indicate that he used the term in its common [scholarly] meaning and not according to his own definition). The second example is not particularly interesting. Weber argues that a socialist state would be as ruthless in its economic dealing with subordinate states, as a capitalist state (Weber, 1978: 919–920). Finally,

More generally, verification of subjective interpretation by comparison with the concrete course of events is, as in the case of all hypotheses, indispensable. Unfortunately, this type of verification is feasible with relative accuracy only in the few very special cases susceptible of psychological experimentation. In very different degrees of approximation, such verification is also feasible in the limited number of cases of mass phenomena which can be statistically described and unambiguously interpreted. For the rest there remains only the possibility of comparing the largest possible number of historical or contemporary processes which, while otherwise similar, differ in the one more decisive point of their relation to the particular motive or factor the role of which is being investigated. This is a fundamental task of comparative sociology. Often, unfortunately, there is available only the uncertain procedure of the 'imaginary experiment' ('*gedankliches Experiment*') which consists in thinking away certain elements of a chain of motivation and working out the course of action which would then probably ensue, thus arriving at a causal judgment.

WEBER, 1978: 10

This passage is followed by another, similarly dense passage of about the same length, in which two examples of this type of "mental experiment" are presented (Weber, 1978: 10–11). One is Gresham's Law or the tendency for bad money to drive out good money. The other is the Battle of Marathon, which was decisive for the emergence of Western culture. If the Persians had won, the course of the West would have been very different (see also Weber, 2012: 174ff).

The next example of a thought experiment is considerably easier to understand and comes from the appendix on intellectual craftsmanship in *The Sociological Imagination* by C. Wright Mills. One of the ways in which sociologists can stimulate their sociological imagination, Mills says, is by positing "an imaginary world":

The release of imagination can sometimes be achieved by deliberately inverting your sense of proportion. If something seems very minute,

---

it is not known why Weber used the expression "*gedankliches Experiment*" and not the term for thought experiment that Ernst Mach had popularised in the German-speaking world, *Gedankenexperiment*. Weber was well aware of Mach's writings, even if it is not known if he had read his famous essay on thought experiments from 1897, "Über Gedankenexperimente" (later republished in a somewhat different form in a book from 1905, *Erkenntnis und Irrtum*; Mach, 1972; e.g. Scaff, 2011: 157).

imagine it to be simply enormous, and ask yourself: What difference might that make? And vice versa, for gigantic phenomena. What would pre-literate villages look like with populations of 30 millions? Nowadays at least, I should never think of actually counting or measuring anything, before I had played with each of its elements and conditions and consequences in an imagined world in which I control the scale of everything. This is one thing statisticians ought to mean, but never seem to, by that horrible little phrase about 'knowing the universe before you sample it'.

MILLS, 1959: 215

The fourth and last example comes from the work of Robert K. Merton (1948, 1968). The description of his thought experiment reads as follows:

It is the year of 1932. The Last National Bank is a flourishing institution. A large part of its resources is liquid without being watered. Cartwright Millingville has ample reason to be proud of the banking institution over which he presides. Until Black Wednesday. As he enters his bank, he notices that business is unusually brisk. A little odd, that, since the men of A.M.O.C. steel plant and the K.O.M.A. mattress factory are not usually paid until Saturday. Yet here are two dozen men, obviously from the factories, queued up in front of the tellers' cages. As he turns into his private office, the president muses rather compassionately: "Hope they haven't been laid off in midweek. They should be in the shop at this hour."

But speculations of this sort have never made for a thriving bank, and Millingville turns to the pile of documents upon his desk. His precise signature is affixed to fewer than a score of papers when he is disturbed by the absence of something familiar and the intrusion of something alien. The low discreet hum of bank business has given way to a strange and annoying stridency of many voices. A situation has been defined as real. And that is the beginning of what ends as Black Wednesday—the last Wednesday, it might be noted, of the Last National Bank.

Cartwright Millingville had never heard of the Thomas theorem. But he had no difficulty in recognizing its workings. He knew that, despite the comparative liquidity of the bank's assets, a rumor of insolvency, once believed by enough depositors, would result in the insolvency of the bank. And by the close of Black Wednesday—and Blacker Thursday— when the long lines of anxious depositors, each frantically seeking to salvage his own, grew to longer lines of even more anxious depositors, it turned out he was right.

MERTON, 1948: 194; 1968: 476

3   Explication of the Four Thought Experiments

There exist different reasons why it is necessary to explicate each of the four thought experiments. In the case of Durkheim, the reader needs for example more information to be able to follow his argument. The example of crimes in a society of saints is part of a more general argument in *Rules of Sociological Method* about the functional role of crime in society. Durkheim's thoughts on crime are also quite complex, and to some extent unclear.

In Durkheim's well-known formulation, crimes are "useful" for society (Durkheim, 1964: 70). One of the reasons he thinks so is that people's reactions to crime keep the values of society alive; and no society can exist without strong and vibrant values. There also exist two other reasons why crimes are useful. A society without crimes would leave no room for progress and change. Many groups in a society are also at different stages of their development, something that prevents uniform behavior from emerging.

Keeping these arguments in mind makes it easier to understand Durkheim's thought experiment. It is set in a society, in which a certain number of crimes are committed. The whole population is then exchanged for one in which everybody is a saint. The result, however, is not what you might have thought, namely that crimes would now disappear. There will still be crimes, Durkheim says, but of a different nature. The reason for this is that a society cannot exist without values, and values cannot exist without crimes. The function of crime, to phrase it differently, is to keep alive the values in which the great majority of the people believe and thereby also help to reproduce them.

In Durkheim's view, a crime is not defined by a certain type of behavior, say the act of theft or committing a murder but by the kind of values that exist in a society. Being rude or blasphemous is not a crime in modern society, but in a society of saints it might very well be criminalised. Durkheim would in other words have sharply disagreed with James Madison's famous statement in *The Federalist* (1788): "if men were angels, no government would be necessary" (Madison, 2017).

Weber's thought experiment is hard to penetrate; it may also seem that his *"gedankliches Experiment"* does not belong in a discussion of thought experiments. Thanks to Carl Hempel's discussion of Weber's *"gedankliches Experiment"* it has, however, become part of the standard literature on thought

experiments.[10] In the next section we shall also try to show that if you explicate Weber's argument and explain what place it has in his overall approach to
sociology, it becomes more accessible.

According to the principles of interpretive sociology, as outlined in Ch. 1
in *Economy and Society*, the action of an individual is driven by a motive. An
action has two parts, each of which is indispensable: an "outer" behavior and
an "inner" meaning that fits the behavior.[11] To verify the nature of an action,
the sociologist needs solid facts about both ("evidence"). It is usually harder to
get evidence about the meaning than about the behaviour.

In an experiment the sociologist can control both the behaviour and the
meaning that goes with it. In most analyses of real life, however, experiments
cannot be carried out, and the sociologist has to resort instead to the method
of comparison. Here one tries to locate two examples which differ on one
point, say the element of meaning.

In some situations in real life, however, the comparative method cannot
be used, Weber says. This is the situation in which the type of action is very
uncommon, in the sense that no other action that is similar in nature exists.
In such a case, the sociologist has to resort to a special procedure, namely, to
make the mental experiment of removing one part of the complex chain of
motives (*Motivationskette*) that drives the action and see what happens when
this is done. The different course in action that results from this way of proceeding, shows the effect of the removed element. Weber emphasises that the
result of carrying out this type of mental experiment does not provide solid
proof; he also argues that there exists no other way to proceed.

Let us now see how Weber's argument fits the definition of thought experiments that is used in this chapter: (I) you begin with an initial state, (II) in
which a specified change is introduced, (III) setting off a social process that is
worked out in the mind of the analyst according to the logic of a sociological
analysis, (IV) until the end state has been reached). The unique phenomenon to
be explained in Weber's case constitutes the initial state. One link in the chain
of motives that has created this situation is then removed, setting off a process that ends up with a different outcome. The difference in meaning-motive

---

10   According to Hempel, Weber's "imaginary experiments" are "intuitive" in nature and not
     "theoretical" (Hempel, 1952: 73–77). In theoretical thought experiments you make deduc-
     tions from covering laws. Weber's intuitive thought experiments, in contrast, are based on
     a kind of empathetic understanding which is faulty. As a result, they can only be heuristic
     in nature, that is, they can be used to suggest, but not prove hypotheses.

11   'Action' is "behaviour" invested with 'meaning' for Weber. For details, see the explanation
     that follows on Weber's definition of sociology in *Economy and Society* on pp. 4–24.

accounts for the difference in social action and outcome. Or to be more precise, it *probably* accounts for the outcome, according to Weber.

Take, for example, the Battle of Marathon. The initial situation consists of the development of Western culture, in which Greece has played a crucial role. Remove now the element of Greek culture by imagining that the Battle of Marathon had been lost and that the Persians had conquered the Greek city states. In this case a process would have been set in motion that would have resulted in a different type of culture in the West. The reason for this is that the Greek city states would probably have been incorporated into the Persian empire and its authoritarian culture. This would probably have changed not only Greek culture but also what we today know as Western culture. This conclusion is reasonable—but we cannot be sure since it is the result of an imaginary operation.

In the case of Weber's second example, Gresham's Law, we begin with European society in the Middle Ages, where we know that coins with a small amount of valuable metal (due to the clipping of coins) were more often in circulation than coins with larger amount. We do not know why this was the case, but let us assume that one of the motives involved was a rational attitude to money making. In short, people clipped the more valuable coins, and traded with the less valuable ones, because they wanted to make money. This constitutes the initial situation for Weber. Let us now make the mental experiment of removing the rational intention and replace it with, say, a more traditional economic attitude, or one in which people did not feel free to clip coins for personal gain. The more valuable coins would then have remained in circulation. The following conclusion is likely: if people have a rational intention toward money-making, bad money will drive out good money. The conclusion is likely, but you cannot know this with any degree of certainty.

Compared to the complex thought experiments of Weber, those of Mills are simple and easy to grasp. It is crucial for sociologists to be imaginative, according to Mills; and there are many ways in which you can exercise your imagination and make it work for you. One of these is to change the number of people in the cases you study. Take, for example, small pre-historic societies, and assume that instead of having very small populations, they have 30 million inhabitants. What changes will this lead to?

The initial situation in this thought experiment is a number of small societies, with one set of institutions. The population is then dramatically changed, something that sets off a series of changes in the structure of these societies. Some institutions may become more complex, to fit the new population; others may split into several new institutions; and so on.

Note that Mills does not spell out which changes will come about; this is something that he wants the reader to do. The point of his thought experiment is in other words *heuristic*, in that it enables the sociologist to discover something new. The purpose of this type of thought experiment is not to prove a specific point but to help the sociologist to come up with new ideas and in this way theorise better. It also has a playful quality to it, that makes it come close to what has been called a thought game (*Gedankenspiel*; Seel, 2018).[12]

Merton's analysis of the bank going bankrupt is well-known in the sociological literature, where it is usually seen as an example of how a social mechanism operates. Merton himself, however, referred to it not as a thought experiment but as "a sociological parable" or the kind of story with a sociological moral attached (Merton, 1968: 476; see Jaworski, 1990). A parable is typically defined as "a usually short fictitious story that illustrates a moral attitude or a religious principle" (Merriam-Webster, 2017). In Merton's sociological parable, the moral message is that a run on a bank damages society and can be stopped through legislation (in the form of deposit insurance).

Whatever Merton's intentions may have been with his example of The Last National Bank, it does have the structure of a thought experiment. Merton begins the analysis by positing a stable, hypothetical situation. He then introduces a change, which he closely follows until a new stable state has been established. In the initial state, the people who keep their savings in the bank feel that their money is safe; and so it is. A change is then set off by a false rumor that the bank is unstable, something which makes some people withdraw their savings. This makes even more people do the same, since they see other people taking out their money. And in the end the bank goes bankrupt, since it has lent out some of the deposits and cannot suddenly give people back their full savings.

4   Exploration of the Individual Cases

Can one say that the four examples of Durkheim et al. are good thought experiments and that they are still relevant? Do they prove some analytical point, or do they rather raise some interesting issues? Can the ideas around which they

---

12   Seel differentiates the thought game from the thought experiment on the ground that it has nothing to do with argumentation (Seel, 2018: 15). This seems restrictive in our view. A mention can also be made in this context of Henshel's suggestion that artificial experiments in sociology may have a heuristic quality that is valuable (Henshel, 1980). The key idea is that you make a number of severe assumptions, similar to the way things are done in natural science experiments; and then try out the results in reality, to see if they are sound or not.

are centred be generalised? These are some questions that are relevant for all of these thought experiments.

Starting with Durkheim, it is clear that it is only possible to accept his thought experiment with a society of saints if you also accept his ideas about crime and how society works. His ideas on both of these topics, however, are controversial; they also lack empirical support. This leads to the dilemma of having either to discard Durkheim's example or to keep it, because it has virtues other than those that were intended by its author.

Regardless of how this issue is decided, it should be pointed out that there exists at least one very important quality in Durkheim's thought experiment. This is that it is distinctly sociological in nature. The process that is set off by exchanging the normal population in a society for one exclusively of saints does not follow just common-sense logic, but also one that is based on a specific sociological theory.

Let us, however, return to the question whether one should discard Durkheim's thought experiment or whether it still has some merit. One obvious answer would be to argue that Durkheim's example can be useful for heuristic purposes, even if this is not how it was originally intended. If you take some organisation (or society or institution) and change its whole population, what will happen?

A move of this type is similar to what Mills suggests, and it does have its value. Our view, however, is that what is most valuable about Durkheim's example is something else. It is, to state it once more for emphasis, that Durkheim, in his discussion of what happens in a society where everybody is a saint, depicts a process that follows a distinctly *sociological* logic. This is a very fine quality, we argue, of Durkheim's thought experiment.

There exists, to repeat, a certain affinity between the thought experiment of Durkheim and that of Mills in that both are heuristic; that of Mills is explicitly so, while that of Durkheim implicitly so (with the help of the reader). Both are also focused on the structure of society, but again in different ways. Durkheim argues that structure trumps individual phenomena, and that a crime is not defined by its content. Mills suggests something else. If you change the number of actors, society's institutions will probably also change. What works in a small society for how to make, say, political and legal decisions, is not likely to work in a huge society.[13] In a pre-literate society, the group of elders may

---

13   This argument is common in the social science literature. For a more elaborate discussion
      of the point, see the work of Simmel on the impact of number of actors on the social
      structure (Simmel, 1959). An isolate differs from a dyad and a triad. This essay also con-
      tains several other examples of how the number of actors influences the social structure.
      An aristocracy can by definition not be too large; the type of democracy that is possible
      depends on the number of inhabitants; and so on.

decide many issues that in a modern society are decided with the help of the state and the legal system.

Note, however, that Mills' thought experiment is not very much developed; it says, for example, nothing about the sociological process that will probably be set off by a change in number. Different institutions also change in different ways. To exaggerate a bit: Mills' example is like an experiment where you just toss something into a petri dish to see if anything will happen. This illustrates both the strength and the weakness of a heuristic thought experiment: something will happen, but you have no idea what. Serendipity rules.

A sign of a useful thought experiment is that it can be generalised. Is this also the case with Mills' thought experiment? Mills himself suggests so. He argues that every time a sociologist looks at a population, the first thing that he or she should do is to decide what the number of actors means for the institutional structure. Again, the reason for doing this is heuristic. Will a minority population, for example, develop one type of institution, if it is size X, but another if it is size Y? The same kind of question can be asked about the majority—and perhaps about any group or society.

Can also Durkheim's thought experiment be generalised? The answer is "yes", at least at one level. The idea that you can replace the population in an organisation or society with a very different population, and see what happens, is clearly useful. What, for example, would happen if all the soldiers in an army were female? This is obviously not what Durkheim had in mind, but proceeding in this way allows you to benefit from Durkheim's thought experiment without having to accept his very special view of sociology.

If we now switch to Weber and Merton, also here there exist some similarities as well as some differences between their thought experiments. Both, for example, focus on the role that the element of *meaning* plays for the unfolding of the social process, as described in the thought experiments. For Weber, paying attention to meaning is central to his project of an interpretive sociology; for Merton, it is something that should be done according to the dictum that people's definition of the situation has consequences for their behavior. To cite from his example of The Last National Bank, "Public definitions of a situation ... become an integral part of the situation and thus affect subsequent developments. This is peculiar to human affairs. It is not found in the world of nature" (Merton, 1968: 477).

But there also exist differences between the thought experiments of Weber and Merton; and these as well have to do with the role assigned to meaning. For Weber, meaning is absolutely central to what constitutes sociology, while this is much less the case for Merton. Weber often wrote on the theme of how social science differs from natural science, in that the former has to take the subjective intention of the actor into account. As we know from *Economy and Society*, Weber also tried to work out exactly what role is played in a causal sociological explanation by the element of meaning. Merton, on the other hand, was much less interested in the notion of meaning. Making a general reference to the definition of the situation was usually enough for him.

In the cases of Gresham's Law and the Battle of Marathon, Weber uses the thought experiment as a tool to construct an explanation in situations when this is especially difficult. In certain cases neither comparisons nor experiments can be used, according to Weber; and this means that you have to proceed in a very special way. This is to remove one part of the chain of motives (*Motivationskette*), replace it with another part, and then see what happens when this is done. The result of proceeding in this way, Weber notes, is never definitive; the suggested explanation is at best a probable one.

Merton's thought experiment is different from that of Weber in that it is less technical and also modelled on a common social situation, namely a run on a bank. Ultimately, this has to do with what has already been mentioned, namely that Weber constructed a version of sociology in which the element of meaning plays a much more central role than in that of Merton. Nonetheless, Merton's thought experiment is very well constructed and exemplary in many ways. He spells out the initial hypothetical situation with precision, as well as the sociological process that is set off by a hypothetical change. The reader also gets to follow how the situation changes step by step, which is a sign of a fully developed and well-constructed thought experiment.

Merton also generalises from his single example and, as part of this, suggests a new social mechanism: the self-fulfilling prophecy. This represents a major accomplishment. Other examples where this mechanism operates are cited and discussed by Merton. Black workers in the United States, for example, are not by nature strike breakers, as some white workers claim. They may, however, become strike breakers in that they have been excluded by white workers from joining unions. The idea of the self-fulfilling prophecy has been used also by other social scientists in a huge number of empirical studies (e.g. King, 1973; Farrell and Swigert, 1978; Merton, 1982: 103–104; 1988: 300–301; Timmermans and Sudnow, 1998).

5   Discussion: Thought Experiments and Thought Exercises

Two key questions remain to be addressed in this chapter: What would a good thought experiment in sociology look like; and What are the advantages of using thought experiments in sociology? In Table 9.1 we have tried to list some

TABLE 9.1   Qualities of a good thought experiment in sociology

	A Society of Saints (Durkheim)	Gresham's Law/ Marathon (Weber)	Reversal of Proportions (Mills)	Run on a Bank (Merton)
Relevance to sociology	Yes	Yes	Yes	Yes
Analytically sharp	Yes	Yes	No	Yes
Quality of surprise	Yes	Yes	Yes	Yes
Element of meaning included	No	Yes	No	Yes
Minimalist structure	Yes	Yes	No	Yes
Transparent process that follows a sociological logic	Yes	Yes	No	Yes
Generalisability	No	Yes	Yes	Yes
Sparks discussion	Yes	Yes	Yes	Yes
Empirically confirmed	No	Not applicable	Not applicable	Yes
Used by other sociologists	No	No	No	Yes

Note: Merton's and Durkheim's thought experiments come the closet to what may be considered the conventional or "classic" thought experiment. Weber's experiment is focused on missing information in one part of what is needed for the causal argument; and Mills' thought experiment lacks a determined end state.
SOURCE: THE AUTHORS.

of the qualities that a good sociological thought experiment should have. They should, for example, be analytically sharp (analyticity) and have a minimal structure. The process that is described should be well developed, transparent and clearly follow a sociological logic. There should ideally also be a surprising quality to the result.

Granted that thought experiments are useful also in sociology, how do you create a good one? As we were writing this chapter, we had this question very much in mind and tried to come up with a few good thought experiments of our own. To do so, we felt, would illustrate the fact that it is easy to construct, and use thought experiments in sociology. To create new sociological thought experiments, however, turned out to be much harder than we had thought. The model we first tried to follow was that of Durkheim and Merton, which we regard as the "classical" model and best suited for sociology (that of Weber seemed too special and that of C. Wright Mills a bit flimsy).

After a number of attempts to create a few good thought experiments we were forced to admit failure and gave up. We could not create even one. This bothered us since the reason for writing this chapter was not so much to advocate the use of thought experiments by brilliant sociologists as to show that the average sociologist might find it useful to use a thought experiment now and then in his or her research and teaching.

At this point we took a second look at C. Wright Mills' argument and decided that it had one very good quality, namely that it was pretty easy to come up with similar ones. It was, however, also clear that Mills' thought experiment was of a special type. While he advocated carrying out an argument in your mind, he did not specify what the result of the experiment would be. His thought experiment, in brief, was, as mentioned earlier, *heuristic*.

We therefore concluded that besides the conventional type of thought experiments, there also exists one that can be called *a heuristic thought experiment*. This is a thought experiment that is used to suggest ideas to the researcher, not to prove a specific point. It is also private in nature, since it will not to be published but used exclusively to come up with ideas during the research process.

If you in this way eliminate the idea of having a fixed result in the thought experiment, is the term "thought experiment" still applicable? An experiment that can end up in just about any way is definitely not a good experiment according to existing standards. Still, there is a quality to Mills' way of proceeding that sets it apart from ordinary empirical research in sociology. A better name for Mills' way of proceeding than thought experiment might therefore be *a thought exercise*, to use a term suggested to us by David Fasenfest. You assume that something will change in a situation you are interested in analysing, and you try to figure out what the result will be—in order to get some good ideas for the main, empirical part of the research—that is all.

If we for a moment forget about thought experiments and instead focus exclusively on thought exercises, it would appear that these can also be used by sociologist in a few other situations. Take, for example, theorising. Karl Weick, whose specialty is organisation theory, has suggested that the process of theorising can be viewed as a series of "imaginary experiments" or "thought trials" (Weick, 1989: 519–523). When you theorise, he says, you try to come up with "conjectures"; and this means that you have to "simulate possible scenarios" (Weick 1989: 520).

Weick does not specify exactly how you simulate these possible scenarios, so a few examples may be helpful. When you theorise, you may for example, want to try out several different social mechanisms in order to see which one can best explain the phenomenon in which you are interested. Or you may want to work through a few different ways of establishing the research object, in order to get a good handle on it. Or you may want to try out different directions in which to generalise, once you have established the research object (or the result).

Thought exercises can also be carried out just to train your mind as a sociologist or to improve your knowledge of the society in which you live. What we have in mind here are predictions, but not predictions of the individual type (will Trump be reelected?) or of the technological type (will there soon be driver-less cars?). Predictions of a *sociological* nature are about something else, namely patterns of behavior, as illustrated by cases such as the following: Will a certain type of crime increase/decrease over the next few years? Will the structure of the family remain the same in the near future?

Making predictions about this type of pattern is useful for sociologists for a number of reasons. For one thing, they make you aware of the assumptions that you bring to an analysis and of the limits to your knowledge about certain topics. In cases where reality proves you wrong, you will now be able to better pinpoint which factor(s) you failed to take into account and that help to explain your failure. This gives a distinctly pragmatic flavor to this kind of thought exercise: you incorporate your errors, as shown by experience, into the next prediction. To cite Peirce, the father of pragmatism: "Experience ... says: *Open your mouth and shut your eyes/ And I'll give you something to make you wise*" (Peirce, 1997: 160).

Finally, both thought exercises and thought experiments, point to the importance of one factor that is usually ignored in sociology. This is *the power of thinking*, or that much work in sociology is not empirical in nature but depends on the power of thought that you bring to an issue or a problem. To train this power strikes us as crucial, both in practising sociology and in teaching it. In fact, much of the future of sociology may depend on it.

References

Brown, J.R. and Fehige, Y. (2017). "Thought Experiments", in N. Edward and N. Zalta (eds.). *The Stanford Encyclopedia of Philosophy*. Available at https://plato.stanford.edu/archives/sum2017/entries/thought-experiment/.

Brown, J.R. (1986). "Thought Experiments Since the Scientific Revolution", *International Studies in the Philosophy of Science* 1 (1): 1–15.

Brown, J.R. (1991). *The Laboratory of the Mind*. New York: Routledge.

Brownlee, K. and Stemplowska, Z. (2017). "Thoughts Experiments", in A. Blau (ed.). *Methods in Analytical Political Theory*. Cambridge, UK: Cambridge University Press.

Chandrasekharan, S., Nersessian, N., and Subramanian, V. (2011). "Computational Modeling: Is This the End of Thought Experiments in Science?", in M. Frappier et al. (eds.). *Thought Experiments in Philosophy, Science and the Arts*. London: Routledge.

Christie, N. (1971). *Hvis skolen ikke fantes* [If There Were No Schools]. Oslo: Universitetsforlaget.

Cohen, M. (2005). *Wittgenstein's Beetle and Other Classic Thought Experiments*. Oxford: Blackwell.

Collins, R. (1981). "On the Microfoundations of Macrosociology", *American Journal of Sociology* 86 (5): 984–1014.

Collins, R. (2018). *Civil War Two*. Maren Ink, format Kindle.

Davenport, E. (1983). "Literature as Thought Experiment (On Aiding and Abetting the Muse)", *Philosophy of Social Science* 13: 279–306.

Du Bois, W.E.B. (1904). *The Development of a People*. Chicago: Redpath Lyceum Bureau.

Durkheim, E. (1964). *The Rules of Sociological Method*. New York: The Free Press.

Ellsberg, D. (1961). "Risk, Ambiguity, and the Savage Axioms", *Quarterly Journal of Economics* 75 (4): 643–689.

Farrell, R. and Swigert, V.L. (1978). "Prior Offense Record as a Self-Fulfilling Prophecy", *Law & Society Review* 12 (3): 437–453.

Florian, E. (2015). "Gedankenexperimente in histeriographischer Funktion: Max Weber über Eduard Meyer und die Frage der Kontrafaktizität", *Berichte zur Wissenschaftsgeschichte* 38 (1): 77–91.

Fogel, R. (1964). *Railroads and Economic Growth*. Baltimore, MD: Johns Hopkins University Press.

Farraro, T. (1989). *The Meaning of General Theoretical Sociology*. Cambridge, UK: Cambridge University Press.

Folger, R. and Turillo, C. (1999). "Theorizing as the Thickness of Thin Abstraction", *Academy of Management Review* 24 (4):742–758.

Galilei, G. (1954). *Dialogues Concerning Two New Sciences*. New York: Dover Publications, New York.

Häggqvist, S. (1996). *Thought Experiments in Science and Philosophy*. Stockholm: Almqvist & Wicksell.

Häggqvist, S. (2009). "A Model for Thought Experiments", *Canadian Journal of Philosophy* 39 (1): 55–76.

Hill, M. (1987). "Novels, Thought Experiments, and Humanistic Sociology in the Classroom: Mari Sandoz and 'Capital City' ", *Teaching Sociology* 15 (1): 38–44.

Hempel, C. (1952). "Problem of Concept and Theory Formation in the Social Sciences", in American Philosophical Association. *Science, Language, and Human Rights.* Philadelphia: University of Pennsylvania Press.

Henshel, R. (1980). "Seeking Inoperative Laws: Towards the Deliberate Use of Unnatural Experiments", in L. Freese (ed.). *Theoretical Methods in Sociology.* Pittsburgh: University of Pittsburgh Press.

Hill, M. (2005). "Sociological Thought Experiments: Five Examples from the History of Sociology", *Sociological Origins* 3, (2, Supplement): 3–19. Available at http://digital-commons.unl.edu/sociologyfacpub/351/ (accessed on August 11, 2017).

Hughes, E.C. (1945). "Dilemmas and Contradictions of Status", *American Journal of Sociology* 50 (5): 353–359.

Hughes, E.C. (1963). "Race Relations and the Sociological Imagination", *American Sociological Review* 28 (6): 879–890.

Husserl, E. (1931). *Ideas: General Introduction to Pure Phenomenology.* London: George Allen & Unwin.

Jaworski. G.D. (1990). "Robert K. Merton as a Postwar Prophet", *American Sociologist* 24 (3): 209–216.

Johnson-Laird, P. (1983). *Mental Models.* Cambridge, MA: Harvard University Press.

Killewald, A. (2013). "A Reconsideration of the Fatherhood Premium: Marriage, Coresidence, Biology, and Fathers' Wages", *American Sociological Review* 78 (1): 96–116.

King, A. (1973). "Self-Fulfilling Prophecies in Organizational Change", *Social Science Quarterly* 54: 384–393.

Kuhn, T. (1977). "A Function for Thought Experiments", in *The Essential Tension.* Chicago: University of Chicago Press.

Landsburg, S. (2012). *The Armchair Economist: Economics and Everyday Life.* New York: The Free Press. The first edition appeared in 1993.

Latour, B. (1998). "Thought Experiments in Social Science: From the Social Contract to Virtual Society", Annual Public Lecture, April 1. Brunel University. Available at http://www.artefaktum.hu/it/Latour.htm (accessed on August 11, 2017).

Le Guin, U. (1969). *The Left Hand of Darkness.* New York: Walker.

Mach, E. (1972). "On Thought Experiments", no source: 449–457. Available at http://emerald.tufts.edu/~skrimsky/PDF/On%20Thought%20Experiments.PDF (accessed on August 1, 2017).

Macy, M. and Willer, R. (2002). "From Factors to Actors: Computational Sociology and Agent-Based Modeling", *Annual Review of Sociology* 28: 143–166.

Madison, J. (2017) [1788]. "The Structure of the Government Must Furnish the Proper Checks and Balances Between the Different Departments", *Independent Journal.* Available at http://www.constitution.org/fed/federa51.htm (accessed on August 4, 2017).

March, J., Sproull, L., and Tamuz, M. (1991). "Learning from Samples of One or Fewer", *Organization Science* 2 (1): 1–13.

Markle, G. and MacCrea, F. (2008). *What if Medicine Disappeared?* Albany, NY: State University of New York Press.

Markle, G. and McCrea, F. (2003). "What If?: Thought Experiments in Sociology", Paper presented at the annual meeting of ASA, August 16, Atlanta, Georgia. Available at http://citation.allacademic.com/meta/p_mla_apa_research_citation/1/0/5/8/6/pages105868/p105868-1.php (accessed on August 11, 2017).

Merriam-Webster (2017). "Parable". Available at https://www.merriam-webster.com/dictionary/parable (accessed on August 2, 2017).

Merton, R.K. (1948). "The Self-Fulfilling Prophecy", *Antioch Review* 8 (2): 193–210.

Merton, R.K. (1968). *Social Theory and Social Structure*. Enlarged ed. New York: The Free Press.

Merton, R.K. (1972). "Insiders and Outsiders: A Chapter in the Sociology of Knowledge", *American Journal of Sociology* 78 (1): 9–47.

Merton, R.K. (1982). "Our Sociological Vernacular", in Robert K. Merton (ed.). *Social Research and the Practicing Professions*. Cambridge, MA: Abt Books.

Merton, R.K. (1987). "Three Fragments from a Sociologist's Notebooks: Establishing the Phenomenon, Specified Ignorance, and Strategic Research Material", *Annual Review of Sociology* 13: 1–28.

Merton, R.K. (1988). "Unanticipated Consequences and Kindred Sociological Ideas: A Personal Gloss", in C. Mongardini and S. Tabboni (eds.). *Robert K. Merton & Contemporary Sociology*. New Brunswick, NJ: Transaction Publishers.

Mills, C.W. (1959). *The Sociological Imagination*. New York: Oxford University Press.

Nersessian, N. (1992). "In the Theoretician's Laboratory: Thought Experimenting as mental Modelling.", in D. Hull et al. (eds.). *Proceedings of the 1992 Biennial Meeting of the Philosophy of Science Association*. East Lansing, MI: Philosophy of Science Association.

Noelle-Neumann, E. (1993). *The Spiral of Silence: Public Opinion – Our Social Skin*. Chicago: University of Chicago Press.

Peirce, C.S. (1997). *Pragmatism as a Principle and Method of Right Thinking*. Ed. by Patricia Ann Turrisi. Albany, NY: State University of New York Press.

Rossi, P. (1986). "How Applied Sociology Can Save Basic Sociology", *Journal of Applied Sociology* 3 (1): 1–5.

Rossi, P. (1987). "The Overlooked Contributions of Applied Work in Sociology", *American Sociologist* 18 (4): 369–374.

Scaff, L. (2011). *Max Weber in America*. Princeton: Princeton University Press.

Seel, M. (2018). *Nichtrechthabenwollen: Gedankenspiele*. Berlin: Fischer.

Shapin, S. and Shaffer, S. (1985). *Leviathan and the Airpump: Hobbes, Boyle, and the Experimental Life*. Princeton, NJ: Princeton University Press.

Sibley, E. (1971). "Sociology at Bay?", *American Sociologist* 6: 13–17.

Simmel, G. (1895). "Über eine Beziehung der Selektionslehre zur Erkenntnistheorie", *Archiv für Systematische Philosophie* 1 (1): 34–45.

Simmel, G. (1959). "Quantitative Aspects of the Group", in K. Wolff (ed.). *The Sociology of Georg Simmel*. New York: The Free Press.

Sorensen, R. (1992). *Thought Experiments*. New York: Oxford University Press.

Stearns, L.B. and Mizruchi, M. (1986). "Broken-Tie Reconstitution and the Functions of Interorganizational Interlocks: A Reexamination", *Administrative Science Quarterly* 31 (4): 522–538.

Tetlock, P. and Belkin, A. (eds.). (1998). *Counterfactual Thought Experiments in World Politics*. Princeton: Princeton University Press.

Thoma, J. (2016). "On the Hidden Thought Experiments in Economics", *Philosophy of the Social Sciences* 46 (2): 129–146.

Thomson, J.J. (1985). "The Trolley Problem", *Yale Law Journal* 94 (6): 1395–1415.

Timmermans, S. and Sudnow, S. (1998). "Social Death as Self-Fulfilling Prophecy: David Sudnow's 'Passing On' Revisited", *The Sociological Quarterly* 39 (3): 453–472.

Weber, M. (1978). *Economy and Society: An Outline of Interpretive Sociology*. 2 vols. Berkeley, CA: University of California Press.

Weber, M. (2012). *Collected Methodological Writings*. London: Routledge.

Weick, K. (1989). "Theory Construction a Disciplined Imagination", *Academy of Management Review* 24 (4): 797–806.

Ylikoski, P. (2003). "Thought Experiments in Science Studies", *Philosophica* 72: 5–59.

CHAPTER 10

Constructing and Researching the Object in Time and Space

Harriet Bjerrum Nielsen

What is time? Things change, and time is how we keep track.
JAMES GLEICK, 2016: 269

∴

1   Introduction

The dimensions of time and space are inherent in sociological inquiry but
are considered in varying ways and degrees in different theories and methodologies. Since the phenomena that sociologists investigate mainly comprise
what the Canadian philosopher Ian Hacking has coined the 'interactive kind'
(1999: 32), they come into existence as patterns or dynamics of human interaction. As these patterns and dynamics are conditioned by time and space, they
are open to change and seldom repeat themselves in exactly the same form. In
national statistics, this ongoing change appears in the well-known problems
of maintaining the same definitions, variables, and values over time, which
need to be rethought and sometimes changed to remain relevant. Conceptual
sociology may experience the challenge through the use of concepts and theories, which also emerge from specific historical contexts and, thus, can be
described as 'chronotopes': particular forms characterised by intrinsic connections between temporal and spatial relations (Bakhtin, 1981). Thus, the objects
of sociological inquiry are constantly in motion: what you observed, described,
and explained yesterday may be gone or at least changed today, including the
relevance of your own research perspective. In the words of Max Horkheimer:

> The facts which our senses present to us are socially formed in two ways:
> through the historical character of the object perceived and through the
> historical character of the perceiving organ.
>
> HORKHEIMER, 1937, in CONNERTON, 1976: 213

The different sociological approaches to the issues of time often follow the micro–macro dualism, that is, changing structures *or* changing acts. In Giddens' theory of structuration, time plays a central role in the effort to bridge this dualism and understand the 'processual structuring' of social structures and the 'dynamic stabilisation' of actors (Giddens, 1984). However, as the Norwegian sociologist Sverre Moe (2010) argued, the actual forward movement of societal structures in historical time tends to be lost as the temporal character of the processes of structuration are seldom given any specificity. The same could be said about Giddens' theory of the modern self and its relationships (Giddens, 1991), which gives attention to the *mechanisms* of self-identity (reflexivity, life narratives, control of time, risk balance, pure relations, and so on), rather than to the historically situated biographical self. The abstract notion of the self makes it difficult to define what actually drives subjects in the processes of structuration and what the outcomes may be. Thus, Giddens' theory helps us to see the temporal connection between structure and self, whereas his concept of time—both in regard to social and psychological structures—stays diachronically weak and analytically tied to the situation.[1]

In this chapter, I argue that a longer perspective on how people interact with the institutional and cultural conditions of their time may reveal more detail of the processes of social change and give a broader perspective on the actions of the present. A premise for my analysis is that psychological and institutional structures represent different *forms* of the social that should neither be radically separated nor reduced to each other. Subjects are historically and biographically formed. Subtle and gradual processes working on the level of subjectivities may provide a psychological readiness for cultural and political change and, thus, be a vital part in social dynamics (Horkheimer, 1937; Williams, 2011; Aarseth, 2008; Nielsen, 2017). The question I want to raise is: what may we learn about subjects as research objects, their historical character, and their way to interfere with historical change if we are more attentive, methodologically as well as theoretically, to different ways in which time enters into the lived experience, including in the sociological quest for knowledge?

---

1   This analytical focus is also evident in the figure of structuration in Giddens (1984), where the relation between the unacknowledged condition of an action, the agent's reflexive monitoring of this action, and the unintended consequences of the action is visualised as a circular movement, not as a forward-moving timeline.

2   Time as Event and Biography

In Oslo, Norway, there is a huge park, Frognerparken, which is home to a permanent sculpture installation by the Norwegian sculptor Gustav Vigeland (1869–
1943). One of the great artworks in this park, it comprises 36 granite sculptures
of human beings together in different situations, ages, and phases of life in the
movement from birth to death, placed in three rising concentric circles, with
twelve sculptures in each circle around a huge monumental monolith. Each of
the sculptures capture an impressively lively moment of relationships between
people, an event characterised by emotional states of joy and laughter, sadness
or boredom, fear and conflict. In one of the childhood moments, we see a circle
of girls with their heads close together in a whispering formation while excluding
a little boy who wants to join in. In other moments, the boys are depicted with
more playfulness, laughter, and more aggression, and no girls try to join in here.
Further on in the life cycle, we see heterosexual couples approach each other in
ambivalence of fear and attraction, including some sculptures with men being
violent towards their female partners. At older ages, the women and men appear
to find their way back to their single-gendered groups and comfort in each other.
    Vigeland's depiction of the different ages and genders are archetypical and
stereotypical, with a focus of the traditional family as a basic unit and life as a
repeating cycle that seamlessly continues at the point of the circle where the
old die and the new are born. There is presence, relationships, and flow in each
sculpture, but no individuality or socio-historical context (Wikborg, 2010). The
historical character of the perceiving organ (cf. Horkheimer) of Vigeland makes
itself very clear: the works were created in 1930s and 1940s Europe, a period
where this type of archetypical depiction of the strong and healthy human—
often, as also the case here, in supernatural size—and a naturalised and het-
erosexualised hierarchy between man and woman, were popular, including in
artistic expression. This universalistic perspective evidently contributes to the
blurring of the *historical character of the object perceived*. However, the sculptures still portray something about how time transcends the dynamics of the
single event. I suggest that the fascinating power of Vigeland's artwork is exactly
this combination of flow and liveliness of action in the situation of each separate sculpture and the biographical timeline they form when seen together and
imagined as depicting a lifeline.[2] How did one event extend into the next? How
does the dynamic of a situation transcend into long-term effects?

---

2   One may also read the sculptures as a cross-sectional sample; however, as they are stripped
    from any historical context, these two readings blend into each other as a story of human life

Event and biography may be understood as representing two different kinds of time in a person's life: the *synchronic* and the *diachronic*. Synchronic time contains the flow of human action/interaction in a given situation, while diachronic time grasps the irreversible movement forward in time, from birth to death. This doubleness of time is captured in Bergson's (1911) distinction between 'durée' (duration, the experience of temporality) and 'temps' (abstract chronological time). Norwegian anthropologist Anders Johansen (2001) suggests the concepts 'time of the action and events' and 'abstract time' to be useful in socio-cultural analyses. The advantage of connecting concrete time to action is that the present is not defined as simply an ever-moving point on the line between past and future, gone before we ever had a chance to notice or describe it, but rather is tied to the meaning(s) of the specific action that we engage in. Johansen describes practical tasks, such as planting, harvesting, or cooking, but as Vigeland's sculptures illustrate, they may also be thought of as situations of play, communication, competition, conflict, violence, love, illness, etc. In short, the present is an event or a social situation, not a chronological moment, and, thus, from a sociological perspective, it is sensible to attach temporality to the present itself, not only to the line from the past into the future.

3   The Arrow of Time

The two aspects of time—the synchronic 'time of the action' and the diachronic 'abstract time'—are not mutually exclusive concepts.[3] The 'action'-type of time is present in all societies, as no society can survive without concrete, practical, and meaningful human action/interaction, but as all known societies also have some kind of understanding of time that exceeds these daily situations, these two time concepts are not mutually exclusive. Still, the emphasis of abstract time has gained importance in complex societies where planning and coordination between different actors and institutions called for greater temporal synchronisation. In modern, capitalist society, the emphasis is on time as a force and a resource to exploit, rather than being an inherent part of the action or the event (Luhmann, 1995; Eriksen, 1999; Johansen, 2001;

---

where generational shifts and individual life courses through the different ages become the same story.

3   Yoga could be an example of how one may simultaneously be engaged in the presence of the action and in a longer forward perspective. One may practise yoga to calm stress and improve the capacity to be present with one's body and mind in the moment; however, one probably also does this because one believes it will be good for the health in the long run.

Moe, 2010). Abstract time may be described as empty, chronological time, as a resource to be used, but also as an irreversible and one-direction 'arrow of time' that no living beings or societies can stop nor escape.[4] As the American physicist Lee Smolin formulated, we have a choice about where we move in space, but no choice about which moment to inhabit (Gleick, 2016: 265). When situated historically, abstract time follows a linear movement, not a circular one, as suggested in Vigeland's cosmology. In the specific modernist concep-tion of linearity, it is connected to determinism, development, enlightenment, progress, and money, but one does not have to subscribe to this logic to agree that time, in the abstract sense, transcends the situation and moves irrevers-ibly and thus in a 'linear' fashion in only one direction.

Even though abstract or diachronic time in this sense is linear, it may, how-ever, also at the same time be *heterogeneous*, involving different temporal strands moving at different paces and in different spaces. Norwegian cultural historian Helge Jordheim (2012a) argues that the synchronic moment is always filled with experiences, objects, and practices that are uncontemporary with each other because they belong in different diachronic contexts and processes. This idea was introduced by historians in the second half of the 20th century[5] and the German historian Reinhart Koselleck further developed these thoughts with the concept of 'Ungleichzeitigkeiten', meaning instances of non-synchronicity or non-contemporaneity: "The diachronic organizes itself in terms of mul-tiple overlapping layers, which run contrary to the conventional periods and opens up for different combinations" (Koselleck, 2010 [2006], cited in Jordheim,

---

4   'The arrow of time' is a concept of astronomy and physics developed in the 1920s and involv-ing the 'one-way direction' or 'asymmetry' of time leading into disorder (entropy). The pop-ular image is that 'one cannot unscramble eggs' or expect an evaporated liquid from a cup to return to the cup by itself. As a theory of energetic outlet and increasing disorder in the universe, the arrow of time does not fit well to historical processes, which appear rather to move towards increasing differentiation and complexity (Eriksen, 1999). However, the arrow of time still makes sense in terms of the distinction before/after and in relation to historical events. It also encompasses the experience that, no matter how they are socially constructed or self-constructed, children become adults, whereas adults do not grow into children, other than in a metaphorical sense. Much of the entertainment value of films like *Big, Billy Madison*, and *The Curious Case of Benjamin Button* lies in our experience of this irreversibility. (Gleick, 2016; Nielsen, 2016).

5   A central name here is Ferdinand Braudel of the French Annales school, who suggested that there are at least three levels of time that make up the historical process: the rapidly chang-ing and shifting event-time, the time of social and economic structures, and cycles with a much slower rhythm in the 'longue durée' of landscapes and geography or slowly changing mind-sets and mentalities (Jordheim, 2014: 502. See also Sandmo, 2016).

2012b: 156).[6] Hence, diachronic time may also be present in synchronic time and give situations "a historical depth, which is not identical with their chronology" (Koselleck, 1972; cited in Jordheim, 2012b: 170). The crossing diachronic lines in the present contribute to creating some of the wider contexts of meaning that are inherent in our acts. In our research on gender in change (see the following section), my colleague Monica Rudberg and I described, much in the same vein as Koselleck, the different and uneven changes in gender identities, gendered subjectivities, and the sociocultural possibilities of young women at different historical moments as 'lacks of contemporaneity' (Nielsen and Rudberg, 1994: 108–109).

The idea of the multi-layeredness of time and meaning is a perspective we can also find within psychoanalytic theories of subjectivity. The singular subject emerges as layers of interpretation from different points in time, as a formative sedimentation in which old interpretations are not just replaced by new ones but exist as possibilities in a person's psychic universe. Incompatible conscious and unconscious interpretations may be seen as pressing towards change or they may emerge as symptoms (see Nielsen, 2016). Thus, subjectivity is here understood as a temporal phenomenon enfolding in the interaction between past, present, and future.

Combining synchronic and diachronic time and awareness of the heterogeneous character of time are also fruitful perspectives for sociological analysis. If linear time is abandoned or reduced to the ongoing synchronic flow in the present, we lose insight into the long-term effects of action and the historical formation of subjectivity. This may happen in sociological case studies on either the micro- or macro-level, or it may be seen in research inspired by poststructuralist epistemology, where any kind of object or subject stability is defied. On the other hand, a purely diachronic view disregards the ways different layers of time are present in the subject or situation. This may lead to an understanding of subjectivity or societal forms as determined and coherent and, in this way, also miss out the tensions and dynamics that may push towards social change. Jordheim (2012a) offers a vivid description of how the separation of the two concepts of time may be seen in the inverse relationship between anthropology and historical research:

---

6   Jordheim (2012b) argues that Koselleck deconstructs the idea of linear and homogeneous chronological time and replaces it with a more complex, heterogeneous, and multi-layered notion of temporality (151). I agree that Koselleck's approach defies homogeneity and linear determinism, but not necessarily the linear direction of time. Also a multi-layered and complex object moves and is constricted by the 'arrow of time'.

To think historically in categories such as development, growth, event, continuity, change, durability, rupture, stability, etc. is a challenge within the fields of anthropology; to think culturally analytically, in categories of equality and difference, identity, insides and outsides, borders, structures, etc. is an equally big challenge within the field of history. Probably it has to do with how scholars of these academic disciplines are accustomed to representing time and space, and not least, the relation between them.

> JORDHEIM, 2012a: 60, author's translation

Arguably, instead of choosing between the synchronic and diachronic concepts of time, it would be better to ask *how these temporalities interact* in a given case. How are the processes of becoming in the present connected to historically and biographically accumulated experience and expectations of the future? What happens if the synchronic situation is seen from a diachronic perspective, and in what ways may diachronic timelines be connected to the dynamics of synchronic situations?

4   Gender in Change: Time as a Methodological Dimension

Qualitative longitudinal research and research on life history and generational transmission all highlight time as an important methodological, empirical, and analytical category, while at the same time immerse themselves in the detailed mapping of spaces where life is lived at different points of time. Since the time dimension in these cases also enters the research process itself, the context for the interpretation of any incident is extended as time passes for the interpreting researcher as well. My point is, of course, not that all social research should be longitudinal, although it would be an advantage to our understanding of many social forms if more was. Investigating the ways in which the synchronic research object can be embedded in diachronic timelines may indicate how time also enters the research process more generally. Thus, I suggest that an increased 'diachronic awareness' could form part of the assumptions made by researchers using synchronic data.

In the following sections, I will illustrate and discuss these points by drawing on my experiences in a longitudinal study of gender in change. To explore gender in change is indeed to enter a space where many heterogeneous timelines run beside each other, sometimes in and sometimes out of sync. Gender is central to divisions of labour and to the structuring of institutions. It is also a profound cultural system of meaning, norms,

conventions, symbols, and myths; a dimension of bodies and physical reproduction, individual identities and personal experience, social relations
and everyday interaction. The impact and meaning of gender are complex,
contextual, and changing over time (McNay, 2004; Adkins, 2004; Aarseth,
2009). Processes of modernity affect all aspects of gendered life, but not necessarily at the same time, to the same degree, or in the same way. Women
may become autonomous subjects with education and jobs and hold leading positions in society, but still be seen as objects or the 'second sex' (De
Beauvoir, 1949). Similarly, both women and men may be engaged supporters
of feminism, but also simultaneously feel attracted to some aspects of traditional gender positions.

In our longitudinal project, we studied gender in change over three generations of Norwegian women and men, born respectively around WW1,
WW2, and in the early 1970s (Nielsen and Rudberg, 2006; Nielsen, 2017). The
project examined how the processes of social mobility and cultural modernisation were related to the psychological project of becoming adults in
these three generations. We sought to understand the interactions between
cultural and personal gender in a process of change, to grasp the historical embeddedness not only of cultural norms but also of subjectivities,
and, more specifically, how generational relationships contribute to these
changes on the psychological level. The data comprised observation in five
classes in two high schools with different social profiles in Oslo in 1990 and
life history interviews with approximately half of the students in each class.
The mothers and grandmothers of the female students and the fathers and
the grandfathers of the male student were invited to similar interviews, and,
in terms of generations, we ended up with 22 female chains and twelve male
chains. The youngest generation, who was around 18–19 years old at the time
of the first interview in 1991, were re-interviewed in 2001 and 2011 when they
were approaching 30 and 40 years of age. Thus, the project operated methodologically with temporality in three different ways: through life history
interviews, through a generational sample, and through a longitudinal study
lasting over 20 years of the youngest generation's life (for more details, see
Nielsen, 2017).[7]

---

7   In the following empirical examples from the project, I will focus on some of the changing
    generational patterns. Of course, not all the interviewees within a generation fit equally well
    into these patterns; however, since the scope of the article is time as a theoretical and meth-
    odological dimension, the individual and cultural variation are not examined here, except
    for some indications of the significance of social class.

5   Time-Bound Research: Blind Spots and Reflections

I will start with some reflections on how time entered the research process itself. Longitudinal studies confront the researcher with diachronic time in many ways, and one of the more troublesome experiences is to realise how one's research questions may appear outdated a decade or two later: What made me ask these strange questions? Why did I have such an odd perspective? Thus, Horkheimer's claim about the *historical character of the perceiving organ* becomes difficult to ignore. There may, of course, be other aspects that are not felt to be outdated, or it may even be the case that some research questions have preserved fruitful perspectives that might have been forgotten because they do not fit with the present academic fashions (see also Hunt, 2008). The point is not that the researcher or the research community always become more enlightened as time passes, but rather that time inevitably makes its mark on the researcher's view and construction of the object in the present, and that this becomes particularly visible in research that spans longer stretches of time. Much methodological attention has been given to the situatedness of the researcher in terms of gender, age, class, ethnicity, etc., and in regard to cultural assumptions and theoretical preconceptions. However, typically spatial metaphors are employed here, for instance, as in 'standpoint theory' (Harding, 1986) or the claim that it is neither possible to view the studied object from 'nowhere' nor from 'everywhere' (Haraway, 1988). What has had less focus is that the researcher is also positioned in time, and, as time is a more absolute dimension than space and conceptual framings (from which it is, at least in principle, possible to move to other places or new perspectives), the position in time may be less accessible to self-reflexivity in the situation. This might be the reason for the numb feeling one can experience when being confronted with the time-boundedness in one's own longitudinal or generational research. However, it simply draws what is, in fact, the case for all research.

In the aforementioned three-generational project, this time-boundedness became particularly clear in some aspects of the sampling and interview guide. In the early 1990's Norwegian society, neither immigration nor sexual diversity received great focus, and without much consideration, we chose a sample consisting only of ethnically white Norwegians, and, as it turned out, only students who identified as heterosexual. Other kinds of variations were secured: social class, divorced/non-divorced parents, and the role the students took in class. In the hindsight of just 10 years, when ethnicity and sexual diversity had gained much greater attention, these choices became conspicuous in a way they were not back then. The exclusion of ethnic variety, however, also interacted with Horkheimer's first dimension, *the historical character of the object perceived*: due to the late immigration to Norway, the overwhelming majority of the students in Oslo high schools in 1991 were, in fact, white and ethnic Norwegian.[8] The choice of not including the one or two minority students in each class was also more deliberate than the exclusion of sexual diversity. Since the focus was on modernisation processes in Norway over three generations, we decided that students whose parents and grandparents did not grow up in the Nordic countries were less relevant for the project. This may be seen as a reasonable argument, but it is also possible to argue that including them would have given us some interesting contrasts to work with. The consideration here is not what would have been the 'best' methodological solution, but to illustrate that had the decision been taken some years later, it might have been different; thus, time puts its mark on what is perceived as interesting and relevant methodological choices.

Sexual diversity garnered less reflection. We did not deliberately exclude queer students, rather, we simply did not reflect over the possibility that there were any. In the pre-queer times of the initial interviews, there was little attention to sexual diversity or fluidity; thus our own unquestioned position as heterosexual women interacted with the widespread cultural blindness of the era. Homosexuality was not illegal but seldom disclosed in classrooms, a scenario that had made it difficult to take into account. Even if we had considered this factor, announcing openly that we were seeking sexual diversity in our interview sample would probably have been seen at that time as an ethical violation, not only by research ethics committees, but also by schools, parents, teachers, and even the students themselves. Still, we might have found ways to circumnavigate this potentiality if we had been more aware of sexual diversity or the research team itself had been more sexually diverse. Again, the point here is not to raise a discussion about what is the right method of strategic sampling for different cases, but to illustrate the mutual dynamic between the changes in the object perceived and changes in the researcher's perception. In Hacking's words, "What was known about people of a kind may become false because people of that kind have changed in virtue of what they believe about themselves" (1999: 34).

By the follow-up interviews of 2001 and 2011, the situation had indeed changed: questions of migration, sexual orientation, racism, and heteronormativity were everywhere. The number of students from immigrant families

---

8   Norway is a small country with a population that was ethnically rather homogeneous (including a small Sámi population in the north) until the late 20th century. This specific demographical history explains why there were very few immigrants and practically no non-white students in Norwegian schools at the time our study was conducted.

had increased radically and there were more openly queer students. Thus, new questions were introduced in these interviews, where we also tried to 'catch up' with what our informants had thought about these issues 10 years earlier. When asked retrospectively about their knowledge and experiences with homosexuality as 18-year-olds, participants' answers illustrated that it was indeed not until the mid-1990s that gay and lesbian rights appeared on the mainstream public agenda. Several of them recounted a 10-year reunion for their high school graduation, where they learned that two girls from one of the classes were in a same-sex civil union, news that came as a complete surprise to everyone. A few had experienced a close friend coming out as gay or lesbian and remembered the awkwardness they had first felt. At 30, this timidity towards the issue had disappeared. Thus, the initial blindness of the researchers to sexual diversity also reflected a time when it was a little-acknowledged phenomenon. However, due to the time span of the research, we also learned that there had, of course, been students with a silent, non-normative sexuality in the classes we observed. How would it have affected our construction of the object of study if we had understood this in 1991?

6   Time-Bound Experiences: Age and Generation

The possibility of filling blind spots retroactively also depends on time in another way, namely, the age phase and cohort of the informants. Whereas the interviewees of the youngest generation had been keen to talk about non-normative sexualities when they were around 30 years old—as they had fresh experiences of this from their own and other's search for sexual identities as young adults—the issue sparked much less interest in the 2011 interviews when the interviewees were approaching 40, a point in time where they were enmeshed in and focused on their families and young children. This indicates that an interview guide may be constructed and trigger information differently, not only according to the moment in history but also in relation to the age phase and generation of the interviewees.

It was already quite clear in 1991 that parts of our interview guide functioned more effectively with the two youngest generations, who shared with us the psychological and individualist approach typical of the culture of late modernity. The oldest generation, especially those who had grown up in rural areas, attempted as best they could to answer our strange questions about adolescence or love: "I can't remember that we had like puberty and all that stuff. I can't say I had that" (Rural woman, b. 1910). Many of the rural women also struggled to describe to us what had attracted them to their fiancés, whereas ready-made romantic stories poured out of their daughters and granddaughters when asked the same question. We also had to tread carefully with some of the more explicit sexual questions when talking to the oldest generation. These mismatches between the construction of the interview guide and the experiences of the interviewees resonate with Koselleck's theories of how concepts, words and the historical realities may become out of sync and operate as a historical dynamic towards change. The temporal displacements in our interviews went both ways: often our elder informants sensed that we, belonging to a younger generation, might misunderstand their words, for instance, in regard to the much stronger class divisions of their childhood worlds. An urban woman, born in 1911 into an upper-middle-class family, recalled her mother's charity work with pride, but realised midway that we would probably misunderstand what she was trying to tell us:

> You should've seen the amazing Christmas care packages mother made for people in the hard 1930s when people were really struggling. Yes. And they weren't pauper's gifts either, far from it (...) Those who were a bit better off, or I don't know how to explain it so you don't get me wrong ... but they also had a huge sense of responsibility.

The time-bound experiences of the interviewees also raise the question of what, logically, can be compared between generations. Due to structural and demographic changes related to increased standards of living, increased levels of general education, and the increased prevalence of divorce, the same experiences in different generations of not receiving an education, being poor, or having divorced parents, attain very different cultural and emotional meanings. Thus, instead of comparing the same items, such as the level of wealth or the number of divorces in the childhoods of different generations, it may sometimes be more apt to compare items that represent the same *kind* of existential insecurity, for instance, the experience of poverty in the oldest generation and the experience of divorce in the youngest. As the oldest generation knew that poverty and the death of parents were calculated risks in life, so was the possibility of parental divorce for their grandchildren. The increased consciousness of the fragility of human relations became the backdrop of life for the youngest generation, and they learned how to handle it much in the same way as their grandparents learned to handle the material hardships of their childhoods.

The construction of the object through the intricate interaction between the time-bound research questions, time-bound experiences and perspectives of the interviewees, both in regard to generation and age phase, is not just a methodological issue to be resolved but represents part of the conditions for undertaking research on the 'interactive kind' of phenomena (cf. Hacking, 1999). For a synchronic study, the aspect to concentrate on is that the time-bound horizon from which we ask and from which the informants' answer may both reflect dimensions of the object itself and the researcher's own construction of the object.

7   Pockets of the Past in the Present

The temporal displacements between concepts, words and realities mentioned in the previous section may also be seen as an expression of the multi-layeredness of time, or, as Koselleck coined it, "the simultaneity of the nonsimultaneous" (cited in Jordheim, 2012b: 162). Memories are always reconstructions in the present of what happened in the past and narratives are, therefore, characterised by selections, linking of memories, interpretations, and chosen perspectives (Josselson and Lieblich, 1993; Bruner, 2003; Rosenthal, 2004). Evidently, the stories of the informants' childhood, youth, and family life are seen through discourses or 'lenses' that belong to different historical moments, some of them dated more recently than the time they were recounting. For the eldest generation, such recent lenses providing narrative perspectives included, in particular, the increased standards of living, possibilities for education, and changed norms of morality. The men tended to particularly emphasise the moral decay in society, whereas the women were more occupied with the increased openness surrounding sex and bodily functions and the diminished social differences among people. Hardly any of the lenses of the older generation were present in the stories of the middle generation. Instead, their retrospective narrative perspectives included increased enlightenment and the norm of gender equality.

Coincidentally, however, we also found older layers of meaning in the way the interviewees talked. Across generations, there were different 'genres' at work in the ways the informants discussed the world and themselves. The oldest generation tended to construct their stories in a rather deterministic 'structuralist' way, often saying, *"That was the way it was back then"*. Many of them were good storytellers. They offered broad and generalised pictures of their family life, their activities, and the community they grew up in, but also included many vivid details that almost evoked a feeling of standing in front of a naturalist landscape painting:

I must say that I grew up in a good home. I must say I did. And father was a carpenter, so we always had skis and ski sticks. I had an awfully long way to school, so in winter we went on our skis if the snow was good. And we had sleighs, too. We lived close to the railway station, so when we went to school, we had to go all the way down into the valley, and across the river—I think we had a 6 km-long walk to school.

Woman, b. in 1910 into the rural lower-middle-class

The outer things are made central here: what one did, what happened, what one had, what one ate, often illustrated through concrete episodes and events. Much more frequently than the following generations, the older interviewees talked in terms of a collective 'we'. This descriptive and non-individualist perspective was also seen in their evaluations, where nuances and reservations were seldom conveyed: things were either good or bad, and criticism of parents and homes was rare.

This deterministic sociological genre was not present in the talk of the middle generation. Their self-presentations drew on a more psychological genre, always problematising their own motives, seeking the answers in childhood experiences, as well as reflecting upon their own reconstruction of memories:

When I think back on my childhood, and as a young adult, I must say I think it was unusually good and, well, fortunate. And I know that it is like you often forget things, and you repress bad memories because nobody is totally happy. I know that. But, really, I found this diary, from when I was 17 years of age, and it reads there, 'I am so happy, everything is so good'. So, I did write that there.

Woman, b. in 1944 into an urban middle-class family

This generation provided lengthy descriptions of family relations and dynamics and was much less focused on material life conditions or the community they grew up in. Recollections of activities and events often slid into interpretations and evaluations of those activities and events. Psychological concepts had become everyday ideas and were used to interpret their lives and feelings (cf. Giddens, 1990), which also seems to imply the removal of a taboo against talking negatively about others—such statements can now be understood within a legitimate field of analytic and interpretative activity, not as finite assertions about how somebody 'really' is.

The youngest generation still made use of this psychological discourse, but it was often simultaneously ironically negated, especially in the first interview at the age of 18. The 'who-am-I?' orientation seemed to permeate everything they said, and instead of a 'story' of their upbringing, they gave us bits and pieces, held together more by the underlying emotional tone than by the actual information or a storyline. It could sometimes be difficult to grasp whether they were trying to convey problems or simply put themselves and their family on the stage:

> Well, mostly we eat at home, but not dinners really. We just have a sandwich system. We make dinners when we feel like it and have sandwiches when we don't feel like it. My mom got quite frustrated. Like every time she had made something, I said 'Ugh, are we having *that* for dinner?!' [laughs] 'Ugh, I don't want that. Phew!', if it looked kind of boring.
>
> Urban middle-class girl, b. 1971

One might say that their perspective on the world related more to the academic genre of 'cultural studies' than to the 'sociology' of their grandmothers or the 'psychology' of their mothers.

Viewed strictly as historical sources, all the interviews are synchronic remnants from 1991; thus, the 'time of the action and events' is the interview situation. The generation-specific genres may stem from both the age phase of the informants and the relationship in the interview situation to us as interviewers belonging to the middle generation. However, the different perspectives and narrative genres may also tell us something about historical shifts and how people come to understand themselves in changing historical contexts. The fact that people from the same generation so clearly tend to pick similar discourses when constructing their memoirs of childhood and youth also makes it feasible to view these discourses as *small pockets of history,* preserved in the individuals, or, to use Koselleck's words, "a diachronic movement through the synchronic moment" (Jordheim, 2012a: 166). The gradual rise of modern reflexivity, for instance, is evident in the narratives across the three generations interviewed in the same synchronic moment. The different genres may also be described as Bakhtinian chronotypes representing the relationship between a specific textual structure and an actual reality (Bakhtin, 1981: 243). The oldest generation's focus on the outer world may be understood in relation to the scarcity in their childhood; the relational interest in the middle generation may be interpreted as a result of new possibilities of leisure and self-realisation; and finally, the observational, ironic style of the youngest generation would be hard to imagine without their extensive access to the media, just as their fragmented stories might be an expression of the actual relational havoc surrounding them. The stories of each generation, featuring many of the same concrete recollections, indicate that there are indeed experiences to be interpreted, not only inventions of the present. Subjects contain different layers of chronological time, which will be integrated in their self-presentation of the present.

8   Seeds of Futures in the Present

It is not only the past that represents an integral part of the present: the same goes for the future. In his work on the psychology of imagination, Sartre introduced a distinction between lived and imagined futures. The former are possibilities for a future that is already present: what we expect will happen, given what we already know. The latter is an imagining of what could come into existence, even though it is not part of our actual experience. The two are related, as the imagination of what is not yet is not arbitrary but always a negation of the world from a particular point of view (Sartre, 1972: 215).

The presence of both lived and imagined futures was evident in the three-generational project when we asked our informants about the dreams they had in life when they were young. The dreams of the oldest generation both presupposed and exceeded their specific situations as young women: a rural girl dreamt of getting a job as a shop assistant, whereas a small-town girl who actually was a shop assistant dreamt of moving to the city or opening her own shop, and some of the city girls dreamt about travelling to some other place to obtain a certain education. Dreams of the impossible need not be formulated too precisely, and they are not so difficult to give up, either. Therefore, poor rural girls dreaming of becoming shop assistants, nurses, or even travelling the world may also say that they did not pursue these dreams very energetically and that they soon adapted to what was possible and just hoped to get married. For the urban middle-class girls, it appears to have been a much more dramatic sense of loss when external conditions suddenly crushed an anticipated educational plan. In the middle generation, where the possibilities for jobs and education actually exceeded what they could imagine, the dreams rather negated the lack of freedom at home: their dreams of the future were to get away from home and start their own family. In the youngest generation, the idea that 'one can become anything one wants' could be said to negate the split in late-modern society between the horizon of expectation and actual possibilities (cf. Beck and Beck-Gersheim, 2002).

Seeds of the future may also be present in a situation (as a lived future) but only realised later, or maybe not accomplished until the next generations. An example from our study is the young women's reframing of gender, body, and sexuality in the public sphere. Seen from a generational perspective, this may be understood as part of a larger historical process of individualisation that gradually detached gender from subjectivities. The shift in normative ideals for young girls in these three generations can be described as a move from the 'nice girl' of the inter-war period, to the 'popular girl' of the after-war period, and the 'autonomous girl' by the end of the century (Nielsen, 2004; Nielsen and Rudberg, 2007). By identifying themselves as nice girls, only out to have some fun, the young women of the 1920s and 1930s could defend their right to be in a public space without damaging their reputation (Søland, 2000). The 'nice girl' lost ground during the Second World War: the sight of unaccompanied young girls in public spaces did not shock or provoke anymore; thus, young women had now gained more freedom and did not have to legitimise their presence by being 'nice'. However, the new freedom and individuality of the 1950s and 1960s also implied a new form of exposure for young women, where they were evaluated by other young people on the basis of their looks and popularity (Breines, 1992). The 'nice girl' had by now become a 'boring girl', whereas the 'cheap girl' was still around. However, this absence of a clear line between 'nice' and 'cheap' girls also meant that sexual morality was on its way to becoming a personal matter and responsibility, not just something to adapt to. Thus, freedom in the public space, carved out by the inter-war generation under the flag of being nice girls, was further elaborated by the post-war generation in a curious blend of increased individualised morality and responsibility on the one side, and a strengthening of the heterosexual script on the other. Towards the end of the century, the contour of the 'cheap' girl was becoming blurred. Young women in the 1980s and 1990s were allowed to experience both desire and ambition as gender-syntonic, and it was now rather the fear of not being self-reliant and independent that tormented them. The popular and boy-crazy girl lingered on the edge of conformity; the danger was no longer that of being 'a fallen women', but rather of being 'a fallen subject' (Nielsen and Rudberg, 2007).

In this analysis, the behaviour of one generation becomes the stepping-stone for the next. What appears incredibly conformist when seen isolated in each generation, may, in fact, be steps in a longer process of change when seen diachronically and over generations. Like Sartre, one may say that each generation has acted on the basis of their own lived future, but, through their imagined future, they have also contributed to extending the lived future for the next generation. One needs generational data to see such processes; however, it is important to also be aware of this ambiguity when analysing synchronic data since there may be layers of meaning that cannot be fully deciphered in the present moment. Single items can be part of bigger movements, and, therefore, the space for interpretation must be kept open.

9   The Past Meets the Present and Creates the Future

My final example of how following subjects over time may render visible their contributions to new social forms is taken from the historical peak of house-wives in Norway in the 1950s. In feminist analyses, the housewife era has been understood primarily as a result of the improving living standards and after-war family politics in combination with the power imbalance between men and women (Hartman, 1981; Oakley, 1990). However, adding a diachronic per-spective through biographical data allows for a wider interpretation than in studies that have had only a synchronic focus. The below example indicates how a specific gendered biographical experience may be formulated into a new life project when it meets a new historical situation.

The oldest generation, in particular, those who grew up in rural areas, described a strict gendered division of work with women inside and men out-side. However, in the struggle to make ends meet, the women would often have to assist the men outdoors. In the interviews, the men of the elder generation remembered how hard their kind and mild mothers had to work. In contrast, the women described their mothers as strong and strict figures and their fathers as more fun and playful. As young couples and parents in the years after the Second World War, this generation chose to organise their lives through a gendered division of work into providers and housewives. This may be seen as a life project, especially for the men from rural poor or backgrounds, the social group who were the backbone of the migration to cities after WW2. They wanted their wives stay at home to spare them the hard toil that their moth-ers had to endure and to secure the best possible childhood for their children. They described it as a deliberate choice and discussed it with pride, expressing gratitude to and admiration for their wives' contributions to the household, including their proficiency as child carers and raisers. One of them, Einar, who had a small shoe repair shop in Oslo in the 1950s, said:

> We had three children and it went really well, she was very capable. She was a very clever girl, very responsible and such a wonderful mother. I never had to think about the kids. I could work and so on. Never needed to worry ... Could trust her one hundred per cent. She took care of the kids ... food and shelter and always well kept. And she didn't have a job outside the house. I wanted her to be home with the kids.

However, Einar also had to work hard to make ends meet. He worked long hours in his shop to provide for his family, which was not easy since he was suffering from severe health issues following his war injuries:

I managed. Had to go to work. I had brought children into the world and had a responsibility, a huge responsibility. And you can't give up. You just have to keep going. Even if it hurts a bit sometimes.

From the perspective of the men in this generation, providing for their families and letting their wives stay home was a gift of love and a way to prove oneself as a 'grown-up' and responsible man. The price they paid, though, emerges in the striking contrast between the proud descriptions of their accomplishments at work and their replies when questioned what had been the most important things in their lives. Asked what had made him most happy in life, Einar said, "It must have been when I became a father, I have to say. That has been my everything". We may understand this as a life project in a specific historical moment where these men's biographically formed subjectivity, including a specific way to feel about gender, matched the new demands of the labour market, the rise in living standards, family policies of the post-war welfare state, and the possibility for most families to survive on one income. Hence, subjective and structural changes reinforced each other to create a social change in gender relations.

Compared to the idealisation of female care and the gratitude towards their wives expressed by the men, the silence on these matters from the women we interviewed is more than striking. Some of them rather questioned the strict rural work division of their childhood and vocalised their feeling that work could have been more of a joint venture between husband and wife. Refining gender complementarity is not an obvious solution here, and, thus, tensions and unrest are built into the new life project of this generation from the very beginning. A blind spot in the new gender arrangement is the implication of the move from a rural to an urban context, which was crucial in this generation. The idea of refining gender complementarity had, for many of the men, been conceived of in a rural context where women's work did not confine them to the house but functioned less well when put into practice within an urban setting, where housewives were expected to do their work within the home. If the refined gender complementarity was given as a gift of love from the men in this generation, it does not appear to have been received in that way (Nielsen, 2017). A synchronic reading of the power imbalance in this situation is not wrong, but it does not grasp the whole picture, particularly how the different biographical pasts of men and women were a condition for their life projects, which was part of the realisation of the new social order. However, the times were definitely on the men's side in a period where it was both ideologically and economically arranged for married women to stay at home.

10   Time and Theoretical Integration

I have presented a number of arguments in this article: that time is always
co-constructing the object of study, often in ways that is difficult to access in
the moment; that time has an influence on what informants of different ages
and generations may be able to express about their situation; that social phenomena may be understood better if synchronic and diachronic perspectives
are integrated; that time has a multi-layered character, both in the sense that
the past may exist as small pockets, and futures as seeds in the present; and
finally, that following subjects over time may render visible their life projects
and, thus, contribute to a more adequate understanding of new social forms.
In doing this, I have also explored what Horkheimer's claim about the historical character of both the object perceived and the perceiving organ may imply
in the research process.

To conclude, I will discuss two ways that understanding the research object
in time and space could also contribute to the clarification of theoretical
issues. The first is that it may help soften some of the many prevailing theoretical dualisms, such as agency and structure, the psychological and the social,
and essentialism and constructivism (see also Giddens, 1984; Luhmann, 1995;
Falmagne, 2009 on this point). Following subjects over time or from different
generations indicates, for instance, the untenability of the poststructuralist
dualism between continuously processual becoming, on the one side, and
what is seen as a static and inherently essentialist humanistic subject tied up in
discourses of progress, rationality, and normalisation, on the other. Including a
time dimension that is connected to biographical experience and to lived and
imagined futures demonstrates it is not necessary to choose between either
studying people's identities as unitary, coherent, and universal, *or* studying
how their identities are constantly changing or linguistically constituted in
the processes of the present. Experiences of interaction are sedimented over
time such that the way a person 'does' gender also becomes an expression of
who the person has become through these actions, and, thus, in that sense
'is'. Further, the dualism between essentialism and nominalism, which makes
it tricky to understand the co-existence of change and continuity in people's
lives, may be lessened by the perspective of the multi-layeredness of time in
the subject as it allows for the coexistence of change and continuity in actions,
as well as in their outcomes. Thus, subjects come into being by sedimentations
of events and experiences over time, brought about by action.

A second way in which understanding subjects in time and space may help
to resolve theoretical disagreements is that it can also locate theories in time.
If the objects of inquiry change historically, so must the theories about them.

Different theoretical perspectives are often discussed as different conceptual accounts in timeless contexts or as a product of newer and more advanced thinking. What happens if they are also seen in relation to the changing object? Could a diachronic perspective on the research object contribute to dissecting when theoretical disagreements are primarily products of different epistemological assumptions and conceptual arguments and when they also reflect changes in the object that call for the formulation of new theoretical perspectives?

The three-generational project indicates that this may be the case. The project considered different psychoanalytic perspectives to understand gender and subjectivity that had emerged as theoretical alternatives in academic debates. The different theories were formulated at different historical points, and the most recent of them was clearly best attuned to modern gender theory. However, the theories may also be seen and used as historical formations, not only in the sense that they reveal the cultural, normative, and theoretical assumptions of their time but as sources of information about empirical patterns that later disappeared or became less poignant. This turned out to be the case when we compared the changing patterns of gender and subjectivity in the three generations of women and men with the different theories: the oldest generation seemed to be best explained by the Freudian Oedipal model (Freud, 1925), with its emphasis on psychological gender complementarity in the patriarchal family and the importance of the split between feelings of identification and feelings of desire. The middle generation had a better match with the gender identity model, where processes of individuation-separation, in connection with asymmetric parenting, lead to gender differences in the development of intimacy and autonomy (Chodorow, 1978). The youngest generation fit best into the gender ambiguity model, which questions the idea of two traces of development and views difference and sameness as a continuous tension in the psychic life of gender as well as in the modern family (Benjamin, 1995). These three psychological gender theories were formulated during or in the aftermath of the childhoods of the three generations, and even if the fits are not seamless, the relatively better match between the model and the childhood from the same period is notable.

This indicates that it is not only the theories that have changed as a result of critical work but also the gendered psychologies they set out to describe, suggesting that the different psychological constellations and tensions described in these models have had different impacts in different historical contexts. It also implies that the reason the theories developed as they did was that they caught the contours of a changed generational pattern in the times in which they were formulated: new structures of feelings related to gender. Maybe gender identities were, in fact, more binary and less fluid half a century ago? In that case, the concept of stable identities is not necessarily theoretically wrong, but such identities appear to have become less frequent. In raising these questions, I am neither positing that we should assume all theories will always be empirically true during the period in which they were conceived, nor that theoretical and normative critique is redundant or worthless, nor even that researchers simply directly reflect the times in which they live. Rather, I am arguing that it may be useful to also include more awareness of time in theoretical debates: as researchers, we must take into account that neither in methodology nor in theoretical work is it possible to move out of time.

References

Aarseth, H. (2008). *Hjemskapingens moderne magi* [The modern magic of home making]. Institutt for sosiologi og samfunnsgeografi, Universitetet i Oslo.

Aarseth, H. (2009). "Situert refleksivitet: Det narrative selv mellom tilhørighet og distanse." [Situated reflexivity: The narrative self between belonging and distance], *Sosiologi i dag* 39 (4): 7–28.

Adkins, L. (2004). "Reflexivity", in L. Adkins and B. Skeggs (eds.). *Feminism after Bourdieu*. Oxford: Blackwell.

Bakhtin, M.M. (1981). *The Dialogical Imagination: Four Essays*. Austin, TX: University of Texas Press.

Beck, U., and Beck-Gernsheim, E. (2002). *Individualization: Institutionalized Individualism and its Social and Political Consequences*. London: Sage.

Benjamin, J. (1995). *Like Subjects, Love Objects: Essays on Recognition and Sexual Difference*. New Haven and London: Yale University Press.

Bergson, H. (1911). *Matter and Memory*. London: George Allen & Unwin.

Breines, W. (1992). *Young, White, and Miserable: Growing Up Female in the Fifties*. Boston: Beacon Press.

Bruner, J. (2003). "Self-making narratives", in R. Fivush and C.A. Haden (eds.). *Autobiographical Memory and the Construction of a Narrative Self: Developmental and Cultural Perspectives*. Mahwah, NJ: Erlbaum.

Chodorow, N. (1978). *The Reproduction of Mothering: Psychoanalysis and the Sociology of Gender*. Berkeley: Berkeley University Press.

De Beauvoir, S. (1979) [1949]. *The Second Sex*. Middlesex: Penguin.

Eriksen, T.B. (1999). *Tidens historie* [The history of time]. Oslo: J. M. Stenersens forlag.

Falmagne, R.J. (2009). "Subverting theoretical dualisms: Discourse and mentalism", *Theory & Psychology* 19 (6): 795–815.

Freud, S. (1925). "Some Psychological Consequences of the Anatomical Distinction between the Sexes", *Standard Edition* 19: 241–258.

Giddens, A. (1984). *The Constitution of Society: Outline of the Theory of Structuration.* Cambridge: Polity Press.

Giddens, A. (1990). *The Consequences of Modernity.* Cambridge: Polity Press.

Giddens, A. (1991). *Modernity and Self-Identity: Self and Society in the Late Modern Age.* Cambridge: Polity Press.

Gleick, J. (2016). *Time Travel: A History.* New York: Pantheon Books.

Hacking, I. (1999). *The social construction of what?* Cambridge, MA and London: Harvard University Press.

Haraway, D. (1988). "Situated Knowledges: The Science Question in Feminism and the Privilege of Partial Perspective", *Feminist Studies* 14 (3): 575–599.

Harding, S. (1986). *The Science Question in Feminism.* Ithaca, NY and London: Cornell University Press.

Hartman, H.I. (1981). "The family as the locus of gender, class, and political struggle: The example of housework", *Signs* 6 (3): 366–394.

Horkheimer, M. (1976) [1937]. "Traditional and Critical Theory", in P. Connerton (ed.). *Critical Sociology: Selected Readings.* Harmondsworth: Penguin Books.

Hunt, L. (2008). *Measuring Time, Making History.* Budapest: Central European University Press.

Johansen, A. (2001). *All verdens tid* [All the time of the world]. Oslo: Spartacus.

Jordheim, H. (2012a). "Øyeblikkets historie" [The history of the moment.], *Norsk antropologisk tidsskrift* 23 (1): 55–65.

Jordheim, H. (2012b). "Against periodization: Koselleck's theory of multiple temporalities", *History and Theory* 51 (2): 151–171.

Jordheim, H. (2014). "Introduction: Multiple times and the work of synchronization", *History and Theory* 53 (4): 498–518.

Josselson, R.E., and Lieblich, A. (1993). *The Narrative Study of Lives, Vol 1.* Newbury Park: Sa.

Koselleck, R. (1972). "Einleitung", in O. Brunner, W. Conze, and R.Koselleck (eds.). *Geschichtliche Grundbegriffe: Historisches Lexikon zur politischsozialen Sprache in Deutschland.* Stuttgart: Klett–Cotta,vol. I, xxi.

Koselleck, R. ([2006] 2010). "Wiederholungstrukturen in Sprache und Geschichte", in C. Dutt (ed.). *Vom Sinn und Unsinn der Geschichte: Aufsätze und Vorträge aus vier Jahrzehnten.* Frankfurt am Main: Suhrkamp Verlag.

Luhmann, N. (1995). *Social Systems.* Stanford, CA: Stanford University Press.

McNay, L. (2004). "Agency and experience: Gender as lived relation", in L. Adkins and B. Skeggs (eds.). *Feminism after Bourdieu.* Oxford: Blackwell.

Moe, S. (2010). *Tid - en sosial konstruksjon?* [Time - a social construction?]. Oslo: Abstrakt forlag.

Nielsen, H.B. (2004). "Noisy girls: New subjectivities and old gender discourses", *Young - Nordic Journal of Youth Research* 12 (1): 9–30.

Nielsen, H.B. (2016). "The Arrow of Time in the Space of the Present: Temporality as Methodological and Theoretical Dimension in Child Research", *Children & Society* 30 (1): 1–11.

Nielsen, H.B. (2017). *Feeling Gender: A generational and psychosocial approach*. London: Palgrave Macmillan.

Nielsen, H.B., and Rudberg, M. (1994). *Psychological Gender and Modernity*. Oslo: Universitetsforlaget.

Nielsen, H.B. and Rudberg, M. (2006). *Moderne jenter. Tre generasjoner på vei* [Modern girls: Three generations on their way]. Oslo: Universitetsforlaget.

Nielsen, H.B. and Rudberg, M. (2007). "Fun in gender—Youth and sexuality, class and generation", *NORA - Nordic Journal of Women's Studies* 15 (2–3): 100–113.

Oakley, A. (1990). *Housewife*. Harmondsworth: Penguin Books.

Rosenthal, G. (2004). "Biographical Research", in C. Seale, G. Gobo, J.F. Gubrium, and D. Silverman (eds.). *Qualitative Research Practice*. London: Sage.

Sandmo, E. (2016). *Tid til historie: En bog om historiske spørgsmål* [Time for history]. København: Hans Reitzels forlag.

Sartre, J.-P. (1972). *The Psychology of Imagination*. London: Methuen.

Søland, B. (2000). *Becoming Modern: Young Women and the Reconstruction of Womanhood in the 1920s*. Princeton and Oxford: Princeton University Press.

Wikborg, T. (2010). *Gustav Vigelands: Kunstneren og hans verk* [Gustav Vigeland and his work]. Oslo: Aschehoug.

Williams, R. (2011). *The long revolution*. Cardigan, UK: Parthian.

CHAPTER 11

Academic Star Wars

Pierre Bourdieu and Dorothy E. Smith on Academic Work

Karin Widerberg

1 Introduction

Not only are Pierre Bourdieu and Dorothy E. Smith critical sociologists, as sociologists are or are expected to be, but they are also critical of the very foundation of our discipline and our craft as sociologists. Their critique and approaches to an alternative sociology have had a major impact within our field, resulting in different 'schools', with each advocating an empirical and theoretical approach (Bourdieu advocating field analysis and Smith institutional ethnography). Their contributions to sociology are profound but rarely compared, even by those of us who have made use of both of their approaches, albeit one at a time or side by side. It is like having best friends that have never met and wishing to introduce them to each other. Here I will argue that the similarities—and also the differences—of the two perspectives are the very reasons why we should try to combine them while undertaking empirical research. I believe that a comparison and combination of the two approaches could contribute to the development not only of each approach but to our discipline as a whole. This will be the very aim of this chapter, where academic work as a research field and topic will be used to compare and discuss these two authors' approaches regarding research design, analysis, and results, illuminating their methodological argumentation.

2 Sister and Brother: Family Resemblances

Pierre Bourdieu and Dorothy E. Smith are of the same generation both chronologically and intellectually. Although educated, trained, and working on different continents—Bourdieu in France and Smith (born and raised in England) on the west coast of the US—their theoretical luggage is strikingly similar, illustrating the more coherent sociological doxa of the first part of the 20th century. The traces of the classics—Marx, Goffman, Merleau-Ponty, Bakhtin, Foucault, to mention just a few—are accordingly profound in Bourdieu's and Smith's critique of dominant sociological traditions, as well as in the alternative approaches they propose. An ethnographic gaze and approach also characterise their works, although, as we shall return to, they are quite differently outlined. Moreover, both authors have explicitly referred to an outsider position in academia—Bourdieu coming from the 'wrong' class and Smith having the 'wrong' gender—to explain their stances. Reflection accordingly represents a question of positionality to both authors, of one's relation to the object of study—a structural rather than personal issue. A major part of their work is devoted to such reflections regarding the sociological discipline so as to ground the alternative approaches they pro- pose, and although they both repeatedly claim the importance of discovery through analytical-empirical descriptions, their argumentation is profoundly theoretical, meta-theoretical, and epistemological. As such their texts are a heavy read, loaded with implicit and explicit methodological references and implications. Fortunately, their texts are also witty. In Smith's case, one is struck by the elegance of the precise language of her approach, while in Bourdieu's work, energy and good humour emit from the pages. Neither of them wastes any time on the other; Smith mentions and discards Bourdieu's concepts *en passant*, while she is made totally invisible in Bourdieu's writing. They have other—some of them shared—enemies on their agenda. Thus, let us begin with a brief presentation of the characteristics of their respective approaches, exemplified by empirical research on the chosen topic: academic work. Since Bourdieu is the most well-known of the two, his approach is pre- sented first and more briefly than that of Smith; however, Bourdieu's voice is also made present during the account of Smith's approach, so as to highlight where they agree and where they differ. Against this backdrop, this chapter concludes with a final discussion of if, when, and how their approaches can be combined.

3   Pierre Bourdieu and His Method of (Field) Analysis

In *The Craft of Sociology* (Bourdieu, Chamboredon, and Passeron, 1991), ini- tially designed for students as a textbook in sociological research, Bourdieu et al. argue against the pitfalls of 'spontaneous sociology' and the illusion of immediate knowledge. Referencing Durkheim, they state that a social fact has to be constructed and that this construction is an epistemological break "that can separate scientific interpretation from all artificialist or anthropomorphic interpretations of the functioning of society" (ibid.: 23). For this to happen, one needs a theoretical understanding of the social, including an understanding of research as social.

3.1   *Relation as an Analytical Category*

To Bourdieu et al., the social is relational to its very core; the real is identified not through substances but through relations (Bourdieu, 1990a: 126), and, accordingly, agency should be understood as such and not as an individuated entity. It is the relation and not the individual that is to be the analytical entity. Nevertheless, when constructing the object of study, which is to be approached relationally, one must avoid another pitfall within the sociological discipline, namely, empiricist sociology. All the operations of sociological practice, such as interview guides, questionnaires, coding, statistical analysis, and so forth, are and should be "theories in action" (ibid.: 39). Claiming a neutral or objective stance will, in the worst case, result in collecting 'nothing more than the fictitious discourses that the subjects devise to cope with the situation of inquiry and to answer artificial questions, or even with the supreme artifice of a lack of questions. In short, whenever the sociologist renounces his epistemological privilege, he sanctions a spontaneous sociology' (ibid.: 38). One has "to question the methods and theories at the very moment at which they are implemented, in order to determine what they do to objects and what objects they make" (Bourdieu et al., 1991: 11).

3.2   *The Theoretical Stance as an Object of Study*

The theoretical stance taken in constructing the object of study also has to be investigated as a social relation, just like the object of study. The researcher needs to *objectify* her relation to the object of study so as not to write into it this very relation as if it were part of the object. As Bourdieu noted:

> By failing to objectify the truth of the objectifying relation to practice, one projects into practices the function of practices as it appears to someone who studies them as something to be deciphered
>
> BOURDIEU, 1990a: 99

That is, sociological and political concepts and categories are positionally constructed; they express how something is understood from a particular position.

3.3   *A Method of (Field) Analysis*

For Bourdieu, the solution to the dilemma of needing theory without wanting to reproduce ideological understandings is to propose, in my terms, 'a method of analysis' that focuses on the relational and makes use of concepts as tools to grasp the relational, which then must be empirically filled with content. The field as a concept and the different forms of capital—economic, symbolic, cultural, and political—that play out there relationally as well as the habitus as its embodied agency, are, to my view, primarily meta-concepts. They must be filled with empirical contents, which Bourdieu himself stresses over and over when these concepts are used by his followers as explanations rather than starting points for exploration.

3.4   *Transcending the Pitfalls of the Sociological Discipline*

By proposing such a method of analysis, Bourdieu aims to transcend the dominant pitfalls of our discipline. In his perspective, the theoretical oppositions between theorists and empiricists, subjectivists and objectivists, structuralists and phenomenologists, and so forth, are not only false but 'completely fictitious' (Bourdieu, 1990a: 34). The issue at stake is rather the gap between the theoretical aims of theoretical understandings and the practical and directly concerned aims of practical understandings. To "avoid giving as the source of the agents' practice the theory that had to be constructed in order to explain it" (ibid.: 60), another view, that is expressed in Bourdieu's terminology, has to be taken, for example; strategies replace rules when investigating kinship. To Bourdieu, the objectivist and subjectivist 'moment' (ibid.: 126) are to be understood and handled as a dialectical relation. Even if the subjective moment in his own approach, when taken separately, might seem nearer to interactionist or ethnomethodological analyses, there is a radical difference. In Bourdieu's method of analysis, points of view are apprehended as such and related to the positions in the structure of the corresponding agents (ibid.: 126). Thus, his method is a way to grasp the structural without taking an objectivistic stance and to look for practical sense without falling into subjectivism. What does such a method of analysis imply to a study of academic work?

4   Homo Academicus

Bourdieu studied academic work empirically, or rather the field of academic work, in line with the critical refection on scientific practice that runs through and parallel to all of his works. *Homo Academicus* (Bourdieu, 1988), a sociological analysis of the academic world, "aims to trap Homo Academicus, supreme classifier among classifiers, in the net of his own classification" (Bourdieu, 1988: xi). Since this is Bourdieu's own playground, objectifying his relation to the object of study demands special attention so as not to domesticate but to 'exoticize the domestic' (ibid.). It is, thus, not his own view of academia that is to guide his empirical investigation and classifications (the way he criticises other such attempts, for example, Aron, [ibid.: xvi]), but rather the views and actions of the players positioned on the field, their *habitus*. That is, one could say, the *practical sense* of homo academicus grasped through 'participant objectification' (ibid.: xviii).

To comprehend this scenario, two sets of relations have to be related: the space of works or discourses taken at differential stances *and* the positions held by those who produce them (ibid.: xvii). That is, positions and views are related, but not in a simple cause and effect manner since a position is determined by the number of different forms of capital (economic, social, political, and cultural), which, when taken together, are the foundations for dispositions embodied as habitus. In making a correspondence analysis, where the attributes for capital (position) and views are summed up for each individual along two axes, a picture of the relational power of each group is given. Since this is the very aim of Bourdieu's approach—to illuminate how power relations within a field are made and fought, in this case, in academia—defining the attributes or indicators of different forms of capital comprising a position is a key issue. In the investigation of homo academicus, he and his fellow researchers used questionnaires, interviews, and written documents. The indicators of academic capital are clearly specified (ibid.: 39–40): 1) inherited cultural and social capital, 2) educational capital, 3) capital of academic power, 4) capital of scientific power, 5) capital of scientific prestige, 6) capital of intellectual renown, 7) capital of political and economic power, and 8) political dispositions, in the widest sense. Under each indicator, a list of examples is given.

Although a massive and fairly systematic gathering of material is hereby envisioned, there is no presentation of how these indicators have found their way into the analysis. They are not the result of an empirical investigation (as they would be in an institutional ethnographic study, which I will demonstrate later), at least none that Bourdieu here documents, but they are the very tools he starts out with when empirically investigating the field. It is as if they were self-evident, yet they must obviously be the result of extensive analytical reflection. Rereading the book almost 40 years later, it is, of course, easy to argue for other factors, such as indicators related to New Public Management and the very ranking of the indicators to be discussed. The material and the analyses in *Homo Academicus* are, however, so overwhelming in terms of both their volume and the depth of their reflections, that, as a reader, one is more struck by the abundance of new knowledge and understanding than by its potential limits and shortcomings.

5   The Power Struggle of the Academic Field

Through Bourdieu's analyses, we learn how power moves within and between disciplines and faculties whose development was triggered by the events of 1968. The student masses entering the field and the corresponding increase of teaching positions and the general political mobilisation, including that of the labour movement, generated new relations that shook the positional power structure of the university. Before this 'critical moment' (Bourdieu, 1988: chapter 5), an understanding of the processes by which academic habitus is maintained and reproduced is presented in much detail throughout several chapters. Here, the analyses reveal, first of all, that the supposed objective qualities of academic discourse are the very by-product of an academic's conformity to university norms and the university hierarchy (ibid.: 29). The disclosed relation between power and knowledge allows us to question how different scholars, methods of research, and intellectual perspectives are endorsed or invalidated by the mechanisms of power located throughout the microcosm of the university's social structure (ibid.: 104–105). An academic's authority and claims to objectivity are, therefore, not inherent qualities of an individual but the result of constructed and academically sanctioned properties that characterise the scholar and their position in the structured space of the university field (ibid.: 19–24). The hierarchical positions of the university domain are then "obtained and maintained by holding a position enabling domination of other positions and their holders" (ibid.: 84).

Second, we learn how this academic power is maintained by rigorous 'selection and indoctrination' processes (ibid.: 40–41). These processes include completing the sequences of career-related achievements, for example, the thesis and publication, so as to achieve academic credibility and consequently access more prestigious positions within the academy (ibid.: 88). These processes also include the presence of a supervisor (ibid.: 94), and such 'relations of dependency' reinforce the academic power and authority of the supervisor (ibid.: 90–95).

To succeed within academia and obtain academic capital of their own, students must respect the hierarchical order of the university and conform to the sanctioned properties of established academics (including the supervisor) within their field. The properties that the aspiring academic adopts are summarised by Bourdieu through the concept of *habitus*; "a system of shared social dispositions and cognitive structures that generates perceptions, appreciations and actions" (ibid.: 279). Students and professors maintain this system by conforming to the established *habitus* and by associating academic capital to positions within the university, thereby, reinforcing the structural power dynamics of the university field (ibid.: 91–95).

6   The Positionality of Intellectual Voices

Such an analysis allows us not only to recognise general patterns and processes, and read ourselves and our academic histories into them, but also to understand the positionality of specific intellectual voices. Internationally well-known French intellectuals such as Althusser, Derrida, and Foucault, incorporated into other countries' curricula as 'classics', are found by Bourdieu to be marginally positioned in the academic field. Not being full professors, which limited their options for teaching, supervising, and research, they were forced to work as more or less free-floating individuals and came to:

> share a sort of *anti-institutional mood* homologous in its form to that of a considerable fraction of students: they are inclined to react impatiently to the discrepancy between their already considerable fame in the outside world, that is outside the university, and also outside France, and the subaltern status which is accorded them inside the French university world, in collusion with the contempt and their rejection, by an institution which, when they were adolescents, had attracted and even consecrated them.
>
> BOURDIEU, 1988: xix

In the case of Roland Barthes, not being one of the institutional elites, his entire mode of thinking and writing is explicated by this outsider's position. As Bourdieu observes:

> Roland Barthes represents the peak of the class of essayists, who, having nothing to oppose to the forces of the field, are condemned, in order to exist, or subsist, to float with the tides of the external and internal forces which wrack the milieu, notably through journalism [. ...] Roland Barthes gives instantaneous expression to all the changes in the forces of the field while appearing to anticipate them, and, in this respect, it is sufficient to follow his itinerary, and his successive enthusiasms, to discover all the tensions which were applied to the point of least resistance of the field, where what is called fashion continually flowers.
>
> BOURDIEU, 1988: xxii

So much for free-floating intellectuals, their (ideological) products, and (ideological) function when taken up in the disciplines.

7   The Homo Academicus of Today

Bourdieu's study of the academic field has, of course, been a great inspiration to others. Michèle Lamont's study *How Professors Think: Inside the Curious World of Academic Judgment* (2009) is but one well-known example. Here, she analyses the criteria of judgment on research studies adopted in six disciplines: philosophy, history, anthropology, English literature, political science, and economics. In contrast to Bourdieu, her analyses are primarily empirically and not theoretically grounded, aiming to explore the meanings of the evaluative terminology employed. That is, even if Lamont and Bourdieu can, in one sense, be said to have a similar aim of studying the habitus of academic judgment, Bourdieu maintains the field of academia and its hierarchal power structure and power struggles as the context and guideline to his empirical analyses. For Bourdieu, academic judgements are seen through that lens, as illuminated in the final chapter of his book, titled, *The Categories of Professorial Judgment*.

The institutional ethnographic study of *Doing the Ideal Academic* (Lund, 2015) also displays striking similarities to the Bourdieu's findings, yet as we shall soon demonstrate, the very difference of the approach also opens up other understandings of academia. It should also be emphasised that, if the study of The Homo academicus was undertaken today, Bourdieu would most likely have given the mainstreaming of academia, in the guise of new public management, more critical attention. There is nothing in his model that hinders such a focus, in fact, quite the opposite. Since a central concern of his is to prevent scholarly knowledge from becoming 'an instrument of power' (Bourdieu, 1988: 16), the mainstreaming of academic knowledge production would be, I believe, at the core of an investigation of The Homo academicus of today.

But now to Dorothy E. Smith and her critique of, and alternative to, sociological research traditions. How does her 'method of inquiry' differ from or add to the approach proposed by Bourdieu?

8   The Approach of Dorothy E. Smith: A Method of Inquiry

The margins of my Bourdieu books, cited above, are filled with exclamations such as 'just like Smith!', 'see Smith', and a few instances of 'wrong according to

Smith!'. In the margins to her books, I have made few, if any, such references to Bourdieu. Her approach and its language appear so self-contained and specific that it seems to stand on its own legs.

Like Bourdieu, Smith finds that the issue at stake lies elsewhere than the ongoing debate between different theoretical and methodological traditions and, again like Bourdieu, she offers an alternative approach that transcends objectivist and subjectivist stances. However, her aim, or rather the aim of her approach, is presented differently in that it proposes 'a sociology for people' and not of or about people. Thus, what is the foundation for her alternative? As noted at the beginning of this chapter, since Smith's approach and work are less known than that of Bourdieu, it will be more extensively presented. Bourdieu is however invited along as an imagined commentator to her proposals, so as to bring the pair into dialogue.

9   Doing Sociology Is Partaking in Ruling Relations

To be a sociologist, Dorothy E. Smith, the founding mother of institutional ethnography (IE) argues,[1] is to be a part of a set of social relations in which specialised knowledge is separated from everyday knowing. Research is made into a general capacity where everything is researchable, which only researchers, the specialists, can do. As a sociologist, one is by definition part of the ruling relations, where actual work is separated from abstract and intellectual work and where the latter is being specialised. Smith claims that this division of labour is the foundation for the development of the conventions of how the social is to be written and made into sociological texts. These sociological conventions, she argues, rely on Durkheim's rules of sociological method (Durkheim, 1982, reprint in English), which still, in spite of the critique of positivism, function as foundational conventions of too much of today's sociology. The Durkheimian heritage, praised by Bourdieu as a way to escape subjectivist sociology, is criticised by Smith for the very establishment of the split between practical sense and theory, giving theory the upper hand. While Bourdieu talks of a dialectic relation between objectivist and subjectivists stances, Smith—as will be demonstrated later—proposes an approach that cuts across and transcends such dichotomies. However, since Smith's alternative is a direct response to her critique of the sociological conventions, we must first present what she lists as elements central to this kind of hegemonic sociology.[2]

---

1   A detailed presentation of Smith and her works is given in Widerberg (2017).
2   Smith, 1999: 54–62.

10   The Sociological Conventions for How to Do Sociology

First of all, the subject is suspended. A new social object or unit (social fact
or phenomenon) is constituted as existing externally to particular individuals.
This is done through, for example, the nominalisation of verbs, as in aggression and depression. Second, agency is reattributed from the subject to social
phenomena. It is the aggression and depression, the attitude or interest, which
are now made into problematics rather than the individual and their relations.
Third, through these preceding steps, the sociological becomes detached from
the actual. These textually constituted realities then become objects of sociological work. By subsequently privileging the order of the sociological discourse
over the order of the actual, the actual is made into an expression of the discursive. Finally, subjects are reconstructed as figments of discourse. The subjects
now enter the text as pseudo-subjects or categories of personages to whom the
objectified attributes (aggression, attitude, and so on) can be assigned.

Thus, sociological conventions are characterised by the establishment of a
position within the text where the social as written is separated from the social
as lived and experienced, resulting in positionless accounts. It is as if society
could be understood in its totality and from above, like the gaze of God, or
rather, like the view of a bird but without the bird. For Smith, these hegemonic
conventions for 'how to do sociology' are objectifying and, as such, are profoundly inadequate. The sociological text is, however, to be understood as not
merely a result of social relations, that is, of ruling relations. By placing the
reader in a particular relation to the reality described in the text, the text also
plays an active part in the ruling process. Through the objectifying conventions, the reader takes the place of the ruler, they are offered 'the gaze of God',
where local positions, perspectives, and experiences are not only subordinated
but also made invisible.

11   The Sociologist and Their Discipline as an Object of Study

Bourdieu's critique of how sociologists tend to write the social is similar to
Smith's.[3] Like Smith, he demands that the position of the observer (the
sociologist) should be the object of the same kind of critical analysis that we
employ when investigating other objects. Sociology and its praxis have to be
understood, he claims, in the context of the relations and positions within the

---

3   See, for example, Bourdieu, 1990b.

academic field as well as in relation to the wider cultural and historical context in which this field is situated. Otherwise, as previously mentioned, there is always the risk that, without being aware of it, we read our own position and ways of relating to and understanding the social into 'the object', as if it were a part of the object itself, instead of a result of our relation to it. Bourdieu, like Smith, advocates that we problematise the relations in which sociology has developed and in which it is practised today. If we do not, we will most likely end up as non-reflective dealers for the ruling apparatus, translating what are actually politically defined social problems (poverty, criminality, and so on) into the terms and conventions of objectivist sociology. Smith and Bourdieu both propose that reflexivity should involve a proper systematic method here, in contrast to the kind of individualised introspection they claim dominates the self-reflective sociological analyses of today. However, and this is important to note, while Bourdieu labels this method 'objectification', thereby implying that we must make our own relations of knowledge the object for investigation, Smith uses the same word to label the very opposite, namely the process of how the social is written from a ruling perspective.

How then do we go about investigating and writing the social if we are *not* to start with an objectivistic standpoint? In listing the steps below that, according to Smith,[4] must be undertaken, I have inserted brief comments of my interpretation as to Bourdieu's stance to facilitate a comparison of their approaches.

12   Steps in a Method of Inquiry

First, the subject/*knower* of inquiry is to be approached as situated in the actualities of their own living, in relation with others, and not as a transcendent subject. This is quite in accordance with Bourdieu's approach.

Second, the actual activities of particular individuals are focused on as the locus of the ongoing meshing and coordinating of their activities. The concern is accordingly not just with what individuals do but also with the social aspect of their doings. The social is hereby not conceived of simply as the aggregate properties of separate individuals or as an entity that is separable from the actual people and activities that animate it. Rather, the concept of the social directs us to focus on how people's activities are coordinated. This step is also in accordance with the approach of Bourdieu:

---

4   Smith, 1992.

> To step down from the sovereign viewpoint from which objective ideal-
> ism orders the world [...] without reducing knowledge to mere recording
> [...] one has to situate oneself within "real activity" as such, that is, in the
> practical relation to the world.
>
> BOURDIEU, 1990b: 52

Third, concepts to express these coordinated activities, such as the categories of social relations and social organization (as with the more general
notion of the social) must not be used as the kinds of discursive entities that
lift the phenomena out of time and place. A social relation or social organization is not first and foremost a thing to be looked at but rather the place
from which to do the looking. Rather, terms like 'social relations' should
direct our attention to people in a given local site and what they are expe-
riencing. More than this, they should direct attention to how these experiences and practices hook into sequences of action coordinating multiple
other such sites.

Here is a step where Smith and Bourdieu diverge. They both understand the
social as relational and as a place to stand when looking 'out' at society rather
than an entity that can be used as an explanation in itself, for example, using
the concept of class as a relation from which to start looking at society rather
than an explanation in itself. However, Smith proposes that instead of summing up experiences and fitting them into theoretical categories and concepts,
such as in Bourdieu's concept of habitus and different forms of capital, we
should link the relations of these local experiences with extra-local relations
to define the role of ruling relations. Smith's aim in her method of inquiry is,
thus, to enlighten ruling relations in everyday life and activities, so as to draw
a map from which the subjects, taken as a starting point for exploration, can
seek guidance for future action. Bourdieu does not state this as the aim of his
approach and concepts but rather presents it as a way to recognise our agency
in terms of (embodied) structured and structuring relations and dispositions
(Bourdieu, 1990b: 52). The 'Aha!' one experiences when reading his investigations of Homo Academicus, and maybe even more so in *Distinction* (Bourdieu,
1984), does not imply a direct understanding of the role of ruling relations in
the habitus of the groups with varying forms of capital. This is not his aim, not
the gaze furthered by his approach.

Fourth, by considering concepts, beliefs, and other categories of thought
and mind in terms of people's actual practices, the traditional theory/prac-
tice split is avoided. Locating the knower in their body and in a lived world
in which both theory and practice occur, implies an understanding of theory
itself as a practice.

Though Bourdieu could agree to an understanding of theoretical work as a practice that could be studied as such (for example, how sociology is done), his very approach is founded on 'the break' (his term) between "the logic of things from the things of logics" (Bourdieu, 1990a: 61). Both logics have to be investigated, independently of each other, yet related so as to challenge our understanding of both practice and theory. Empirically investigating habitus, for example, will explicate the agency of the relational position of different forms of capital. These concepts then guide the 'looking' but do not provide us with the content, which will have to be discovered. When discovered, this content can tell us something about these very relations and about the struggles in the field in question. Bourdieu begins with a theory of practice, which states, "... as practice insists, contrary to positivist materialism, that the objects of knowledge are constructed, not passively recorded ..." (Bourdieu, 1990b: 52). One could claim that Smith also has a theory of practice guiding her approach, though she instead talks of an ontological foundation for her method of inquiry (Widerberg, 2015a). Smith states that the human is born social and that the craving for social contact is just as fundamental as the craving for food. 'Socialization' as a concept for something that in the interest of society is done *to* the individual (by parents and institutions), is accordingly an *institutional capture* (Smith's concept) of the sociological doxa illustrating its ruling relations to the object of study. As such, it directs our gaze away from the fact that the human, as a social being, seeks to learn and know through others, in relations. If that is how humans learn, we as sociologists should investigate this very process; how individuals as knowers seeking knowledge come to know of the workings of the situation in which we are interested. The 'recording' is meta-theoretically directed into searching for relations and the role of ruling relations in what is known and how it is known. Contrary to Bourdieu, these relations are not theoretically conceptualised but something that needs to be discovered empirically and mapped so as to enlighten how and when ruling relations enter the scene. Further, ruling relations, defined by Smith as objectification, are not an entity or a particular set of relations, but rather a specific way of relating what has to be 'discovered' and given content empirically. Summing up, we could say that Smith and Bourdieu's approaches are both analytically guided: Bourdieu theoretically and Smith meta-theoretically and both founded on epistemology and social theory in the wider sense.

Their divergence regarding the role of theoretical conceptualisation will, however, cause them both to raise and answer research questions differently. Yet, as I intend to argue in my final discussion, each approach has merit if combined with the other: while Bourdieu claims that his theoretical model is characterised by its capacity for breaking with appearances and for generalisations (Bourdieu, 1990b: 54), Smith could claim her method of inquiry achieves likewise, only in a different way, resulting in a different kind of knowledge. To me, these are the very reasons we need to use their two approaches together to develop a sociology both for us (Smith) and about us (Bourdieu). Nevertheless, before embarking on the final discussion, there remain some steps on the IE path, as well as some empirical illustrations, that should be presented.

Thus, fifth, in understanding theory as practice, texts, text mediation, and textuality become central. The text is the bridge between the actual and the discursive, between the local actualities of our living and the ruling relations. As a material object, it can be read in many settings and by many people, at the same time or at many different times. As such, texts are the primary basis for abstraction and, hence, for developing critical analyses of the actualities of living. Since text-mediated relations are the forms in which power is increasingly generated in contemporary societies, sociological investigation of texts is a means of opening up ruling relations to critical interrogation. Bourdieu would most likely agree to this step, but, due to the fact that illuminating ruling relations in Smith's sense of the word is not on his agenda, texts do not play as vital a role in his approach as they do in Smith's.

Sixth, the politics of a method of inquiry of this kind is not aimed at explaining people's behaviour or in any other way at making them the object of research. It is instead focused on explaining to them, and to ourselves, the socially organised powers in which our lives are embedded and to which our activities contribute.

One could say that Bourdieu's empirical work is about people's behaviour, which is made into the object of research by investigating the practical sense of what they do. The aim of his approach can in many ways be expressed as in this sentence above. Yet, people's behaviour is still explicated through a theory of the field (its different forms of capital embodied as habitus), which is not the aim of an IE approach. It is the explication of ruling relations from the perspective of knowers that is the agenda there.

13   Summing up the Steps to a Method of Inquiry

By commencing with our actual activities, the method of inquiry proposed by Smith makes the relational context of our daily lives visible. This is a context in which ruling relations can be found, often in text-mediated forms. The increased use and importance of texts as ruling devices has made the sociological investigations of texts a key issue for Smith, and here she gives a sociological answer to the challenge from the poststructuralists and their approaches to texts.[5] Printed or electronic texts are indefinitely replicable, and this allows identical forms of meaning to be activated in multiple local settings. This materiality of the text, Smith argues, creates a situation in which it can seem that language, thought, culture, formal organisation, and so on exist independently and outside time and the actualities of people's lives. However, even though texts are mediators of discourses and ruling relations, they are also always occurrences in time and space. Texts 'happen', as Smith puts it; they are constituents and organizers of actions, activated when read at specific times and places. The replicability that texts make possible is essential to the kind of organisation that is characteristic of contemporary society. We could not have the existence of corporations, for example, without replicable texts and their discourses.

14   A Sociological Investigation of Texts

Texts, accordingly, represent a possibility for sociologists to explore how the trans-local and extra-local are brought into local settings where people are, into their bodies and particular activities, activities which can be connected with each other. The fact that we are reading the same text does not mean that we all read it the same way. Smith places emphasis on the notion of the text–reader conversation, acknowledging the insights of French poststructuralists such as Roland Barthes (1977), who stresses that a text only becomes what it is in the reading of it. The meaning of a text is, thus, not fixed. Smith's specific argument, however, is that in order to establish the significance of different readings, one has to be able to recognise a text as a specific text. A faithfully replicated text is identical to the text that was copied, and this fact is crucial in establishing the significance of different readings of it—otherwise, the idea of different readings would be of no interest. A text can, in this way, be treated ethnographically. In other words, it is possible and illuminating to explore the variety of ways that particular texts enter into the organisation of any corporation or other powerful and significant institution.

---

5   In her 1996 article, 'Telling the truth after postmodernism', Smith develops in detail both her critique of the poststructuralist approach to texts as well as an alternative sociological understanding and approach.

15   A Research Program for Sociology

The term 'institutional ethnography' signals a kind of research program for sociology.[6] Here, a sociology is proposed that explores the institutional order and ruling relations from the point of view of those who are in various ways implicated and participating in it. It does not aim to understand the institution, organisation, and so on as such, as is the case in systems theory, for example. IE only takes the social activities of the institution as a starting point. Latching onto activities and relations, both horizontal and hierarchical, the approach is never confined solely to the institution or organisation immediately under investigation. The purpose is rather to highlight the connections between the local and the extra-local, thereby making visible the workings of the wider society as they impinge upon activities in the here and now. Conversely, exploring how texts mediate, regulate, and authorise people's activities also expands the scope of the ethnographic method beyond the limits of observation. By dismantling institutional captures through the use of work knowledge, an institutional ethnographer has the 'capacity for breaking with appearances', as Bourdieu would put it, without leaving the actual or transcending it to theoretical concepts. Further, by focusing on the work knowledge and its relations, and not on the knower as a person, an institutional ethnographer 'has a capacity for generalisations', a claim for sociology demanded by Bourdieu.

16   Studying Academic Work Using the Institutional Ethnographic
         Approach

Here, I will briefly present two studies where institutional ethnography was used to illuminate the role of ruling relations in the undertaking of academic work. The first study focuses on the task of teaching (and supervision), while the other focuses on the research (and publication) task. In both studies, the role of texts to regulate these activities is highlighted, and, taken together, they can give us a picture of the role of ruling relations in academic work in the university of today.

---

6   In her 2001 article, 'Texts and the ontology of organizations and institutions", Smith develops
    the perspective of institutional ethnography and gives empirical illustrations of its use; this
    is the very topic of her book, *Institutional Ethnography: A Sociology for People* (2005). In the
    introductory chapter of a book I edited (Widerberg, 2015a), I presented the approach of institutional ethnography in a Scandinavian context.

17   Teaching and the Role of Ruling Relations

A couple of years ago, I decided to carry out an institutional ethnography of the implications of new public management (NPM) in academic work. Following IE guidelines, I did *not* start with sociological concepts and understandings of either NPM nor academic work but with an ethnographic study of everyday academic work and the role of NPM texts therein. An example of such an NPM text is the *accounting of work hours* (*timeregneskap*, in Norwegian). At the end of each semester, each scientific staff member is required to document the teaching work done by completing a form for the accounting of work hours. Since this form and the texts regulating how the counting is to be done have been much debated during the nearly two decades it has been used in my own department, the Department of Sociology and Human Geography (part of the Social Sciences faculty at the University of Oslo), I decided to make that text central to my ethnography, in fact performing a kind of ethnography of the text.

18   'What Do You Do as a Professor of Sociology?'

If asked about my job by someone from outside of academia, my first answer would be that I teach and supervise, carry out research, and perform administration. Most likely, I would then add that the teaching and supervision task amounts to 50%, administration 10%, and research 40%. Any member of my university's academic staff could have answered almost the same, with the correct figures being 47%, 6%, and 47%, which is the official picture of the duties of a professor at a Norwegian university, manifested in general rules and regulations and translated into different departments' local texts, such as the forms for the accounting of work hours. My first answer is simultaneously both a formal one—how it looks from the outside and from above (from a ruling perspective)—and a (partly) honest one since this time apportionment is a framework to which I am obligated and by which I am controlled. By making me *accountable* (Smith, 2005: 113) to this objectified (Smith, 2005: 27–28) job description, I reproduce the *ruling relations* (Smith, 2005: 13–20) that have generated it in the first place. Of course, beneath my obedient compliance, a strategic and tactical practice might hide very different activities or prioritisation of activities.

To quantify my actual everyday work, I recorded all of my work tasks (how long they took and which relations were involved) for a whole month; however, as I found that some tasks and relations were spread out over a very long period, I needed to use my notes and organiser for the whole year. Although

I registered all daily activities, I placed a special focus on those that were to be translated into the accounting of hours, that is, activities that count.[7]

18.1   *IE Steps and Conceptual Tools*

Summing up my study in terms of its IE steps and conceptual tools, the following should be highlighted:

- I began by investigating the *work knowledge* of me as *the knower* of academic work.
- This work knowledge was recorded ethnographically, focusing on teaching and supervision. The place, time, and relations of the tasks were described in detail.
- How all this work was translated into a *text* regulating these activities, in other words, the accounting of hours, was then investigated. The *institutional captures* of the categories and of the text in itself, that is, the institutional understanding of the activities, was revealed as differing from the work knowledge of the knower. Being *accountable* in terms of these institutional captures, however, also make them more or less come true, individually and collectively. Thereafter, how this text—the accounting of hours—is taken up in horizontal as well as hierarchical relations, linking local to *trans- and extra- local relations*, is then described and analysed. Mapping all these relations finally illuminates 'how it is put together'. Thus, *ruling relations* become visible, that is, how one objectifies, views, and evaluate one's own work as well as the work of colleagues (employees and employer) in ruling terms and from a ruler's perspective.

So, if this was 'the method of inquiry', that is, the IE steps I used to uncover the ruling relations within my daily activity as a professor, what were the empirical substance and results of such an approach? Let me be brief and highlight just some of the major empirical findings.

19   Empirical Findings from the IE Study

It is easy to conclude, *first of all*, that there are activities related to teaching and administration that are not registered as such and are thus not recognized as

---

7   Research activities, expressed as publications and research money, were also registered and counted but much more roughly, and the consequences (i.e. the awarding of money) are more directed towards the institutional than the individual level. A full description of this ethnographic study can be found in Widerberg, 2014, and Widerberg, 2015b. The latter also features ethnographic studies from other positions..

work duties. *Second*, the hours allotted to tasks (i.e. their rating) bear little if any relation to the actual amount of time used on the task in question; in this system, there is no way to know if one, on the whole, uses more or less hours than one is credited for. *Third*, the way a task is rated affects how one reports it. *Fourth*, the changes in my work situation experienced over the past decade (longer semesters, more students, more demanding courses, and more administration) are not reflected in the accounting of hours. That is, the form could have been completed in a similar way ten years ago, and *the actual increase of my workload* that has occurred in the intervening period *is not revealed*. The ethnographic data as a whole illustrate that *the accounting of hours affects not only the tasks you do and how you do them but also your whole state of mind. You become or are expected to become one who counts and reports everything, and, if the tradition of counting and documenting is based on the individual as a unit, individualisation will increase at the expense of a more collective work culture.*

This, however, is a picture drawn from an employee perspective. The use of the accounting of hours at the department, faculty, and university level will, of course, affect its further workings, even for its employees. It is, therefore, necessary to shift from the perspective of the employee to that of the employer[8] in order to analyse the employer's reaction to the employees' use of the time-bank. Grasping this dialectic of ruling is important if we wish to fully understand the workings of NPM.

The research reveals that the individual account is used by those in charge at each level in the chain of command to supervise the level below, with the ultimate aim of supervising the work situation of the employee. By this means, the work of staff members is made 'proper', in relation to rules and regulations, and mainstreamed. Nonetheless, this is, of course, not the only use of the accounting of hours.

At the departmental level, accounting of hours is also used to gain insight into the amount of time—and thus money—that is being spent on different tasks. Such insights are used in discussions of future action, and, at staff meetings, these facts and figures for both teaching and research are presented in such a way as to include and make the whole staff accountable in the running of the department. The accounting of hours presents a picture of the department as the truth; figures based on our own accounting reports are used to draw a picture that is hard to reject. However, this process produces a picture of how it should be, not how it is. On paper, time and money can be saved,

---

8 I also undertook ethnographic studies from other positions. A more detailed description of these studies is presented in Widerberg, 2015b.

and the accounts can be balanced on all levels. This ideal is then made true by affecting both one's understandings and actions. We try to live up to the norms and interpret our failure or success as issues for the individual. Of course, we all know that this picture does not tell the whole truth, but we have not developed, either individually or collectively, alternatives that we can present. *The accounting of hours and the research registration accordingly make the employee accountable not only for their own actions but also for the actions of the collective. They are tools through which the employee—in a democratic organization such as my department—is made accountable to management at all levels.*

To summarise, the empirical findings of these institutional ethnographic studies illuminate how local and trans-local relations are linked into ruling relations, activated in the everyday work of academic employees and employers. The picture and map hereby given is a foundation for future actions regarding teaching—but what about research, the other part of academic work?

20   Research and Ruling Relations

In her doctoral dissertation, *Doing the Ideal Academic: Gender, Excellence and Changing Academia* (2015), Rebecca Lund focuses on the role of gender when academic knowledge is targeted to profound changes through the neo-liberal marketisation of universities. Will neo-liberalism contribute to a decrease or an increase in gender-equality within universities? Can gender-equality, conversely, contribute to a change in neo-liberalist ideology and practice? These questions are translated by Lund into the research objective to understand how academic quality and excellence, manifested in the 'ideal academic', is constituted in social and gendered relations. Two research questions guide Lund's empirical investigation and analyses: "How are gendered social relations of academic work organised and enacted among scholars in changing academia?" and, "How are the social relations coordinated and shaped by texts in and around the practices that define and evaluate the quality and potential of academic work?"

21   Choosing a Standpoint as a Point of Departure

Junior female scholars at Aalto University in Finland were chosen as the point of departure in Lund's research as they are the group most likely to be vulnerable to the rupture between stated ideology (gender-equality and neo-liberalism) and the demands and doings of everyday life, due to the present gender structure found in universities as well as in family life. That is, both men and women in different university positions might experience this rupture, but junior female scholars are positioned to make this rupture most visible and, accordingly, are a voice most worthy of our attention. Focusing on Aalto University (a new university formed along the lines of neo-liberalism), how they do the 'ideal academic' institutionally, and how all this is experienced by a group trying to get in, is strategic. By using the institutional ethnography approach in highlighting such a concentrated and focused case—Aalto, the 'ideal academic', and junior female scholars—we are able to draw conclusions from this case that can be more generalised to other universities 'on the move'.

21.1   A Method of Inquiry as a Guideline
In understanding how academic quality and excellence, manifested in the 'ideal academic', is constituted in social and gendered relations, the steps and concepts of institutional ethnography were followed in Lund's study. The *standpoint* (point of departure) was junior female scholars; it is their *work-knowledge* of how quality, excellence, and the ideal academic is done that is explicated, and the *local-, trans-, and extra-local social and gender relations* that these women's activities are connected to. Here, *texts* play a central role in linking the local to the extra-local. How ruling relations enter the everyday life and work-knowledge of the women in their gendered relations—in terms of *institutional captures*—the objectifying discourse defining quality, excellence, and the ideal academic reveal how the ideal academic becomes gendered. Three themes are herein picked out to illuminate the process in praxis: *the work of becoming excellent* (chapter 5), *the work of boasting* (chapter 6), and *the work of love* (chapter 7).

On the first theme, *the work of becoming excellent*, Lund demonstrated how texts and people's experiences intertwine to produce a certain kind of ideal academic, who should realise a certain kind of masculinity (egocentrism, careerism, and informality), age (young), sexuality (heterosexuality), and internationality (speaking fluent English). People express a belief in the existence of gender equality, while at the same time presenting gender inequality in their own lives. These inequalities are then expressly understood as located in individuals rather than in institutions or organisations.

As for *the work of boasting*, meaning exaggerated promotion or branding of the self or the organisation, the focus is on what is boasted about and how it is done. Boasting is present in everyday work, such as completing applications, reading strategic texts, or participating in occasions filled with proud and boastful language. The institutional and organisational language of excellence includes cruel optimism, which disables rather than enables people's work in academia. In spite of the apparent neutrality, the language of promoting excellence includes 'doing' gender, particularly doing masculinity. Ironically, this situation may also provide legitimation for women's boasting.

The *work of love*, finally, is related to writing and publishing. The passion to write and publish in academic journals, which here are defined as high-level journals, are partly contradictory aims. Review processes, standardisation of the structures of articles, and a variety of methodological and theoretical standpoints cause disturbances for researchers and force them to adopt trans-local criteria for publishing. However, love and passion are not free sources of motivation to publish. They are also "shaped within social and ruling relations" (ibid.: 239). Lund shows that passion and trans-local relations of ruling become intertwined and support each other, demonstrating "how social relations of gender place people differently in terms of activating this love" (ibid.: 254).

In conclusion, one could say that Lund's study demonstrates not only that the academic habitus is gendered but also that the entrance of neo-liberalistic ruling relations will imply a further masculinisation of academic work, in spite of an explicit gender equality ideology and a gender-neutral language. The implication of this main- and male-streaming of academic work for the production of knowledge is explicitly highlighted and questioned in her work.

22   Coupling the Approaches of Smith and Bourdieu: A Final Discussion

22.1   *From Institutional Ethnography to Field Analyses*

Beginning from below, from the local, like an institutional ethnographer, limits the field of investigation, no matter how generalisable the results might be to other local positions and relations similar to those studied. Taking my own study as an example, it cannot tell us about how academic teaching (and supervision) is done, or documented into an accounting of hours, in other disciplines, such as the sciences or medicine. It might not be experienced as an issue to such scientific staff due to the way they teach and supervise (in the lab, to groups, on one's own research project or theme, and so forth). They might not even fill out any such reports. Their work knowledge is accordingly different and maybe, in turn, so is the role of ruling relations. Analyses of the work knowledge emanating from different disciplinary positions are required if we are to understand the role of ruling devices such as the accounting of hours for the functioning of the university institution. A field analyses á la Bourdieu, focusing on the power structure and struggle between the disciplines, could explicate the role of such ruling devices in different disciplines; if it results in change, or reactions, or the opposite. These kinds of ruling devices are more likely in accordance with the way work is done in some disciplines than in others, that is, their effects will be more dramatic to the work done in particular disciplines. A field analysis could accordingly elucidate the results of the institutional ethnography by positioning them on the field, and this would broaden our understanding.

The same kind of arguments can be made regarding Lund's study of how the ideal academic is done. The ruling devices for how the ideal academic is to be done might more or less accord with the traditions of the disciplines. A field analysis here could also uncover the role of such ruling devices in different disciplines, and just as in the case of teaching, the ruling devices are likely more in accordance with how research is done and published in some disciplines than in others. Further, the consequences of such ruling for the knowledge produced will thus vary with the disciplines.

22.2   *From History and Theory to* IE

The argument above indicates the importance of analysing an IE study in light of historical and theoretical understandings, not only field analyses, so as to contextualise the findings. In my own study, presented above, an understanding of the potential specificity of *public welfare-state ruling relations* could and should have informed an understanding of the role of new public management. This would have enabled me to understand more fully the ambivalence I encountered in my study but also given me a chance to question the general concepts and understandings of NPM as well as of the welfare state. Not searching for historical and theoretical specificity of ruling relations might cause us to miss a chance to see both specific variations, as well as specific fundamental relations informing ruling devices and their implementation. It might, for example, be argued that in *public welfare management*, the extensive ruling from above is more dialectic, allowing for feedback from below (giving new content to categories, setting them aside, inventing new categories, and so forth). Professional judgment and discretion might consequently play a more vital and different role during public welfare management. *Institutional circuits*—a concept that captures how a category or concept, for example, publication scores within academia, is used as governance from global relations to the local and back again (Griffith and Smith, 2014: 12–13, illustrated on page 301)—might actually be a part of the parcel in public welfare management, although the very fact of ruling in the name of welfare might also make opposition less likely. On the other hand, one could argue that welfare ideology might be the very foundation for such opposition. Does welfare ruling and public management imply more obedience or more resistance, or maybe both? We obviously need to know more about if and how specifying ruling relations, such as welfare state ruling, make a difference, and this theoretical and historical question also needs to be raised within IE studies. A lack of such a background might result in empirical IE studies from different societies being quite alike, as variations on a theme, when, in fact, the very theme might be in question.

Along these lines, an understanding of the welfare state challenges our understandings of ruling relations. Objectification in the name of welfare, aiming at equality of class, gender, and ethnicity—that is, *public welfare objectification*—results in specific experiences and reactions that are characterised by ambivalence and insecurity. In the Nordic context of today, such ruling permeates all aspects of everyday life to an extent that is unheard of in most democracies elsewhere. As such, *Nordic public welfare objectification* presents a case where the more general patterns and implications of ruling can be highlighted and discussed. This is not to underestimate the differences between the Nordic countries regarding the design of welfare ruling in different spheres, for example, in higher education; academic work is ruled in quite different ways in Finland, Denmark, and Sweden. Still, it seems as if the good intentions of welfare state ruling 'make it work' smoothly in the Nordic context, whereas, in other countries, such ruling might be taken as the brute force of the market that silences opposition and guarantees compliance. The methodological consequences of an approach like this, as to *which local and trans-local relations we start and end our studies with*, will always need to be problematised and discussed, but within these frames, an IE approach can provide content to studied local and trans-local relations that, in turn, might challenge the theoretical concepts and understandings we commenced with.

New public management must thus be approached as part of the welfare ruling relations—as *new public welfare management*—due to its functioning within the welfare context. In the name of welfare, through aiming towards equality regarding both treatment and distribution of resources (in terms of class, gender, and ethnicity), objectification can be made legitimate in the eyes of its citizens in their daily activities at work and at home. The ambivalence and insecurity demonstrated, not only in my study presented above but also in other IE studies of NPM, for example, in Ann Christin Nilsen's work on daycare personnel and how their gaze towards children at risk (2015; 2017), is constructed. Such studies can be interpreted as illuminations of how objectification is experienced and handled in everyday work. *Public welfare objectification*, then, is it to be considered a specific form of ruling relations, resulting in specific reactions (ambivalence and insecurity) or non-reactions.

Taking *public welfare objectification* as a starting point is perhaps the key to understanding why NPM works 'everywhere' but for very different reasons.

Compliance in response to brute force or good intentions are vastly different situations, calling for different political actions.

22.3   From Field Analyses to Institutional Ethnography

If an institutional ethnography could be argued to merit from being incorporated into a field analysis or other theoretical and historical understandings, would the opposite also be true? What would field analysis gain by making use of the approach of institutional ethnography?

When undertaking field analysis, a standpoint (a position where people are situated) is *not* chosen by unravelling local and extra-local relations, as in an IE study, as a map of relations to explicate the role of ruling relations in everyday life and work. However, such a position could also have been chosen as a starting point, without abandoning the approach of the field analysis. Hereby, a discovery of how things are done, from the perspective of the knowers, which is not theoretically predetermined, would be made possible. Other issues and relations than those emanating from a 'pure' field analysis might materialise, changing the gaze and understanding of the field. Gender can serve as an obvious example: taking a standpoint implies taking gender into account, the way Lund did in her study of the doing of the 'ideal academic'. Not taking a standpoint, like Bourdieu in *Homo Academicus*, implies not taking gender into account throughout the analysis, hereby masking the gender aspect of the academic field, its gendered power structure, and its struggles. Besides taking a standpoint as a starting point for empirical exploration, there is nothing in the approach of field analysis that would not allow for a study of ruling devices, such as my study of the accounting of hours. The focus on ruling relations and their textual expressions within institutional ethnography help us to see the role of ruling relations in everyday life and work. To also maintain this focus when carrying out a field analysis á la Bourdieu would imply a greater concentration on the role of new public management within the university. Moreover, as earlier argued, a field analysis could elucidate how new public management is handled in the power structure of the field.

Finally, it is generally accepted that different approaches generate different questions and answers, which legitimate a particular choice of approach, facilitating the research process. Of course, this also holds true for the approaches of Bourdieu and Smith and represents the very reason for the lengthy empirical examples given in this chapter to illuminate the empirical implications of each approach.

Thus, in spite of their shared and profound methodological foundation— investigating and problematising the researcher's relation to the object of study, the relation not the individual as the analytical entity, an ethnographic approach, a focus on power/ruling and emphasising discovery through empirical investigations—the goals of Bourdieu and Smith, and consequently their approaches, are quite differently outlined. For Bourdieu, the goal is to illuminate social hierarchies where people are relationally positioned in the power struggle of the field. The habitus of his homo academicus is, therefore, explained through the different forms of capital acquired positionally within and between disciplines. It is the power structure and struggle of the academic field that is the target of Bourdieu's approach. However, while habitus, understood as embodied habits acquired in specific relations, can be said to be a result (although not the only one) of the Bourdieu approach, it would, in fact, be the starting point of one of Smith's IE investigations, where the aim is to illuminate the work knowledge of the academic so as to uncover the role of ruling relations. This implies a directed investigation of the work-knowledge (that is, a specific way of investigating habitus), focusing on the role of trans- and extra-local relations, often in the form of texts and activated in the local relations. The aim of this linking and mapping of relations is to explicate to us how we are connected with ruling relations in our everyday life and work, and it is precisely here that I believe that the IE approach can offer a contribution to Bourdieu's field analysis approach. Simultaneously though, the lack of focus on social hierarchies, power structures, and struggles when undertaking IE might make the research results from such studies more contestable. As I have argued above, a field analysis á la Bourdieu, or other historical and contextual understandings of ruling relations, can shed new light on the results of an IE study like my own.

To conclude, there is a need for both approaches and for them to be as fully developed and explored as possible so as to make 'epistemological distinctions'. As I have tried to argue here, each of these approaches would benefit from the use of the other, without abandoning the approach as such. New public management and the international mainstreaming of academia call for such an approach, where the indicators of academic power are clarified through institutional ethnography, hereby founding a platform for analyses of an academic field, as well as a platform for textual analyses illuminating the international academic field. It is demanding but possible and, I believe, most fruitful to the development of sociology as a discipline.

References

Barthes, R. (1977). "From work to text", in *Image, Music, Text: Essays*. Glasgow: Fontana Press.

Bourdieu, P. (1984). *Distinction*. London: Routledge

Bourdieu, P. (1988). *Homo Academicus*. Cambridge: Polity Press.

Bourdieu, P. (1990a). *In Other Words: Essays Towards a Reflexive Sociology*. Cambridge: Polity Press.

Bourdieu, P. (1990b). *The Logic of Practice*. Stanford, CA: Stanford University Press.

Bourdieu, P., Chamboredon, J.-C., and Passeron, J.-C. (1991). *The Craft of Sociology: Epistemological Preliminaries*. Berlin: Walter de Gruyter.

Durkheim, É. (1982). *The Rules of Sociological Method*. New York: The Free Press.

Griffith, A.I. and Smith, D.E. (eds.). (2014). *Under New Public Management*. Toronto: University of Toronto Press

Lamont, M. (2009). *How Professors Think: Inside the Curious World of Academic Judgment*. Cambridge, MA: Harvard University Press.

Lund, R.W.B. (2015). *Doing the Ideal Academic: Gender, Excellence and Changing Academia*. Doctoral dissertation. Aalto University: Aalto University Publication series, 98/2015.

Nilsen, A.C.E. (2015). "På jakt etter styringsrelasjoner ved «tidlig innsats» i barnehagen" [In search of ruling relations in "early effort" in the institution of daycare centres], in K. Widerberg (ed.). *I hjertet av velferdsstaten. En invitasjon til institusjonell etnografi* [In the heart of the welfare-state: An invitation to institutional ethnography]. Oslo: Cappelen Damm.

Nilsen, A.C.E. (2017). *Bekymringsbarn blir til. En institusjonell etnografi av tidlig innsats som styringsrasjonal i barnehagen* [Problem children are 'made up': An institutional ethnography of early intervention in the institution of daycare centres]. Doctoral thesis: University of Agder.

Smith, D.E. (1992). "Sociology from women's experience: A reaffirmation", *Sociological Theory* 10 (1): 88–98.

Smith, D.E. (1996). "Telling the truth after postmodernism", *Symbolic Interaction* 19 (3): 171–202.

Smith, D.E. (1999). *Writing the Social: Critique, Theory, and Investigations*. Toronto: University of Toronto Press.

Smith, D.E. (2001). "Texts and the ontology of organizations and institutions", *Studies in Cultures, Organizations and Societies* 7 (2): 159–198.

Smith, D.E. (2005). *Institutional Ethnography: A Sociology for People*. Oxford: AltaMira Press.

Widerberg, K. (2014). "In the best of interests? New public management, the welfare state, and the case of academic work: An ethnographic exploration", in A. Blok and P. Gundelach (eds.). *The Elementary Forms of Sociological Knowledge*. Department of Sociology, University of Copenhagen, Copenhagen

Widerberg, K. (2015a). "En invitasjon til institusjonell etnografi" [An invitation to institutional ethnography], in K. Widerberg (ed.). *I hjertet av velferdsstaten. En invitasjon til institusjonell etnografi* [In the heart of the welfare-state: An invitation to institutional ethnography]. Oslo: Cappelen Damm.

Widerberg, K. (2015b). "Akademia. Om styring i den akademiske hverdag" [Academia. On ruling in academic everyday life], in K. Widerberg (ed.). *I hjertet av velferdsstaten. En invitasjon til institusjonell etnografi* [In the heart of the welfare-state: An invitation to institutional ethnography]. Oslo: Cappelen Damm.

Widerberg, K. (2017). "Dorothy E. Smith", in R. Stones (ed.). *Key Sociologial Thinkers*. Basingstoke; New York, NY: Palgrave Macmillan.

CHAPTER 12

Living Theory

Reflections on Four Decades of Teaching Social Theory

Michael Burawoy

It's January 1977.[1] I've won the lottery. Through a series of unlikely events, I've landed a job at Berkeley—a dream come true. It was an exciting time in sociology and especially at Berkeley, the flagship campus of what was claimed to be the greatest public university in the world. The campus hosted 29,000 students, 1,200 faculty. In 1964, Mario Savio, leader of the Free Speech Movement, in a famous speech, had assailed the university's bureaucratic machine, calling on the students "to put your bodies upon the gears and upon the wheels ... upon the levers, upon all the apparatus, and you've got to make it stop!" Clark Kerr, the President of the University of California, mastermind of the masterplan for free college education for all who desired it—today in tatters—was fired by then Governor Reagan for not putting out the fire. Indeed, the Free Speech Movement inaugurated a decade of political turmoil on campus, with sociology one of its epi-centres.

When I arrived, the department was still in shell shock, dispersed in fragments. Neil Smelser, then department Chair, had determined that I should teach the required one-quarter course in social theory—never mind the B's and C's I'd gotten for my papers in social theory at the University of Chicago. Was he punishing me or the students? It wasn't clear. Whatever you want, Professor Smelser, I'm at your service. When I asked Art Stinchcombe, why he had 'incomprehensibly' (or so I thought) moved from Berkeley to the University of Chicago, he told me that he couldn't stand teaching Berkeley undergraduates, who looked on so bored and uninterested. At Chicago he wouldn't have to teach any undergraduates. As for my new colleagues at Berkeley, they never seemed to talk about teaching. They just complained that undergraduates didn't know anything and were not interested in knowing anything.

Not knowing much myself I didn't know what to expect. With some trepidation I diligently prepared for the course, blessed with two wonderful teaching

---

1   This chapter was stimulated by a seminar organized by Johan Fredrik Rye at the Norwegian University of Science and Technology at Trondheim. I'm especially grateful to Johan for his interrogation of the way I teach forcing me to reflect and conceptualise what it is that I do.

assistants. That January, I walked into the classroom of some 60 students, scattered among the seats, and gazed up at their fresh and nonchalant faces. I told them I was new to teaching, never even been an undergraduate in the US. I was going to tell them about social theory from the perspective of the division of labour. I then had the presence of mind to ask them what they thought was the meaning of 'division of labour'. As the seconds ticked away and they found the silence unbearable, someone proffered an answer, and then someone else, and soon they were competing for my attention. And, as they say, the rest is history.

Mario Savio's words were prophetic. Today, over the 43 years I've been teaching the university has been transformed—it stutters from one financial crisis to the next, it is now a revenue seeking machine, not least through increasing student fees; it has a bloated administration trying to run the university as though it were a private corporation. With 43,000 students, the campus is bursting at the seams and the costs of attendance are soaring. Students are paying more for less. My theory classes are no longer 60 students but anywhere between 200 and 300; they come from very different backgrounds; so far, the number of teaching assistants has grown proportionately but it's not clear how long that will last. The required theory course has also grown, not just in size but also in length, from one quarter to two quarters to two semesters. Yet, at the chalk face—I still use chalk—things are much the same as I scramble for student attention, competing with the internet rather than newspapers, cajoling them into studying difficult texts between their extensive subsistence labours and the demands of other courses. I like to think that social theory lives on as strongly as ever, but I do face new challenges, in particular a healthy scepticism toward the menu of canonical thinkers.

1   Living Theory

What should we do with those "dead white men" of the 19th century—Marx, Weber, and Durkheim—whose work we teach as the "classics" and whom we regard as the 'founders' of sociology? Sociology is unusual in our continual embrace of founding figures. As Arthur Stinchcombe (1982) reminds us, they inspire us to raise profound questions, to provide exemplary research, to offer models of theoretical thinking, to bring unity to our fragmented discipline, to help to define our identity. If we do need them, can they be brought back from the dead? Can they be resuscitated? Can we turn them into living theory? In this chapter I will suggest a way of doing this, what I call the 'ethnographic approach' to the teaching of theory that I contrast with the 'survey approach'.

There are two meanings to 'living theory', two ways to make theory live. On the one hand, one can make 'theory' live by giving it new energy in the way we read and reconstruct those original texts. Teaching social theory is a relation to old texts, and that relationship has to change as we face new historical challenges in the present. What makes a work classic or canonical is the way it transcends its own time. Yes, Adam Smith refers to '10,000 naked savages' but his ideas about the division of labour and the market still capture the imagination of so many. Yes, Émile Durkheim talks about the relative brain size of men and women, but his understanding of how the division of labour can lead to solidarity still inspires our thinking. Yes, Marx and Engels overlook the divisive forces of race and gender in the formation of the working class, but still their writing on capitalism endures. Not only does the reading and rereading of canonical texts bring new insights and new life to old works but the relation *among* these canonical texts also changes. The canon as a set of relations is itself a living entity.

But there is a second meaning of 'living theory'. Our relation to theory gives new energy to old texts, but in so doing it gives us new energy. As we make theories live, so we inhabit them and give ourselves new lives. This is the difference between *making theory live* and *living in theory*. We are all theorists, we all have cognitive maps of the world, that's how we live in the world. That is the double meaning of common sense—a shared theory but one that we don't think about because and despite dictating our lives. Being explicit about theory offers us new ways of living in the world. Adam Smith tells us that specialisation is good, we are not destined from birth to occupy a certain place, but we can change that place, and if we are diligent, whether we are janitors or entrepreneurs everyone will benefit through the sharing of a 'universal opulence'. Many still believe this. Marx, on the other hand, attunes us to a very different notion of the world in which we live—instead of universal opulence he thinks the division of labour leads to the polarisation of wealth and poverty based on an account of capitalism, its dynamics, and its possible supersession. Durkheim, on the other hand, is less interested in the economic consequences of the division of labour and instead focuses on the conditions under which the division of labour gives rise to solidarity. Adopting a theory is like picking up a new language; it leads us to think differently but also behave differently. So, theory has a life of its own but also propels our own lives.

Well, you might say, this is all very well in 'theory' but what about 'in practice'? In the remainder of this chapter I will try to elaborate the meaning of living theory through teaching social theory to undergraduates. My practice has become 'common sense' as it has evolved intuitively and spontaneously over 40 years, but now I attempt to make it explicit, turning that practice into theory—a theory of practice.

By convention, teaching comes in two stripes. There is the lecture format in which pearls of wisdom pour from the orator into empty, waiting minds as opposed to the dialogic format which works through the active participation of the student. These are less hard and fast types and more a continuum between extremes. Paulo Freire (1970) famously distinguished between a banking model in which knowledge is ingested and accumulated and problem-oriented education that embarks from the lived experience of student. I lean toward the latter, only I don't join the lives of my students as Freire did, but try to bring their lives into the classroom by putting them into conversation with great texts. A tall order, indeed. In reflecting on what I have been doing for the last 43 years, I revise and elaborate Freire's model by distinguishing between the more conventional 'survey' approach to teaching social theory and what I call the 'ethnographic' approach.

2   The Survey Approach

I began teaching social theory as a survey of so-called, collectively-agreed-upon great theorists. That's how social theory is generally taught. One "great" theorist follows another, usually chronologically; the dilemma and debate are not about how to teach but what to teach—which theorists to teach, which to include, and by the same token which to exclude. Inevitably, in my first attempts I introduced far too many candidates as I hopped from one theorist to the next. This survey approach offers students a broad panorama of the mountain range. Different instructors will paint different panoramas, but a distant mountain range it remains. It is useful for students to catch a glimpse of the mountain range to be conquered, an enticing invitation to the nooks and crannies, the escarpments and ravines of each mountain. But that's for a later time that usually never comes.

The survey approach has its drawbacks. I use the word 'survey' in the technical sense as it derives from the methodology of survey research. It involves collecting excerpts from different theories or from secondary summaries, assembled in textbooks. They are treated as discrete data points, a sample from the population of possible theories, a population of great works understood as such by convention. The idea is to be inclusive and representative. If the first question is how to draw the sample of theories, the second question is how to classify them: conflict theory vs. consensus theory, macro-sociology vs. micro sociology, structure vs. agency are three popular classifications.

As in the social survey, this approach suffers from a double decontextualization: the theories are severed from their historical production and they are also separated from one another as though they are independent entities. The dialogue between context and theorist and between successive theorists is muted. Students are easily overwhelmed by both the scope and the decontextualization, that can be overcome by substituting superficial summaries for the original theories. They may capture the mountain range, but they don't experience the gruelling climb up the mountain or enjoy the stupendous view from the top.

If the text-book survey is flawed, then what are the alternatives? There are, of course, modifications of the survey giving it a more interpretive slant. First, theory and theorists are brought into a relationship with one another by examining the world in which they lived. However, if it is to be more than an introductory background that places theory and theorist in their lives and times, this approach requires a lot from the student: command of a sophisticated theory of knowledge as well as a knowledge of history. Done properly, this can be a slippery slope away from the survey to the study of a single theorist lying at the intersection of history and biography.

A second modification of the survey is to select excerpts from great thinkers of the past, based less on a representative sample and more on the teacher's own theoretical vision. In their monumental two-volume *Theories of Society*, for example, Talcott Parsons and his colleagues (1961) compiled a compendium of excerpts, interpreted as steppingstones to his own theory. Theorists are connected to one another in a teleological manner, culminating in the architectonics of structural functionalism.

These more interpretive approaches break from the survey approach in two contradictory directions: the first underlines the singularity of theories as the production of specific contexts while the second strips away the context and instead draws theories together around a common theme or project. But it's still a survey.

When all is said and done, the survey approach assumes a unique reading of a text that has classical status whose rudiments the student has to "learn". If there is context it is usually relegated to some historical background. The student digests the theory and absorbs its content. Students are then supposed to regurgitate the theory in examinations calling for summaries that are right or wrong. It assumes that the student is a passive recipient into whom knowledge is poured. The students are not living theory, nor does theory live.

Over time dissatisfaction with the survey approach led me to an alternative ethnographic approach. Here the central feature is dialogue. Rather than empty vessels, students come to class as actors in a collective drama—they re-enact their own lives through theory. They do this not through passively imbibing texts but by actively building theory in a collective project orchestrated by the teacher. Students not only build theories out of their separate parts, but they build relations between theories, what one might call a theoretical tradition, actively comparing theories to one another and to their own common sense. As they actively participate in building, students enter into the theory as though it were a language to be spoken, and a new common sense arises through their engagement with the world. They are not observers of a distant mountain range but participants in the making and following of cognitive maps of the world around them. They become theorists of their own lives. In their hands, those dead white men come alive as they live in and through theory. In the remainder of this chapter I elaborate the ethnographic approach to theory.

3   Building Theory

In opposition to the survey, the ethnographic method focuses on a series of carefully chosen *extracts* from the original texts of each theorist, extracts that students can manageably study in the allotted time—from a few paragraphs to 10 or more pages per class, depending on their difficulty. That's easier said than done as it is always tempting to assign more than students can absorb. These extracts are like pieces of a jig-saw puzzle that are slowly assembled in the course of a dialogue between teacher and taught. Like the ethnographer's field notes, the extracts are read and reread as they are put into relation with previous extracts (from the same theorist). Each extract is interpreted in the light of what came before and is later re-interpreted in the light of what follows. Slowly but surely, piece by piece, we create a picture of the whole—a picture that is dependent on the original extracts chosen by the teacher.

Once the theoretical architecture is built, we subject it to systematic critique, what I call 'ransacking'. Just as ethnography advances through crises in the field, so theory advances through the challenges it faces, both external anomalies and internal contradictions. External anomalies, misfits between theory and data, derive from historical analysis, but, just as important, from the lived experiences of the students themselves. When the world surprises theory—when the division of labour does not give rise to universal opulence, when the working class is not revolutionary—we are led back to contradictions, false assumptions, erroneous logic. Excavating the text reveals the contradictions. Thus, at one point, Smith says the division of labour leads to innovation, at another (subsidiary) point to stupefication; at one point, Marx says class struggle is the grave digger of capitalism, at another (subsidiary) point its saviour.

Great theories harbour great contradictions that feed their continued relevance and animate debate. The point, therefore, is not to use anomalies and contradictions to dismiss a given theory, but rather to try to resolve them through *reconstructing* the theory on its own terms, that is on the basis of its core assumptions rather than by adding arbitrary postulates. The goal is to refute the refutation. Students gradually master this technique of reconstructive critique, coming up with their own imaginative solutions. This is building theory.

4   Enacting Theory

The ethnographic method has its performative side. If surveying social theory calls for the formal lecture, the commanding authority of a great intellect that impresses and inspires with its lofty message, making a compelling case for each theorist, the ethnographic method calls on the teacher to step down from the lectern and join the students. Pedagogy is organized on the basis of student participation, which follows its own rules, especially important when student enrolments get into the hundreds. All dialogue in the classroom is limited to the text in hand, which students are required to bring to class. But later, at certain points other theorists (but only those who have been assigned in the course) and the personal experiences of students can be invoked. Before the class begins, I write out the questions and reading for next time as well as the plan for the day. I begin the class by summarising where I think we are, where we have come from, and where I hope we are going. We then launch into a collective discussion structured by the questions that were raised in the previous class, always in reference to the text in hand.

Thus, the classes are conducted Socratic-style in which a presumptively known answer is elicited from students through an expanding discussion based on specific quotations from the text, often represented visually in the form of an accumulating diagram on the board—yes, so far, I've resisted PowerPoint. This allows anyone to participate without unduly advantaging those who claim to have prior knowledge of theory. This is education for all, not just those well-endowed with cultural capital. When someone hesitantly sticks up his or her hand for the first time, it is up to me to affirm the student's contribution. That can often call for a certain agility in bringing the student's contribution into line with the on-going discussion. Compulsive-participators are given participation quotas. In principle, any student can contest what the instructor says, which the students invariably do. Indeed, they discover flaws in my arguments, give alternative interpretations of the texts, and in the second semester, they often have me on the ropes as I vainly try to defend each theorist in turn. The presumptively known end point is never reached; having learned how to think theoretically, students have collectively taken the course in new directions. Uncertainty of outcome draws students into creative engagement.

The lecture hall becomes a theatre of participation in which the students become actors with names, real or fictitious, developing their own characters as the plot unfolds. Students become orators as they are called on to read from Marx or Lenin, from Durkheim or Weber, from Beauvoir or Patricia Hill Collins, thereby injecting life into complex texts. Elaborate symbolic incentives—such as affirmation through awarding BB s (Bloody Brilliant)—and public humiliation when rules are violated (students not bringing their books to class) induce but also set limits on participation. The drama is intensified as the class develops its own idioms and customs. I explain to them that Social Theory (ST) is a powerful drug that can be imbibed anywhere, disrupting their lives, turning them in directions the students never anticipated. Student worlds tangle with the evolving conversations within and among theories.

5   Engaging the World

Social theory is difficult. It's not an assemblage of facts. Each theory is a language unto itself that can be learned only with discipline and practice. One learns by speaking, by applying theory to the everyday. To facilitate engagement with the world, but also to make comparison among theories feasible, we need to find a key concept that will orient the course and guide the selection of extracts. I have tried a number of key concepts but have always returned to the idea of the division of labour, because, in principle, it is simple, because the concept is at the heart of so much social theory, because everyone is familiar with it and has participated in the division of labour whether at work, in the classroom, in the sports team, or in the home, and because I was interested in it, being a sociologist of work. If 19th century social theory can shed light on this everyday phenomenon, then living theory can advance. A set of orienting questions, then, drive the course, questions that derive from Adam Smith's apparently simple theory of the division of labour:

- What is the division of labour? What are its different forms?
- What are the origins, mechanisms of development and future of the division of labour?
- What are the conditions of existence of the division of labour?

- What are the consequences of the division of labour (a) for individuals and (b) for society as a whole?

With these questions students can easily tie theory to their daily lives, further encouraged by teaching assistants. Apart from the 'lectures' twice a week, there are also discussion sections, 20 students in size, meeting twice a week for 50 minutes, and led by devoted and creative graduate students. That's where the real learning takes place. They are there to make theory live in the day-to-day world, but also to impose the discipline of reading, writing, and thinking. Along with one-page reading memos due every week, each semester students have to write a 'theory in action' paper (one thousand words) that puts a theorist to work on a current event or their own experiences. Mid-term and final exams are a series of 750-word take-home papers (once again less is more) that challenge them to put theorists into conversation with each other over some empirical phenomenon or an application of a theory to current events as described in an article from a newspaper or magazine.

At the end of the first semester, I try to broaden their historical imagination by supplying students with a series of short but pointed journalistic pieces on a single concrete episode of attempted social change—the revolutions of Cuba, Russia, and Nicaragua or liberation struggles in South Africa, Palestine, and the United States. They are asked to examine the event in question through the successive lens of Marx, Lenin, Gramsci, and Fanon, each sketch being no more than 750 words. They have to be clear in order to be concise and they have to be concise in order to be clear.

At the end of the second semester, the course culminates in a 20-minute oral examination with the students' teaching assistant in which each student has to create a vision of social theory by reconstructing the entire course as a conversation among the theorists. They create their own jigsaw with the pieces at their disposal. They bring images, pictures, drawings in a poster presentation. In preparing for the oral they demonstrate how theories can become part of their mindsets that that they will take with them into their future lives.

The success of the course depends on the devotion of the teaching assistants, all PhD students in the department. The labour of preparation, of delivery, of consultation, of grading generally takes more than the 20 hours for which they are paid. My goal is to develop their commitment to a joint project that I lay out in a manual I have created over the years. At the end of every week, on Thursday evenings, we meet for two hours in my office to discuss administrative issues, to dissect texts that they have poured over, to normalise the grading of student papers, to discuss problematic students, but above all to exchange ideas of teaching techniques, what works, what doesn't. This continues in a more informal way when I take them out to dinner. Their sense of vocation as future teachers has already been instilled before they begin and hardly requires these rituals of solidarity, but it is my recognition of how integral they are to the teaching project.[2]

6   Connecting Theories

The Socratic method presumes I have it all worked out. The final goal is all worked out, but in getting there we take false turns, follow unusual digressions, deal with unexpected disruptions, such as strikes, that become theatrical opportunities for living theory. I take the class out onto the picket line where armed with a megaphone we proceed to conduct a discussion of how our theorist will assess the situation, sometimes with interruptions and contributions from the assembled strikers. Still, despite and through these diversions I do have a vision of where we are going even if it is not always clear how we are going to get there.

To be specific. The course begins with Adam Smith's famous celebration of the division of labour. Critical interrogation of those early pages in *The Wealth of Nations* leads to three key but unexamined questions concerning the division of labour: Marxism's question of *exploitation*: who controls the surplus produced by increased productivity? Durkheim's question of *solidarity*: can self-interest hold society together? Weber, Foucault, and Beauvoir call attention to the question of *domination*: what's its form and how is it sustained? Accordingly, the first semester shows how Marxism is a living tradition that develops successively from Marx and Engels to Lenin to Gramsci and to Fanon, each theorist working off anomalies and contradictions found in previous theorists and highlighted by specific historical challenges. Specifically, the deconstruction of the genius of Marx and Engels gives rise to three shortcomings in their account of the division of labour: an undeveloped theory of the state, a flawed theory of class struggle and a largely absent theory of transition. These shortcomings are tackled, in turn by Lenin, Gramsci, and Fanon, each making contributions and, by the same token, leaving us with new problems.

You might call this an internal dialogue of theory reconstruction as opposed to an external dialogue of critique that takes place in the second semester where Durkheim faces off against Marx, Weber against Lenin, Foucault against Gramsci, and Beauvoir against Fanon. These critical dialogues do not lead to

---

2   Teaching assistants have written essays describing how they have taught this course, including a recently published article. See Herring, Rosaldo, Seim and Shestakofsky (2016).

the conquest of one theorist over another or a progressive theoretical tradition, but to the clarification of what makes each of them so special, viz., their assumptions about human beings that allow them to conceive of society, their vision of history that allows them to project an alternative future (or the dangers of doing so), their explanation of social reproduction that allows them to understand social change, and their innovative methodology that allows them to put their theory to work in empirical studies.

We end with feminist theory—and we read MacKinnon and Collins after Beauvoir to obtain an intimation of a feminist tradition—not only to follow a chronology, not only to develop a critique of classical theory for overlooking gender, but to bring theory home, forcing students to reflect on their own lives and their own place in the (gendered) division of labour. Feminism turns the theory of the division of labour back on the theorist, calling attention to the social location of the theorists we studied. Classical theory constitutes the theorist as manufacturing theory from outside society, which, as feminists insist, is an impossible place to inhabit. Marx, Durkheim, and Weber were part of the society they studied—the theorist cannot be separated from the world they study, but nor can the student.

As the conclusion to the course, feminism is the most vivid expression of the significance of social theory, namely, to question the entrenched common sense we develop as participants in the world, to underline the presence of theory not only in disembodied texts but also in our embodied lives. In denaturalizing our lives and challenging common sense, social theory shows that the world need not be the way it is and explores what it would mean to inhabit a better world. In their different ways it is the utopian impulse that motivates and inspires social theory, infusing energy and meaning into the substantive fields of sociology. In the age of the internet, distance learning, and on-line courses, in the face of the degradation of higher education, it is especially important to uphold the idea of living theory: living with theory, living in theory, and even living for theory.

7   Teaching Theory: Living or Dying?

In trying to elucidate my pedagogy, I'm in danger of freezing it, and once frozen it cannot live, it can only die. The course has begun to atrophy. While trying to resuscitate those dead white men, I have myself become old if not yet dead. A certain ritualism has entered the theatre; students are playing along without really being engaged. The distance between myself and students has grown. Passions forged in the 1970s are out of tune with the present. How many students were even born when I began teaching in 1977? And it's not just a matter of age but it's a matter of class and race. My increasing salary, after all, is made possible by their increasing fees.

I've become complacent, if not arrogant, and, perish the thought, perhaps even condescending. The intense anxiety that suffused my performance in the early decades has ebbed away. No longer is there impatience when students don't do the reading. I remain calm, coaxing them rather than scolding them. My provocations and humiliations secure attention; they no longer incite guilt, but more likely resentment. I watch my evaluations as I've never watched them before—the numbers sink if ever so slightly, and complaints creep in about minor matters, concealing a rising distrust. Without trust all teaching collapses but especially the ethnographic method.

I've changed, but students have also changed. 40 years ago, I would gaze out onto a sea of whiteness, but today students are far more diverse, from different countries, from different races, from different genders and sexualities, from different ages. Single mothers, undocumented students, formerly incarcerated students announce their presence with aplomb. They challenge me to make the course relevant. Now over half the students have transferred from two-year community colleges—for them arriving in the big Cal is exciting, mesmerising, but daunting. They are determined to meet the challenge, but the challenges take their toll, emotionally, physically, and materially.

Students are paying for their education as they never did. If tuition was about $630 a year when I began, it is now $16,000. Many don't pay because their family income is less than $80,000 a year but still, they face escalating costs of attendance as rents hit the roof. Students double up, triple up, some are homeless, and many have become commuters, have moved out to distant places where rents are less. It means that students work longer hours in their jobs and take out loans. They want to get out quickly; so, they take more courses than they should—all to enter an ever more precarious labour market—and from there to support children, siblings, and parents also trying to make their way in the world. Yet still they manage to pay attention, come to class, do their assignments, cajoled into taking theory seriously by overworked and underpaid, but devoted teaching assistants.

When the field site becomes repetitive and predictable, it's time for the ethnographer to intervene, disturb the relations around them. So, it is with teaching. For too long I have insisted on competing for their attention with my body and my soul—no quizzes, no roll call, just me and the text and of course the looming papers. I'm devoted to the white chalk and the black board, furiously drawing pictures that unfold with theories. I'm one of the last. It's time to move on, to succumb to the digital world in which my students live, to draw on PowerPoint to bring a new dimension to teaching. Where the blackboard was an extension of myself, the screen will now be a third person competing for attention. Students will no longer have to squint and puzzle over what I've drawn in the distance, the PowerPoint will be in their faces. But it projects an air of predictability. We will all know that the PowerPoint has decided where we are going and how we are going to get there. From the hidden laws of classroom anarchy, we move to the planned economy. Still the best plans can be subverted.

But that's the form, but what about the content? For almost 20 years, the content of the course has remained static. I had designed a jig-saw puzzle which we slowly put together, manufacturing the pieces as we go, carefully laying them in relation to each other until we came up with the final picture that students express in their extraordinary posters. I loved that final picture, its aesthetics, its logic, but it belies the idea of living theory. The point of a jig-saw puzzle is that the end is predetermined, at least to me if not to the students. We have to put it into motion if theory is to really live.

Students are always asking why we don't read this or that theorist— especially when they learn what my colleagues are teaching in their theory courses. In the survey approach you can simply add another theorist, no big deal, but in the ethnographic approach adding another theorist requires re-evaluating and reassembling the whole. I can't just add another piece without rejigging the whole, revising the picture. So, under pressure from students, instead of adding another piece, I add an elective third semester for those who are addicted to theory. With 30 committed students, I devote myself to a single topic (theory of pedagogy, theory of the university) or to a single theorist (C. Wright Mills, Pierre Bourdieu, and most recently W.E.B. Du Bois).

It is long overdue to redesign the jig-saw puzzle, giving W.E.B. Du Bois a central place. He is an endlessly fascinating sociologist, for so long excluded from academia—both he and his writing—for whom race is central but not to the exclusion of class and gender. In contrast to Marx, Weber, and Durkheim he is from and writes about the US, but in global colours. His writing is often poetic as well as sociological and historical, challenging the theorist to construct analytical frames, concepts out of his lyrical prose. Putting him in dialogue with Marx, Weber, and Durkheim illuminates the different stages of his own life just as the way he places himself in the world he is analysing recalls the contributions of feminists. It takes, at least, an African American to breathe new life into the 19th century masters from Europe. With the help of Marx, Weber, and Durkheim his history speaks directly to students.

Whether I can recapture the students by revamping the course, or whether they are lost forever remains to be seen. But at least I have recovered the anxiety that is *sine qua non* of teaching, the excitement of learning along with those I am teaching. Whether successful or not in reversing my failings, those failings should not be used to indict living theory—a real utopia in a sea of degradation.

References

Freire, P. (1970). *Pedagogy of the Oppressed.* New York: Herder and Herder.

Herring, C., Rosaldo, M., Seim, J., and Shestakofsky, B. (2016). "Living Theory: Principles and Practices for Teaching Social Theory Ethnographically", *Teaching Sociology* 44 (3): 188–199.

Parsons, T., Shils, E., Naegele, K.D., and Pitts, J.R. (eds.). (1961). *Theories of Society: Foundations of Modern Sociological Theory.* New York: The Free Press of Glencoe.

Stinchcombe, A. (1982). "Should Sociologists Forget Their Mothers and Fathers", *The American Sociologist* 17: 2–11.

CHAPTER 13

Postscript

Peter Sohlberg and Håkon Leiulfsrud

Our theory-project has been structured as a triptych with overlapping borders between the construction of the research object, the functionalities of theory, and concept development. The rationale for this being that we wanted to highlight different angles of theoretical and methodological constructions in social science. In Volume I (Sohlberg and Leiulfsrud, 2017), we focused on constructions and active uses of theories based on different examples of creative usage. In Volume II (Leiulfsrud and Sohlberg, 2018), meanwhile, our primary focus was on the elements of theory construction, i.e. the concepts (cf. Swedberg, 2017). In this volume, we concentrated on the construction process in more general terms. In contrast to those who argue in favour of strict formulas for dealing with theory, our claim is that a variety of construction work permeates most of the activity in the social sciences (Hacking, 1999). Theory construction is not helped by a dogmatic view of theory and concepts that is confined to a specific school of thought or paradigm, something that is also reflected in the contributions of our three volumes, where we illustrate varieties of construction work applicable in different paradigmatic settings.

Based on our project discussions over a period of several years, we conclude that it is impossible to establish very strict borders between the construction of the research object, and the construction of theory and concept development. There are also sound theoretical arguments for this. Concepts can never be conclusively studied as isolated elements but rather are always related to what we have labelled a 'conceptual space' (see Sohlberg and Leiulfsrud, 2017) and generally integrated into what we refer to as 'theoretical vocabularies' or into theories (ibid.). By distinguishing between conceptual spaces, theoretical vocabularies, and theories, we aim to identify a continuum concerning the degree to which concepts are interrelated. A conceptual space, as it is referred to here, means that concepts are loosely linked by tradition and habit in the social sciences. Examples discussed in Volume II include 'family', 'social class', 'gender', 'race', and 'recognition', while, at the other end of the continuum we find more formalised theories, where concepts are clearly and explicitly linked in a specific way (see, for example, Erik Olin Wright on class analysis, inspired by Eric Roemer's rational choice framework in Volume II).

Robert Merton's formulation of the ideal of 'middle-range theories' is highly problematic if we search for a stringent, coherent structure and receipt for theory construction (see Sohlberg, 2017). Merton's overall theoretical strategy, which avoids substantial universal theories is, however, fundamentally and profoundly sound. It is characteristic of most of the chapters in our three volumes that the contributions have been formulated on a middle-range methodological level, which means that, in most cases, we have not focused on theories as totalities but on middle-range theoretical operations and conceptual formations. One of our interests has, for example, been to explore how concepts may operate as 'door-openers' within and across conceptual spaces.

Erving Goffman's theatre metaphor, which uses the ideas of 'backstage' and 'frontstage' as varied settings for social interaction, is not just a powerful metaphorical device but also an illustration how a shift of stage may change the play of the game and its sociological connotations (Goffman, 1990). Harriet Bjerrum Nielsen's chapter (in this volume) on time and space is another effective illustration of how concepts are highly interactive, context-dependent, and contingent on the historical period they are framed within. The very concept of the metaphor in a theoretical context could well be an indicator of sloppiness and inaccuracy, as argued by John Scott and Johs Hjelbrekke in this volume. In line with this, throughout this project, we have also emphasised that the break with commonsensical notions could be a fundamental aspect of theoretical creativity. The relationship between metaphors and scientific language is, however, also complex. If one could imagine an antonym to metaphors concerning concept formation, we may find the answer in the operationalist tradition of 'exact' measurable variables.

Notwithstanding the problem with vague and inaccurate metaphors, there is another approach to be considered: the case that concepts that can often be identified as metaphoric can sometimes be understood in terms of their potentially wide applicability in the social science vocabulary (Blumer, 1931). This applicability concerns how the concept in question has a general function that is conducted in different ways in specific cases. When, for example, Göran Ahrne used the metaphor 'social bond' in this volume, the general function is 'binding together' in a social context. The interesting and non-metaphoric part of the analysis is when he investigates the substantial variety of how this is done. Without the metaphor of a social bond, we would not have a common label for the various ways in which this function (binding together) is executed.

An analogous metaphor is again used when Jon Elster, in more structural terms, describes 'the cement of society' (Elster, 1989), a term identifying a basic function that can possibly be fulfilled in a variety of ways. One obvious question here is in what way this quality of cement (binding together) is or can be substantiated. This is also an illustration of how we viewed the seemingly eclectic idea of homeless concepts in the project, that is, concepts that have a rich potential for possible uses in a variety of contexts. The specific applications could be more exact and specified than the overall characteristics or the role the concept plays in a variety of settings. The case that a concept as, for example, a 'mechanism' can be considered a metaphor with potentially very wide applicability does not disqualify it from being productive in different types of social science application (Hedström and Swedberg, 1998).

1   The Non-programmatic Approach

Much of the sociological discourse is programmatic, emerging in the form of declarations regarding the nature of social reality, the nature of power, and the nature of knowledge, etc. This is the positive, clarifying side of the programmatic approach; however, another considerable part comprises declaring what reality, power, and knowledge, etc. are not. This negative approach has manifest, as well as latent, functions to delineate borders, which can, in turn, be a matter of clarity or academic tribalism. This academic tribalism may be motivated by a strong urge not to share a specific worldview or methodology with opponents: if the proportion between negative distancing and positive formulation leans towards the negative side, it could potentially be an indicator of what we here refer to as academic tribalism.

The French sociologist Pierre Bourdieu was not just an astute observer and analyst of academic tribalism within French academia but also a significant player in the academic field in his own right. *The Craft of Sociology* is rich and full of programmatic and distancing statements and standpoints. The concept of 'distinction' is obviously relevant to both the social space and social fields in general, as well as to analyses of the sociological discourse. In the concluding interview with Bourdieu in this book, he seems almost proud to be the only French sociologist of importance who did not attend Lazarsfeld's lectures when he visited France. Despite this rhetoric and self-confidence, Bourdieu et al.'s work in *The Craft of Sociology* has inspired us from the very beginning of our project with its numerous examples of highly creative and innovative ways of building upon and developing the sociological canon, including those of Marx, Weber, and Durkheim. When summarising our project, it is fair to say that throughout the 13 chapters, we have spent little energy on purely programmatic positioning, and even less on declaring what we are not. This is not a matter of mystique and diffuseness, but rather a consequence of our striving to argue through *positive* examples.

2   Ontologisation vs. Construction(ism)

By focusing on the construction of sociological objects, we have attempted to avoid what could be labelled as the 'ontologisation' of social science, which refers to the tendency to search for the essence of a social phenomenon rather than concentrating on its construction. Ontologisation can be illustrated in the way Hans Joas and Jonas Knöbl formulated three basic sociological questions: What *is* action? What *is* social order? What *determines* social change? (Joas and Knöbl, 2009: p. 18, our emphasis). The very phrasing of these questions suggests an ontological approach to the answers, focusing on 'what is' and 'what determines'. The alternative and constructionist approach to these themes would be how action, social order, and social change are constructed. Our focus on the theoretical and methodological construction processes is not intended to deny the reality of social phenomena. Stating that something is 'merely' a social construction is to underestimate the firmness of social realities, as Durkheim observed when he regarded external and constraining qualities as essential aspects of social reality (Durkheim, 2014). Almost regardless of whether we agree with Durkheim or not, or how we regard the ontological qualities of social reality, it is not possible to approach them without conceptual and theoretical constructions.

3   Anything Goes? The Question of Eclecticism

In our earlier discussion of the metaphor of the 'theoretical eye' (see Volume 2, Introduction), we argued that there is no contradiction between creativity and stringency. Expressed in conventional terms, creativity is a quality of the context of discovery, whereas stringency is a quality of the context of justification. One can dispute this simple dichotomy between discovery and justification, but the fact that we consistently concentrate on tools for generating knowledge, rather than iterate a number of social facts, is important. When these tools are used to generate knowledge, it should be possible to scrutinise the outcome through the established criteria used in the scientific community. When we present tools for generating knowledge, the question arises about the order of this toolbox, including the important question of eclecticism. What tools is it possible to combine? Continuing with the metaphorical language of a toolbox for a moment, it is never the case that a carpenter sees their tools as being in some kind of opposition; rather, they are complementary. However, when we view the toolbox of social science, this complementary situation is seldom the case; instead, we find confronting paradigms, theories, and even concepts, and it is often the case that more energy is spent on discussing the correct content of the toolbox than actually using it.

Thus, much of social science is trapped in positioning and demarcations against rival paradigms. In the field of sociology, eclecticism is often discussed in terms of the incompatibility between paradigms or theories representing fixed entities. Whether we interpret this as an integral social logic of academic fields or in terms of functional differentiation, we find a paradoxical situation when it comes to research methodology and actual analysis procedures, where the borders between paradigms are much fuzzier and more unclear.

Most of the contributions in the three volumes in this series have deliberately been written in a relatively eclectic manner to illustrate that sociological theorising does not necessarily need to follow strict predefined rules, as long as it is coherent, transparent, and productive in research practice. This is *not* to say that we, in any way, object to rigorous theory-building within a specific field, research school, or paradigm, but instead is primarily in line with our project belief that theory construction in practice is helped by a more, explorative, and creative attitude towards how to use theory in social research. Just as we, as researchers, have found inspiration in the many innovative ways of thinking about various theoretical objects that appear in *The Craft of Sociology* (Bourdieu et al., 1991), we hope that our example may be used as a door-opener for students and other scholars.

4   Constructions of the Theoretical Object Are Linked to the Potential to Ask Interesting Research Questions

As mentioned in the introduction to this volume, productive theory not only represents a more pragmatic way of seeing or a conceptual structure—it also offers a potential avenue to make sense of the world. In the field of sociology, with its rich tradition of theory and theory development, it is easy to 'fall in love' with theory but harder to find useful guidance on how to work with theory as a methodological tool (see both Swedberg's and Burawoy's chapters in this volume). This is particularly challenging if we ask what the 'theoretical object' in a specific enquiry is and how has this informed the research questions.

It could, of course, be argued that 'constructing the object' and a variety of 'constructionisms' (theoretical and conceptual) are simply a pretentious way of re-naming conventional methods of social science. Our answer to this argument is rather pragmatic: the success or failure of a project such as ours depends on how it can be put into practice. As teachers with the responsibility to teach and supervise our university students' philosophy of science and sociological theory, we have had ample opportunities over several years to test the main ideas and programme of this and previous volumes. We have learnt that both undergraduate and advanced graduate students have benefitted tremendously from actively working with this more pragmatic and methodological approach to theory, as opposed to the simple theoretical replication of what is reported in textbooks or in a designated research field. We have experienced that students who learn to work with this active and 'instrumental' approach to theory construction and concept formation are better equipped as independent minds. None of this is without objections, of course, but as an attempt to make theory into a question of theory *application*, we hope that our examples may continue to be of inspiration and practical use.

References

Blumer, H. (1931). "Science without concepts", *American Journal of Sociology* 36 (4): 515–533.

Bourdieu, P., Chamboredon, J.-C., and Passeron, J.-C. (1991) [1968]. *The craft of sociology: epistemological preliminaries.* Berlin: Walter de Gruyter.

Durkheim, E. in Durkheim, E., Lukes, S., and Halls, W.D. (2014) [1895]. *The rules of sociological method: and selected texts on sociology and its method. Free Press trade paperback edition.* New York: Free Press.

Elster, J. (1989). *The cement of society: a study of social order.* Cambridge: Cambridge Univ. Press.

Goffman, E. (1990) [1959]. *The presentation of self in everyday life.* London: Penguin.

Hacking, I. (1999). *The social construction of what?* Cambridge, MA: Harvard University Press.

Hedström, P. and Swedberg, R. (eds.). (1998). *Social mechanisms: an analytical approach to social theory.* Cambridge: Cambridge University Press.

Joas, H. and Knöbl, W. (2009). *Social theory: twenty introductory lectures.* Cambridge: Cambridge University Press.

Leiulfsrud, H. and Sohlberg, P. (eds.). (2018): *Concepts in action. Conceptual constructionism.* Leiden & Boston: Brill.

Sohlberg, P. and Leiulfsrud, H. (2017): *Theory and theoretical operations.*in P. Sohlberg and H. Leiulfsrud (eds.). *Theory in action. Theoretical constructionism.* Leiden & Boston: Brill.

Sohlberg, P. (2017). "A thick description of Robert K. Merton's middle range theory – Manifest properties and latent ambivalence", in P. Sohlberg and H. Leiulfsrud (eds.). *Theory in action. Theoretical constructionism.* Leiden & Boston: Brill.

Swedberg, R. (2017). "On the heuristic role of concepts in theorizing", in P. Sohlberg and H. Leiulfsrud (eds.). *Theory in action. Theoretical constructionism.* Leiden & Boston: Brill.

Index

CPSIA information can be obtained
at www.ICGtesting.com
Printed in the USA
JSHW021953080422
24696JS00002B/2